VICTORIAN PRELUDE

VICTORIAN PRELUDE

A HISTORY OF
ENGLISH MANNERS
1700 - 1830

BY

MAURICE J. QUINLAN

HAMDEN, CONNECTICUT
ARCHON BOOKS
1965

Library of Congress Catalog Card Number: 65-17408
Printed in the United States of America

TO MY MOTHER AND FATHER

PREFACE 1964

WHEN THIS BOOK was first published—ironically it appeared the day following Pearl Harbor—the reappraisal of nineteenth-century England had already begun. A scholarly assessment of its vast literary output was in process. The so-called complacency of the Victorians was receiving a more careful scrutiny. Their emphasis on the prudential virtues and their social conservatism were being judged anew and in contrast with the freer code of the Twenties. Consequently, though it was unquestionably poor timing to have a book first appear on the day when banner headlines were announcing our entry into World War II, the publication of *Victorian Prelude* at this stage did accord with the trend that directs every age to reevaluate the preceding one.

Since the end of World War II the reinterpretation of the Victorians has continued on a broad scale. As a result, in some ways we are now able to understand our grandparents better than they did themselves. They may still strike us as strange and sometimes amusing, but, with a clearer understanding, the laughter at their seeming absurdities has grown less loud. Among the books that in recent years have contributed to a more substantial knowledge of the Victorians, to mention only a few, are: Richard D. Altick's *The English Common Reader,* Jerome H. Buckley's *The Victorian Temper,* and Walter E. Houghton's *The Victorian Frame of Mind, 1830–1870.* Through these and dozens of other works we appear to have reached the position prophesied by Leslie Stephen when he wrote: "Our descendants will be able to see the general characteristics of the

Victorian Age better than we, who unconsciously accept our own peculiarities, like the air we breathe, as mere matters of course."

In this book my purpose has been, not to analyze the Victorian Age itself, but rather to determine how its distinctive milieu developed from an earlier period in which predominating tastes and values were vastly different. In brief, then, this is a study in the transition from one culture to a sharply contrasting one. When I wrote the book, I was fascinated by what then seemed to me an unparalleled change in the views, the standards, and the way of living that occurred within a generation or two. Now, standing on a higher plateau of the twentieth century, I marvel less at the transition from the age of Fielding to the age of Thackeray than I do at the changes in this country between the time of Coolidge and that of President Kennedy. Better than ever before, however, this book may serve as an illustration of the inevitability of social change, a phenomenon that in a scientifically orientated society becomes constantly more rapid and more complex. What future historians may write about our time, which has coined the new adjective "forward-looking," is a subject to ponder. While it would be rash to make detailed predictions, one may safely surmise that a later age will view the peculiarities we tend to accept as mere matters of course with much the same astonishment and amusement as we experience when reading about the early Victorians.

ACKNOWLEDGMENTS

I WISH to express here my gratitude to various people who have contributed to the making of this book. Mr. Albert Coote, whose good taste is equaled only by his kindness, has helped me immeasurably by his numerous suggestions for improving the text. I am also indebted to Professor John G. Gazley for directing me to sources of information and for letting me draw upon his thorough knowledge of English history; and to Professor James Dow McCallum, who first aroused my interest in the subject of manners.

I am grateful for the grant of a Columbia University Fellowship, which enabled me to do most of my research in England, and for the assistance I have received at Columbia University from members of the faculty. Professor Marjorie Nicolson has made several suggestions for improving the first chapters of this book. The criticisms of Professor Emery Neff have been particularly valuable, because of his wide acquaintance with the Victorian period. Finally, I am especially indebted to Professor Ernest Hunter Wright, who encouraged me to investigate the beginnings of Victorianism and who has, with unfailing interest, directed my studies and advised me in the preparation of this volume.

M. J. Q.

West Hartford, Connecticut
September, 1941

CONTENTS

INTRODUCTION

SIR WALTER SCOTT, weaver of medieval tapestries, was scarcely less interested in the fabric of nineteenth-century society. He was among the first to realize that the habits of the people of his time were undergoing a profound change, a revolution marked particularly by a growing strictness of manners and morals. What we know as "Victorianism" had developed several years before the accession of the queen whose name was to become the symbol of a remarkable era. In 1826, eleven years before Victoria came to the throne, Scott told the following incident.

A great-aunt of Scott, Mrs. Keith of Ravelstone, had asked him if he could get her the works of Aphra Behn, the popular authoress of the late seventeenth century. Scott replied that he could but that he did not think she would find this old writer "quite proper reading." Mrs. Keith persisted, however, saying that when she was a young woman she had found Mrs. Behn's novels very entertaining and that she would like to look at them again. Scott yielded to her request, though when he sent her the books he took the precaution to mark the package "private and confidential." The next time he saw the old lady she thrust the books into his hands and recommended that he consign Mrs. Behn to the fire. "I found it impossible to get through the very first of the novels," she said, and then added reflectively, "but is it not very odd that I, an old woman of eighty and upwards, sitting alone, feel myself ashamed to read a book which sixty years ago I have heard read aloud for large circles consisting of the first and most creditable society in London?" [1]

The most creditable society of Scott's day, though fond of the

[1] *Letters of Sir Walter Scott*, London, 1936, X, 96.

pastime of listening to someone read aloud, would hardly have selected for an evening's entertainment the novels or plays of Mrs. Behn. If the family library contained a set of her works, they would probably be kept under lock and key, for Mrs. Behn, Congreve, Wycherley, Vanbrugh, and various other Restoration writers were now considered improper. The same stricture was applied to many authors of the eighteenth century. The frank language of Fielding and Smollett and the indelicate situations created for their characters offended the prevailing taste. Sterne, less obviously vulgar, was deemed sly and salacious. Even Richardson, the most moral of all eighteenth-century novelists, had his detractors. Having developed a strong preference for polite circumlocutions, readers were particularly shocked by the unvarnished Anglo-Saxon terms of the Elizabethans. Shakespeare was widely read, though for the most part in versions thoughtfully emended by Mr. Thomas Bowdler. Even his painstaking deletions fell short of perfection. For the ultrascrupulous the Reverend John Rogers Pitman had managed to provide a still purer text.

What accounted for this change? Scott thought that it was "owing to the gradual improvement of national taste and delicacy," [2] and with this opinion many of his contemporaries would have agreed. One thing was certain—the stricter literary code merely reflected a general stiffening of manners. Since the time of the French Revolution the upper classes had taken what they called a more "serious" view of life. Gambling, masquerades, and revels, the prevalent pastimes of the previous century, were losing their popularity. There was a noticeable increase in piety. At service time the churches were crowded, and many families had restored the custom of saying grace before meat and prayers before bed. Social gatherings were often sober and dull affairs. Men spent less time over their port and, when they joined the ladies, the conversation was more edifying than lively. The quips and sallies of fashionable discourse in Dr. Johnson's time had given way to discussion of such respectable but prosy matters as

[2] *Ibid.*

the activities of the various tract, missionary, and charitable societies which had been established in the past few decades. Almost every woman of some social standing belonged to one of
these organizations, and whether her allotted task was to distribute religious pamphlets, to collect money for the missionary
funds, or to visit the homes of the indigent, she was professedly
happy to have some share in the task of reclaiming the wicked
and ministering to the poor.

Equally remarkable were the changes which had occurred in
the lower ranks of society. Even among the poor a good many
had acquired respectability. Not that their economic status had
improved, for, if anything, the problem of poverty was still more
appalling than it had been in the previous century. Nevertheless, thousands among those who constituted the lowest class of
society had definitely bettered their social standards. They were
neater in their homes and in their appearance, they had given up
such brutish pastimes as bear-baiting and cockfighting, and the
class as a whole was much better educated than the poor at any
previous time. As compared with their eighteenth-century ancestors, who were inclined to the belief that to pick a pocket was
as good a deed as to drink, they were notably more law-abiding.
Walking through even the worst slums of London, one could now
feel fairly secure of life and property. The streets no longer resounded with bawdy ballads, and on market night hawkers sold,
not the penny histories of famous criminals which had delighted
the populace of Johnson's day, but urgent tracts containing some
pointed moral lesson or the account of a sinner's conversion.

It was clear, from these and a thousand other instances, that a
revolution in manners had occurred during the first quarter of
the nineteenth century. Older people who could recall the period just prior to the French Revolution were amazed at the
change. Most of them rejoiced in the thought that low taste and
coarse habits were fast disappearing. Only the exceptional person
regretted that a certain honest and hearty vulgarity had also
vanished.

Not until the period of the Great War of 1914–18 did similarly rapid social changes occur. But at the beginning of the nineteenth century the tide was flowing the other way. Where the present generation discarded the trammels of convention, unmasked the emotions, and adopted an unprecedented degree of frankness in literature and conversation, the people of Scott's day acquired taboos, introduced strict rules of propriety, and became reticent about sex and the emotions. Both generations were revolting from the customs of their elders.

Almost anyone over thirty can recall the time when certain Victorian conventions were still observed, for Victorianism survived, for a decade or two, the death of the queen in 1901. To be sure the term "Victorian" is sometimes applied, in a strictly chronological sense, to the sixty-four-year period of Victoria's reign, a complex era, distinguished by cross currents of thought, various philosophies, and contradictory creeds. But in another meaning, and the one here employed, this term is synonymous with a peculiar form of social conservatism which, though predominant during the regnancy of the queen, existed both before and after that time. In other words, the dynasty of Mrs. Grundy was even longer than the reign of Victoria.

While she ruled, Mrs. Grundy was an extremely strict arbiter of manners. But she ruled by public fiat, for, despite the jibes of a Dickens or a Thackeray, the Victorians were proud of their social conservatism. This is particularly observable in the works of the minor writers, who, like the forgotten authors of other periods, sometimes reflect the temper of their age better than the major literary figures. Most Victorians felt that their customs and habits were notably superior to those of former times. Although they were sentimental about many things, they did not hanker for a return of "the good old days" of their ancestors. To them the eighteenth century was a wicked era. At other periods in history nations have boasted of their tolerance, their wisdom, or their progressiveness. It was a distinguishing feature of the Victorian age that people gloried in their moral superiority.

The circumstances that produce social change are complex, and there is probably no key, no single set of conditions to explain a revolution in manners. On the other hand, it is naïve to assume that a nation alters its customs as simply as a pendulum swings. Although no attempt will be made to trace to its root every vine or tendril that formed part of the Victorian mesh-work, the purpose of this volume is to show that the social pattern changed as a result of changes in opinions and convictions. Hence we must first take into account the influence of various books and events and the efforts of certain persuasive individuals who managed to convert people from the customs and beliefs of the preceding period.

PART ONE: THE EIGHTEENTH CENTURY

CHAPTER ONE

HARDY RECUSANTS

SAMUEL JOHNSON loved the busy stir and the full tide of existence in eighteenth-century London. Nevertheless, he knew that crime was as common and rancid as the open sewers of the great city. All measures to reduce lawlessness seemed to fail —even the device of parading condemned criminals before the public on the way to the gibbet. In "The Idle 'Prentice Executed at Tyburn" Hogarth vividly pictured this commonplace scene, and in his "London" Johnson wrote:

> Scarce can our fields, such crowds at Tyburn die,
> With hemp the gallows and the fleet supply.

For the London masses, a public execution was a holiday event. Hours before the condemned were to pass, people took their places along the way, filling the windows of houses, jostling one another in alley entrances, or obtaining, for a small fee, the privilege of standing in one of the drays which were drawn up in the middle of the streets to accommodate the curious. The criminals, sometimes followed by their relatives and friends, usually rode to the gibbet in carts. As the procession passed, the spectators scanned the faces of the condemned for some sign of emotion. If a culprit appeared indifferent to his fate or made a show of bravado, they might cheer or applaud. Occasionally a person darted out from the crowd to proffer to the men in the carts a pint of beer or a measure of gin. Other spectators seemed to find a peculiar pleasure in pelting the unfortunates with offal.[1]

Hucksters and "pye men," bawling out their wares, passed

---

[1] Tyburn Fair is described in various works. The details used here are taken from the notebooks of Francis Place, British Museum, Additional Manuscripts, 27,825, III, 97. (Hereafter cited as B.M., Add. MSS 27,825.)

among the crowd with oranges, gingerbread, and spirits. Sometimes the hawkers, anticipating the death of a famous highwayman or murderer by a few hours, sold sheets containing what purported to be the last words of one who had yet to pass in the procession. For a halfpenny one could buy a bawdy song or a ballad describing the life and deeds of some notorious criminal. These songs were very much in favor with the populace, especially at Tyburn Fair or on market night, when a crowd would gather to hear them sung by the professional street singers or by children of the slums. According to Francis Place, the distinguished political reformer of the early nineteenth century, ballads of this kind remained popular until the period of the French Revolution. As a boy, Place had frequently heard them sung, and some years later, when the public had forgotten them, he recorded the words of those which he could remember from his youth. Among them was the following lusty bit of doggerel:

> To the hundreds of Drury I write
> And the rest of my flashy companions,
> To the buttocks that pad it all night,
> To pimps, whores, bawds, and their stallions.
> To those that are down in the whit,
> Battling their darbies with pleasure,
> Who laugh at the rum culls they've bit,
> While here they are snacking the treasure.
>
> Moll Spriggins came here t'other night,
> She tipp'd me a jorum of diddle.
> Gamish is the prisoner's delight;
> We footed away to the fiddle.
> Her fortune at diving did fail,
> For which she did change habitation.
> But now the whore pads the jail
> And laughs at the fools of creation.[2]

Only the rank and file, of course, favored such songs, but members of the upper classes, though less likely to stand gaping at the Tyburn procession, were not above relishing an execution.

---

[2] *Ibid.*, I, 155. Place supplies the following glossary for words in the above song: buttocks, prostitutes; whit, prison; darbies, irons; rum culls, those who have been robbed; diddle, punch; diving, picking pockets.

Horace Walpole, glass of fashion and son of a prime minister, lingered over the details with obvious pleasure when he described the beheading of two rebel lords who had participated in the Stuart uprising of 1745. Lord Kilmarnock, he wrote, died like a gentleman. Once on the scaffold, "he took no notice of the crowd, only to desire that the baize might be lifted from the rails, that the mob might see the spectacle." Having prayed and delivered a speech to the sheriff, Kilmarnock took off his coat and waistcoat and donned a napkin-cap. "At last the earl knelt down, with a visible unwillingness to depart, and after five minutes dropped his handkerchief, the signal, and his head was cut off, only hanging by a bit of skin, and was received in a scarlet cloth by four of the undertaker's men." Walpole, adding many further details, next described the last moments of the second rebel, Lord Balmerino. "As he walked from his prison to execution, seeing every window and top of house filled with spectators, he cried out, 'Look, look, how they are all piled up like rotten oranges.' " [3]

It was typical of the eighteenth century to derive amusement from an execution. Not that people were without compassion at the sight of human suffering, for they had founded numerous charitable institutions to relieve want and misery. Nevertheless, it was a notably calloused and cynical age. English society had relaxed its standards of manners and morals, and corruption could be found in all walks of life. The best society, despite its wit, elegance, and learning, was much preoccupied with drunken routs, foppery, and seduction. The clergy, among whom there were many fox-hunting and play-writing parsons, were inclined to neglect the moral and spiritual directorship of their congregations to engage in abstract speculation upon the nature of man and the universe. In other professions there was an unusual lack of integrity: London swarmed with shoddy attorneys and quacks who lived by blood money, bloodletting, and the peddling of nostrums.

[3] *Letters of Horace Walpole*, ed. by Mrs. Paget Toynbee, Oxford, 1903–5, II, 235 ff.

In the lower brackets of society conditions were still worse. Uneducated, undernourished, and ungodly, the poor were often degraded in their habits and barbarous in their inclinations. Many, having no regular occupation, lived precariously upon the proceeds of crime. From this group came most of the prostitutes, highwaymen, and cutthroats that roved the countryside and the byways of London. There was no distinct criminal class, however, for in this lawless age almost anyone among the poor might pick a pocket or filch clothes from a line. Because the police were notoriously inefficient, felons often escaped detection. But those who were arrested faced inordinately harsh treatment. Penned up in foul prisons, they might have to wait months before coming to trial. Many of them, when convicted, were sentenced to the Tyburn gallows, for, under the laws of the land, even certain forms of petty thieving were punishable by death. Thus the laws, in many instances, were more barbarous than the offenses they were intended to penalize, and a government that employed the pillory, floggings, and public executions might be deemed no less calloused than the hardened multitude.

Despite its many faults, however, the eighteenth century possessed one eminent virtue—a certain frankness about itself. No one denied that the age was corrupt. Writing to a friend in 1749, Horace Walpole observed, "I think what you call flagrancy was never more in fashion." [4] The same view of the eighteenth century may be found in the novels of Fielding and Smollett, and in the novels, diaries, and letters of virtually all English writers of the period. Moreover, if one examines the commentaries of foreign visitors, the public records of the time, and, of course, the pictures of Hogarth, one finds further evidence that manners and morals were unusually corrupt—more corrupt, it may be, than in any other era of English civilization.

There is no need to extenuate the faults which the eighteenth century freely acknowledged. Nor is it necessary further to elaborate upon them, for the social historians have faithfully described

[4] *Ibid.*, II, 324.

the prevailing tone of manners. But to say that loose standards prevailed is not to deny the fact that certain forces were, at the same time, trying to alter these conditions. No decade of the eighteenth century was without its reformers, despite the general complacence of the age, and these hardy recusants were continually striving to improve public morality and to introduce new creeds and customs. Although many of their efforts were doomed to failure, as the century wore on the reformers were more successful, and by the end of the period some of the worst abuses were disappearing.

Having awakened the public conscience, the reformers, who had always been inclined to confuse manners and morals, determined not only to suppress various flagrant and recognized vices, but to prohibit many traditional forms of amusement and to introduce strict standards of decorum. Circumstances favored their cause, and within a surprisingly short time they had succeeded in creating public opinion in support of their strict beliefs. They could not have made such rapid progress in the first quarter of the nineteenth century, however, if the groundwork had not been laid by earlier reformers. These hardy recusants, undaunted by the opposing spirit of the times, were already at work when the eighteenth century dawned.

EARLY EIGHTEENTH-CENTURY REFORMERS

During the Restoration period the nation had thrown off most of the restrictions imposed by the Puritans, but many people, feeling that manners had been relaxed too far, objected to what they called the license of the age. Much as they wanted to reform conditions, they did not dare to take any definite public measures so long as Charles II and his brother James were the monarchs, for these rulers had no use for meddling reformers. But the accession of William and Mary inspired the malcontents with the hope that the country might be ripe for a revolution in manners. They were further encouraged when the new monarchs issued several proclamations in which the magistrates were ordered to deal severely with all "profane and debauched" persons. Armed with these decrees, the reformers inaugurated a vigorous campaign to rid the country of vice.[5]

The first interest of the reformers was to enforce certain vice laws that had been passed from time to time since the reign of Elizabeth. Because they interfered with personal liberties, these statutes had always been difficult to put into effect, and the Restoration magistrates had apparently not insisted very strongly upon their observance. But now, believing that the neglect of these laws was largely responsible for public immorality, certain indignant citizens determined to assist if not compel the magistrates to prosecute offenders. For this purpose they organized at London, in 1692, a Society for the Reformation of Manners.

As a reminder to constables, the society published the following description of the offenses punishable under the vice laws:

A constable may stop any persons that he shall find driving horses, carts, cattle, etc. on the Lord's Day, and carry them before a Justice of Peace, to convict them of offending against the statute 29 Car. 2, cap. 7.

He may do the like to such as he shall find at any sports or pastimes on that day, contrary to 1 Car. 1.

If he find any shop-keepers or other persons, selling or exposing to sale, their wares on the Lord's Day, he may carry them before a Justice of Peace, to convict them upon the statute of Jac. 1, cap. 22.

He may take any that he shall find drunk or blaspheming, prophanely swearing, or cursing, contrary to Acts of Parliament . . . and carry them before a Justice of Peace to convict them.[6]

These laws were so strict that any group attempting to enforce them would naturally be unpopular with the masses. The Society for the Reformation of Manners therefore did not publish the names of its members, though one of its publications affirmed that it had enrolled several eminent lawyers, justices of peace, and members of Parliament.[7] Its chief supporters appear to have been substantial middle-class citizens. In that respect, this early

[5] Josiah Woodward, *An Account of the Society for the Reformation of Manners*, London, 1699.

[6] *The Oath of a Constable*, London, 1701.   [7] Woodward, *op. cit.*, p. 10.

society was like the great voluntary organizations which were to serve as the vertebrae of the Victorian social structure.

In order to detect offenders, the Society for the Reformation of Manners appointed several of its members to act as a vigilance committee. It also employed professional informers to spy upon and report lawbreakers. A person who had been arrested and found guilty received a fine or some other punishment. At the same time, to caution him against further violations of the law, he was given various pamphlets called dissuasives from vice. In addition to these publications, the society printed an annual *Blacklist* of the names of those who had been convicted during the past year and described their offenses. These *Blacklists*, concerned only with violations of the law in the City of London and its immediate suburbs, show that the members of the organization were extremely diligent. In the year 1700, besides "many notorious cursers, swearers, Sabbath-breakers, and drunkards," they convicted "843 lewd and scandalous persons . . . as keepers of houses of baudry and disorder, or as whores, night-walkers, etc." The culprits, many of whom appeared several times before the magistrates, were punished "either by carting, whipping, fining, imprisonment, or suppressing their licenses." [8]

The Londoners who had organized the Society for the Reformation of Manners, hoping to make moral reform a national issue, encouraged the establishment of similar societies in other communities by widely circulating an account of their purposes and the plan of their organization. As a result, several cities in England instituted vice societies modeled after the original at London. How many separate associations were thus formed it is impossible to say, but they appear to have been numerous, for Archbishop Sharp, of York, wrote to another prelate:

The truth is the societies of London have been so industrious in spreading their books, and the success they have had (as they say) in this way, has made such a noise everywhere, that the whole nation almost has taken the alarm. And so eagerly in many places are the

---

[8] *A Sixth Blacklist*, London, J. Downing, 1701.

minds of the people set upon these methods, that it may be justly doubted whether it be in the bishop's power to stifle or suppress these societies, though he should use his utmost endeavours to do so.[9]

Sharp's objection to the societies was based upon the pharisaical attitude of the members. "As for reforming themselves or improving one another in holy living," he said, "there is little provision made." [10] Many people, agreeing with this opinion, believed that the only way to improve public morality was to increase virtue and piety among the upper ranks of society. This was the stand taken by Jonathan Swift. In his *Project for the Advancement of Religion*, published in 1708, he remarked that whoring, drunkenness, cursing, and blasphemy were common faults of the upper classes and that almost as many women as men were guilty of these offenses. According to Swift, the vices of the age resulted largely from the incompetency and corruption of men in responsible position. Particularizing, he said that the clergy were an ignorant lot, officeholders venal, and the magistrates the most tainted of all people in public life. Many of them, he wrote, enriched themselves by forcing "all the bawds of the ward" to pay "for shelter and protection from the laws." By doing so they increased immorality, "for these infamous women are forced upon doubling their work and industry to answer double charges of paying the justices and supporting themselves." As for the reform societies, added Swift, though they had started with good intentions, it was commonly said that they had "dwindled into factious clubs and grown a trade to enrich knavish reformers of the meanest rank." [11]

Defoe, though an assiduous reformer himself, was even more bitter than Swift in his denunciation of the vice associations. In his *Poor Man's Plea*, while admitting that morals were extremely corrupt, he contended that the societies could effect no improvement so long as they singled out the poor as their victims. The vices of the upper classes were equally notorious, said Defoe, but no one dared to carry a wealthy drunkard before a magistrate or

[9] Thos. Sharp, *The Life of John Sharp*, London, 1825, I, 283.
[10] *Ibid.*, p. 175.   [11] *Works*, New York, 1812, IV, 152 ff.

to set a profane merchant in the stocks. Continuing his attack upon the societies in a satire called *Reformation of Manners,* he wrote:

Yet Ostia boasts of her regeneration
And tells us wondrous tales of reformation:
That none but men of quality may swear:
How public lewdness is expell'd the nation,
That private whoring may be more in fashion.
How parish magistrates, like pious elves,
Let none be drunk on Sundays but themselves.
And hackney coachmen durst not ply the street
In sermon-time, till they have pay'd the state.

In these lines Defoe undoubtedly expressed the view of the great mass of people. For the vice societies, paying little attention to corruption in high life, were chiefly interested in whipping the lower orders into a state of virtue. Those upon whom the lash fell showed their resentment by seizing some of the reformers and maltreating them, and at least two members of the society at London were killed in street fights while trying to make arrests.[12]

Despite all opposition, the societies continued for several decades to prosecute people under the vice laws, and the London organization, at least, lost none of its initial zeal during the reigns of Queen Anne and George I. According to its published statistics, in the thirty-three years ending in 1725, it made a total of 91,899 arrests.[13] Thereafter the number of prosecutions decreased, but the members continued to issue annual reports of their activities until 1738, when, it would appear, the Society for the Reformation of Manners died an unlamented death. It was to be a phoenix, however, which rose successively under other names until, in its final resurrection, it was to find the nation genuinely disposed to moral reform.

Another agency designed to improve manners and morals was instituted in 1698. It was called the Society for Promoting Chris-

---

[12] Garnet V. Portus, *Caritas Anglicana,* London, 1912, pp. 69 ff.
[13] *Thirty-first Account of . . . Societies for Promoting a Reformation of Manners,* London, 1726.

tian Knowledge (hereafter referred to as the S.P.C.K.). Several
of its original members, notably Robert Nelson, William Mel-
moth, and Josiah Woodward, also belonged to the Society for
the Reformation of Manners. But the two organizations, while
having many interests in common, differed in various respects.
The S.P.C.K., unlike the other association, required that its
members be communicants of the Established Church. Essentially a religious organization, it sought not merely to eradicate
vice, but to cultivate virtue. Believing that corruption was chiefly
due to ignorance of Christian principles, the members undertook to educate the nation by establishing schools, instituting
parochial libraries, and circulating Bibles, prayer books, and
tracts. The S.P.C.K. soon became an important reservoir of religious literature, and today, after almost two centuries and a
half, this society still holds an eminent position in the publishing
field.

The early pamphlets of the society were frequently admoni-
tory. Upon its lists appeared such gently nudging titles as *A Caution against Drunkenness, A Persuasion to Serious Observation
of the Lord's Day,* and *A Kind Caution to Profane Swearers.*
Special groups were appealed to in publications like *A Soldier's
Monitor* and Kettlewell's *Office for Prisoners.* The society
also printed, chiefly for the upper classes, various diatribes on
the theater, including Collier's *Dissuasive from Play-houses* and
Tillotson's sermons on the stage.[14]

Because the masses were generally illiterate, however, the circulation of books and tracts was necessarily very much restricted.
In some communities almost no one below the degree of a gentleman could read. There were, at the beginning of the eighteenth century, approximately 1,000 endowed primary schools,
which provided instruction for probably not more than 30,000
children. Even where free schools existed, children of the poorest sort were less likely to attend them than children of petty
tradesmen and those belonging to families which managed to

14 W. O. B. Allen and E. McClure, *Two Hundred Years; The History of the
Society for Promoting Religious Knowledge,* London, 1898, pp. 166–68.

keep off the parish rates. The poorest inhabitants, or the vast majority of them, remained in a questionably blissful state of ignorance.[15]

The S.P.C.K. had two specific reasons for wishing to give this group some form of elementary instruction. At the beginning of the eighteenth century the question of the Protestant succession had raised a fear of popery again, and the first purpose of the society was to erect a bulwark against Roman Catholicism by instructing the masses in the doctrines of the Established Church. The second was to promote a reformation of manners.[16] Whether or not they realized it, the members of the S.P.C.K. were also putting into effect two ideas that had developed during the seventeenth century: the first, Locke's theory that moral principles must be taught, since children have no inherent predilection for them; the second, a belief that education must be made more practical and brought home to the masses.

Even those who had no acquaintance with recent theories of education were convinced that there was a close relationship between the ignorance and the profligacy of the lower orders. Uneducated, the masses were frequently unemployed; idle, they not only burdened the parish rates but were more inclined to vice. The founders of the S.P.C.K. decided, therefore, that, to secure moral reform, it was necessary to fit poor children for some humble and useful occupation and, at the same time, to teach them moral and religious principles. For this purpose, the society instituted what were known as charity schools, defining its aim in the following form which was used to pledge contributors:

Whereas prophaneness and debauchery are greatly owing to gross ignorance of the Christian religion, especially among the poorer sort; and whereas nothing is more likely to promote the practice of Christianity and virtue than an early and pious education of youth; and whereas many poor people are desirous of having their children taught, but are not able to afford them a Christian and useful

---

15 David Salmon, "The Education of the Poor in the Eighteenth Century," *Educational Record* (Oct., 1907).

16 M. G. Jones, *The Charity School Movement*, Cambridge, 1938, pp. 28 ff.

education; we, whose names are underwritten do agree to pay yearly . . .[17]

The S.P.C.K. not only raised funds to support the schools, but appointed agents to supervise them and supplied the books used in classes. It also regulated the curriculum, which, in addition to religious instruction, consisted of lessons in reading, writing, and arithmetic, as well as practical training in spinning, knitting, and sewing. The main emphasis was placed upon religion. In charity schools children learned to read, not from primers, but in catechisms and the Bible. Apparently they read virtually nothing but religious works, for the only nonreligious book on a list recommended by the S.P.C.K. was a speller called, preposterously, *The Anatomy of Orthography*.[18]

During the first years of their existence the charity schools gave rise to great expectations. Queen Anne praised them "inasmuch as the pious instruction of children is the surest way of preserving and propagating the knowledge and practice of true religion." [19] Richard Steele, calling them "the greatest instances of public spirit the age has produced," declared that the schools would serve as nurseries for a race of honest and dependable servants.[20] Addison was even more enthusiastic:

I have always looked upon this institution of charity schools, which of late years has so universally prevailed throughout the nation, as the glory of the age we live in, and the most proper means that can be made use of to recover it out of its present degeneracy and depravation of manners. It seems to provide us an honest and virtuous posterity. There will be few in the next generation who will not be able to write and read, and have not an early tincture of religion.[21]

Addison's prediction has an ironic ring, for social conditions in the next generation showed no improvement. More might have been accomplished by the charity schools, however, had they increased as rapidly during the rest of the eighteenth cen-

[17] *The Methods Used for Erecting Charity Schools*, London, 1715, p. 30.
[18] *Ibid.*, p. 36.
[19] R. Nelson, *An Address to Persons of Quality and Estate*, London, 1715, pp. 43 ff.
[20] *Spectator*, no. 294.　　　　　[21] *The Guardian*, no. 105.

tury as in its first fifteen years. Later, as time would prove, popular education and the literacy of the masses would have an important share in effecting a change in the tone of manners. But, although the charity schools prefigured the development of future educational systems, there were not a sufficient number of these institutions in the eighteenth century to raise the standards of more than a small section of the common people.

The country was not yet ready to accept the idea of schools for all. While a number of people had endorsed the charity schools, others asserted that the poor, if educated, would become discontented with their lot and unwilling to engage in humble occupations. According to Bernard Mandeville, it was folly to educate the masses above their station, inasmuch as the nation needed a large group of people to perform unpleasant and laborious tasks. If the founders of charity schools wished to encourage virtue, added Mandeville, they should let the poor remain ignorant, for "as to religion, the most knowing and polite part of the nation has everywhere the least of it . . . and vice in general is nowhere more predominant than where arts and science flourish." [22] There was considerable truth in what Mandeville had to say about the upper classes, but he erred in thinking that promoters of charity schools wished to elevate the masses to a higher social level. Nothing was further from their minds. They considered the rigid stratification of society not only necessary, but divinely ordained. Isaac Watts, a staunch supporter of the schools, expressed the common attitude of the founders when he said:

I would persuade myself that the masters and mistresses of these schools among us teach the children of the poor which are under their care to know what their station in life is, how mean their circumstances, how necessary 'tis for them to be diligent, laborious, honest and faithful, humble and submissive, what duties they owe the rest of mankind and particularly to their superiors.[23]

---

[22] "Essay on Charity Schools," *The Fable of the Bees*, ed. by F. B. Kaye, Oxford, 1924, I, 269 and *passim*.
[23] *An Essay towards the Encouragement of Charity Schools*, London, 1728, p. 26.

Although the charity schools did not fail to teach these principles, the initial enthusiasm which had led to their establishment was dampened in 1715 when some of the trustees and teachers were accused of being Jacobites. Apparently there was some
truth in these charges, but the time was rife with intrigue, and
Low Churchmen and Whigs probably exaggerated the number
of Stuart sympathizers among the charity school managers. At
any rate the suspicion fastened upon these institutions served
to thwart the development of popular education. Most of the
schools already established managed to survive, and it is estimated that approximately 40,000 children were annually educated in these institutions throughout the eighteenth century.
But the charity school movement, like most reforming schemes
of the time, fell short of expectations, and the masses, for the
most part, remained illiterate.[24] Nevertheless, by introducing
the idea that popular education could serve to improve manners
and morals, the S.P.C.K. had blazed a trail which later would
prove an important avenue of social reform.

In the meantime the S.P.C.K. lost much of its initial vigor.
Several of its founders had been inspired by evangelical zeal,
but, as they died, enthusiasm wilted in the unspiritual climate
of the eighteenth century. Though the society continued to circulate the Bible and other religious works, it had grown somewhat apathetic in the promotion of Christianity. Not until the
religious tone of the nation revived did the S.P.C.K. again become a vigorous organization.

One more concern of the early eighteenth-century moralists
remains for consideration—the attempt to reform the theater.
Both the S.P.C.K. and the Society for the Reformation of Manners had some part in this. The first in its pamphlets attacked
the immorality of the stage, and the vice society appears to have
prosecuted some actors for using profanity.[25] But these efforts
to improve conditions in the theater were probably of less con-

24 Jones, *Op. cit.*, pp. 110 ff.
25 J. W. Krutch, *Comedy and Conscience after the Restoration*, New York,
1924, pp. 167 ff.

sequence than those made by numerous writers who, in dozens of pamphlets, denounced the Restoration dramatists.

The best remembered of these attacks is Jeremy Collier's *Short View of the Immorality and Profaneness of the English Stage.* Although he pretended to object only to the corruptions of the theater, Collier no doubt would have liked to see the complete suppression of the playhouses. Several other writers were equally intolerant. Defoe, who had opposed the vice societies, strongly objected to the opening of a theater in London, and when a company of players visited Oxford, he protested that they would "debauch the morals of the sons of our chief families, and the young generation of the nation's instructors." [26] Like Collier, he censured not only the plays of the Restoration dramatists, but those of Shakespeare as well. William Law, who continued the controversy in his *Absolute Unlawfulness of the English Stage,* was more frank than either Collier or Defoe. Asserting that the theater was completely contrary to Christian principles, he condemned it without qualification.

The attitude of these opponents of the stage differed little from that which had resulted in the closing of the theaters in the time of Cromwell. Inasmuch as these latter-day puritans were eager to seize upon any argument to convince their readers that theatrical entertainment was pernicious, it is not surprising that they should have termed many Elizabethan and Restoration plays obscene. But they can scarcely be accused of Victorian squeamishness. Like Swift and Pope, and, indeed, like most of their contemporaries, they themselves commonly wrote with unrestrained freedom of language. Even in his *Short View,* in which he had condemned the use of bawdy allusions in plays, Collier employed a good many coarse expressions.[27] And when the morally indignant Defoe attacked the theater, he damned it in terms of this sort:

> A lay-stall this, Apollo spoke the word,
> And straight arose a play-house from a t - - -.

[26] W. Wilson, *Life and Times of Daniel Defoe,* London, 1830, II, 461 ff.
[27] Krutch, *op. cit.,* pp. 119 ff.

Here whores in hogstyes vilely blended lay.
Just as in boxes at our lewder-play;
The stables have beeen cleans'd, the jakes made clear.
Herculean labours n'er will purge us here.
Some call this metamorphosis a jest,
And say we're but a dunghill still at best.[28]

Addison and Steele, to be sure, generally avoided such coarse expressions, and their criticisms of the stage were much more temperate. But then the authors of the *Spectator* were reformers of a different stripe from the puritan pamphleteers. They wished to improve the drama, not to destroy it. Purged of its faults, the theater might "even contribute its assistance to the advancement of morality," said Addison.[29] What they objected to was its excesses—its unrestrained language, its cynicism, its flagrant characters, and its Rabelaisian themes. Instead of making the typically puritanical onslaught upon the stage, therefore, these writers appealed to what the eighteenth century prided itself upon—its good sense and superior taste. Thus when Steele denounced *Sir Fopling Flutter,* he called the play "a contradiction to good manners, good sense, and common judgment." [30] And when Addison discussed the immorality of contemporary plays, he reminded his readers that dramatists who represented vice in an amiable light failed to write according to the traditions of the Greek and Roman theater.[31]

Such criticisms were more effective probably than the bitter denunciations of Defoe and Collier. But a still more effective influence upon public taste was the new type of comedy which Steele introduced. In his plays, he carefully avoided cynicism and ribaldry, and, by giving prominence to characters who were remarkable for their noble motives and lofty sentiments, he created a new fashion in the theater. Audiences liked his moralizing strain, and other writers, taking their cue from Steele, turned to producing sentimental comedies. In the meantime, the Restoration dramatists had died or had stopped writing for the stage.

[28] "On the New Play-house in the Haymarket," *Review,* II (May 3, 1705), 103.
[29] *Spectator,* no. 446.　　　[30] *Ibid.,* no. 65.　　　[31] *Ibid.,* no. 446.

Thus, for various reasons, the drama became more circumspect than it had been in the late seventeenth century, and for this change the moral reformers might claim a share of credit.

They could not, however, point to many achievements. The upper classes, despite their interest in moralizing plays, showed no evidence of greater rectitude, and the manners and morals of the lower ranks appeared to be as corrupt as ever. In short, social conditions in the reign of George II seemed no better than at the opening of the century.

A NEW VOICE

Reformers have generally been of two sorts. The first are the system-makers who believe that, in order to improve man, it is necessary to change his environment or the conditions under which he lives. Acting upon this presumption, they have formulated different theories at different times, but in most instances the system-makers have believed that the well-being of mankind depends upon certain laws or a certain type of political or economic organization. Reformers of the second sort believe, on the other hand, that laws and systems have little effect upon the happiness or welfare of mankind. Samuel Johnson expressed this opinion when he wrote:

> How small of all that human hearts endure
> The part that kings or laws can cause or cure.

Those who hold this view are convinced that the nature of society is determined by the character of the individuals who compose it, and that the character of individuals is decided by their innermost convictions. Most religious leaders have been reformers of the latter sort, and to this class belongs John Wesley.

Eighteenth-century England produced many hardy recusants, but none so resolute as Wesley. For more than fifty years he crusaded against vice and irreligion, hoping to convert the nation, not from the Church of England, but from religious torpor and sin. What he wanted was a recovery of former zeal, a renewed emphasis upon certain doctrines, a revival of Christian principles. Although his followers were eventually to break from the Established Church, Wesley had no desire to create a schism. As a reformer he was concerned less with institutions than with the convictions of individuals, for he believed that a change in the inner conscience of men was necessary for salvation.

In emphasizing individual conversion, Wesley differed from most divines of the eighteenth century. Some of them, to be sure, had maintained that a spiritual awakening was necessary both for personal salvation and for the reform of public morality. But most clergymen wanted neither the ardent piety of Puritan times nor the scrupulous concern for conduct that had accompanied it. To have appealed to the inner convictions or the emotions of man, moreover, would have marked them as "enthusiasts," and to the age of reason enthusiasm was at least an intellectual heresy. The typical divine was therefore not inclined to insist upon the zealous practice of religion. As a result the majority of people paid but casual observance to religious forms and possessed no more than a lukewarm faith. Believing only half-heartedly, they might compromise upon a half-hearted performance of works. They were not inclined to stake all upon salvation. Then came Wesley, preaching that men could be saved only by the strongest kind of inner conviction. They could not compromise, he told them, for mere nominal Christianity would result only in damnation.

At the core of his teaching was the doctrine of salvation by faith. Wesley believed that no matter how pious or moral a man might be, he was naturally depraved. Neither infant baptism nor the performance of good works could rescue him. He could be saved from damnation only by experiencing a sudden and supernatural conviction that through the Atonement of Christ his sins had been expiated. Once he had gone through this process of illumination, the convert would hate sin and, hating it, he would be armed against it. This belief was not new to Protestantism, but when Wesley began to preach it as the cardinal principle of Christianity, he gave it a significance which it had not been accorded in England for decades.

In reviving the doctrine of justification by faith, Wesley proved to be not only a great religious leader, but a great moral reformer. Although he believed that strict conformity to moral laws could not itself effect salvation, he constantly asserted that one who had been saved by the new birth would and must abandon vice. If one continued to lead a sinful life, it probably meant that one had not been saved. Reasoning thus, Wesley undertook to reform men in a manner very different from that of the early eighteenth-century moralists who had tried to discipline them without altering their convictions. By his exhortations that those who led sinful lives were eternally damned, Wesley gave men a strong motive for refraining from vice and by making conduct a test of one's regeneration, he placed the burden of discipline upon the individual.

This method of promoting a reformation of manners and morals was to prove much more effectual than the earlier one. However, when Wesley, in 1738, started the Evangelical revival, the advent of a new social order lay in the dim future. No thorough change in standards of conduct could come until a large section of the population altered their views, and the process of converting eighteenth-century England was a difficult one.

Wesley did not underestimate the task which he undertook, but, having a passionate desire to save men's souls, he resolutely pursued his mission. Because he appealed to the emotions and preached the necessity of sudden and dramatic conversion, many people considered him a fanatic. Clergymen frequently denied him the right to speak in their churches, the press constantly satirized him, and upon more than one occasion mobs treated him with violence. But when Wesley was barred from a church pulpit, he preached under the open sky, giving sermons in the market place, on a hillside outside a town, or at the entrance of a mine. To the written attacks upon himself and his fellow

Methodists Wesley often replied, and he was a forceful controversialist. He was also a persuasive speaker, and frequently those who came to scoff remained to pray.

A firm Arminian, Wesley taught that anyone, no matter how sinful, could attain salvation. In this respect he differed from the Calvinistic Puritans of the previous century, who held that only the elect could be saved and that the rest of mankind were irrevocably damned. Because other clergymen had largely neglected them, Wesley made the lower classes his special charge. But, unlike the early eighteenth-century harriers of vice, he never hounded the poor nor treated them with condescension. To Wesley poverty was a sign of man's unconcern with the things of this world. Consequently, he not only drew most of his followers from the humbler ranks of society, but exhorted them to share their possessions and to rejoice in their poverty.[32]

Those who were converted usually remained Methodists, for Wesley was an excellent organizer. Realizing that it was necessary to keep his followers active in the observance of their religious beliefs, he divided them into various groups. There were, first, the religious societies which brought the members together for weekly prayers and devotion. From the societies were formed smaller units called "bands," composed of Methodists who were striving for spiritual perfection. Wesley also instituted "class-meetings," each of which consisted of about twelve persons under the direction of a leader who advised, rebuked, and consoled the members as occasion might require, led them in devotional exercises, and interested himself in their temporal welfare. Occasionally members of different societies met at large gatherings called "love-feasts," at which they partook of simple refreshments, sang hymns, and made avowals of faith. By the help of these various organizations, Wesley bound his followers together in close ties of fellowship, provided a bulwark against

[32] The Quakers, like the Methodists, were interested in the welfare of the poor, and the eighteenth-century Quakers, though not a strongly proselyting group, appear to have had a civilizing influence upon the masses, similar, in many respects, to that exerted by Methodism. See, for instance, Isabel Grubb, *Quakerism and Industry before 1800*, London, 1930.

the scorn of a hostile world, and made Methodism the most vigorous religion in England.[33]

Eager to win adherents, Wesley and his clergymen, many of whom were eloquent speakers, traveled up and down the country, preaching to large audiences in all parts of the kingdom. To promote a national revival of religion, however, Wesley knew that he should not rely solely upon the power of the spoken word, but must attempt to arouse his countrymen by supplying them with exhortative literature. Despite his busy and itinerant life, therefore, he managed to find time to write and edit a good many works.

Wesley was particularly concerned to put cheap and simplified books upon the market. Though the masses, for the most part, were illiterate, thousands of poor people had learned to read in free schools. But what were they to read? Having barely enough for food and shelter, they could not afford a subscription to the *Gentleman's Magazine* or calf editions of the poets. Furthermore, since their education was meager, it was difficult for them to read anything but relatively simple English. Yet this group, as Wesley realized, constituted a potentially significant section of the reading public. He began, therefore, to publish a series of works especially designed for uneducated readers. One of these was a cheap pocket-sized dictionary "to assist persons of common sense and no learning to understand the best English authors." [34] Although it was called *The Complete English Dictionary,* it was neither comprehensive nor scholarly, but it was admirably suited to the purses and the understanding of poor readers.

In order to simplify the text, Wesley frequently revised, abridged, and expurgated the works of well-known writers. Sometimes he felt that he was improving the original by his editing, but his chief purpose was to help the barely literate person to extend his reading range. When he edited Young's *Night Thoughts,* he explained:

[33] *A New History of Methodism,* ed. by W. J. Townsend, H. B. Workman, and George Eayrs, London, 1909, I, 284 ff.
[34] *The Complete English Dictionary,* Bristol, 1764, "Preface."

My design in the following extracts is: 1. To leave out all the lines which seem to me either to contain childish conceits, to sink into prosaic flatness, to rise into the turgid, the false sublime, or to be incurably obscure to common readers. 2. To explain the words which are obscure, not in themselves, but only to the unlearned readers.[35]

In compliance with his second purpose, Wesley appended a glossary to the poem in which he explains such words as "domain," "dreary," "column," and "knell."

As a self-appointed reviser of *Paradise Lost* and other classics, Wesley may appear to have taken undue liberties with the works of great writers, but as an editor of popular editions he was helping to create a new reading public. When he altered the books of older writers, moreover, he was merely following what was a common practice of his age. Having no great reverence for original texts, eighteenth-century editors frequently published imitations, extracts, and adaptations of earlier works. Sometimes, with the permission of the authors, they even changed the texts of their contemporaries. Wesley, for instance, having decided that he would like to publish a revised edition of Henry Brooke's *Fool of Quality,* wrote to the author's nephew, with whom he was acquainted, suggesting his plan. The nephew replied that his uncle was too ill to write himself, but "says he most cheerfully yields the volumes you mentioned to your superior judgment to prune, erase, and alter as you please." [36] Shortly afterwards Wesley published his own version of the novel, deleting at least a third of the original text, omitting the author's name, and changing the title to *The History of Henry Moreland.*

It was unusual for Wesley to publish a novel. While he wished to acquaint new readers with the best English writers, he was concerned that they should read nothing but works which would contribute to their moral or spiritual improvement. *The Fool of Quality* he admired, because it contained numerous homilies and encouraged generosity to the poor, but most novels he con-

---

[35] *An Extract from Dr. Young's Night-Thoughts,* Bristol, 1770, "Preface."
[36] *Arminian Magazine,* X (March, 1787), 166–67.

sidered of little value. He had more esteem for poetry, though he was careful of the selections he placed before his followers. When he published his *Collection of Moral and Sacred Poems* in 1744, he explained that such a work was badly needed:

It has been a common remark for many years that poetry which might answer the noblest purposes has been prostituted to the vilest, even to confound the distinction between virtue and vice, good and evil. And that to such a degree that among the numerous poems now extant in our language there is an exceeding small portion which does not more or less fall under this heavy censure, so that a great difficulty lies on those who are not willing, on the one hand, to be deprived of an elegant amusement, nor, on the other, to purchase it at the hazard of innocence and virtue.[37]

Dedicating his anthology to the Countess of Huntingdon, who had encouraged him to prepare it, Wesley added, "There is nothing therein contrary to virtue, nothing that can offend the chastest ear, or give pain to the tenderest heart." [38] But Wesley was a son of the eighteenth century, and there was little or nothing in any of his works that could be called Victorian prudery. When he expurgated a text, as he frequently did, his chief object was, not to delete coarse terms, but to simplify reading and to remove sentiments which were contrary to his teachings. Most of the poems in his collection, such as Prior's "Solomon," Parnell's "The Hermit," and Roscommon's "Paraphrase of the 148th Psalm," were sufficiently orthodox to need no alteration. When Wesley included poems of which he could not approve in their entirety, however, he customarily omitted the lines that he considered unsuitable. Pope's "Essay on Man," for instance, appeared in the collection with some three hundred lines deleted, for the editor had freely excised not only the deistical views of the poet, but various passages that seemed difficult to interpret. Upon other lines he made certain observations, in order to keep readers from thinking in terms which he considered false. When he came to Pope's

Man never is, but always to be, blest,

[37] *A Collection of Moral and Sacred Poems*, 3 vols., Bristol, 1744, "Dedication."
[38] *Ibid.*

he remarked, "Yes, blessed is the man whose iniquity is for-
given and his sin covered." [39] This sort of editorial comment
was perfectly in accord with Wesley's purpose in providing literature for the masses. He was interested in their improvement,
but he believed that their religious and moral views counted for
more than the mere development of the intellect.

In addition to his revised texts, Wesley published various other
works. About 1745 he issued a series of dissuasives from vice,
similar to those circulated by the S.P.C.K., and with titles such
as *A Word to a Drunkard* and *A Word to a Sabbath-Breaker.* He
also published extracts from his *Journals*, several of his sermons,
and various hymn collections. One of his most ambitious projects
was his "Christian Library." Intended chiefly for Methodist
preachers, this five-foot bookshelf contained sermons, meditations, and numerous biographies of famous divines and religious
laymen from the time of the Reformation.[40] More important,
however, especially for the dissemination of Methodist teachings, was the *Arminian Magazine.* Instituted in 1778, this
monthly periodical was particularly designed to defend the belief that salvation is possible for all, and to refute the doctrines
of election and predestination, which the Calvinists, with renewed vigor, were again promulgating. The *Arminian Magazine* also printed religious poetry, testimonials of faith, and
biographies of various people whose lives had been remarkable
for holiness. Wesley was particularly pleased with the success of
this periodical, and very successful it was, selling many hundreds
of copies more than he had expected.[41]

Works of this kind were bound to reach the Methodists, but
Wesley and his associates wanted to create a more general interest in religious literature. In 1779, therefore, they founded
the Naval and Military Bible Society, to provide pocket Bibles
for sailors and soldiers.[42] A few years later they instituted a sec-

[39] *Ibid.*, I, 301 ft.
[40] Richard Green, *The Works of John and Charles Wesley—A Bibliography,*
London, 1906.
[41] *Arminian Magazine,* Vol. I, "To the Reader."
[42] L. Tyerman, *The Life and Times of the Reverend John Wesley,* New York,
1872, III, 314–15.

ond organization called the Society for the Distribution of Religious Tracts among the Poor. In return for a fee of half a guinea, each member of this association received a quota of tracts for free distribution. Among the works thus circulated were some of Wesley's sermons, extracts from Baxter's *Call* and Alleine's *Alarm,* and various pamphlets cautioning readers against swearing, Sabbath-breaking, and similar practices.[43]

These societies, like the S.P.C.K., were forerunners of the great Evangelical associations of the Victorian period. They were but miniatures of the later ones, however, for religious enthusiasm, though slowly reviving, was not yet much more current than it had been in the Queen Anne period, and with the majority of people moral reformers were still extremely unpopular. In fact, when a second Society for the Reformation of Manners was instituted in 1757, it was even more strongly opposed than its predecessor.

The second vice society, though composed of churchmen and dissenters as well as Methodists, drew its strongest support from the followers of Wesley and Whitefield. Wesley, believing that the organization served a useful purpose, gave it his unqualified approval. In 1763 he preached a sermon to its members, and upon this occasion he mentioned that the society had, in the past five years, prosecuted more than ten thousand persons for swearing, Sabbath-breaking, prostitution, and keeping disorderly houses. The prosecutions ceased shortly after this time, however, for some unnamed enemies of the association trapped its members into making an arrest upon false testimony. This resulted in an expensive suit for damages, which left the second Society for the Reformation of Manners bankrupt and forced its members to disband.[44]

Wesley, writing in his *Journal,* expressed strong regret that the organization had been tricked into dissolution.[45] He had favored it as he favored every plan to promote moral reform, but it was not really in accord with his own methods. Vice societies con-

---

[43] Green, *op. cit.,* p. 217.   [44] Portus, *op. cit.,* pp. 243–50.
[45] *Journal of the Reverend John Wesley,* ed. by N. Curnock, London [1910–17], V, 154.

verted no one, and Wesley's policy was to reform people by converting them. It was a slow method, but it succeeded. Even non-Methodists had, in honesty, to admit that the conduct of Wesley's followers was noticeably superior to that of the masses in general. Wesley never let them forget that the actions of one who had received an assurance of salvation gave evidence of his regeneration, and he constantly exhorted his followers to self-discipline. By their close association with one another in the religious societies, moreover, the Wesleyans were able to keep careful watch upon the conduct of their neighbors, and no doubt fear of censure further helped to discipline their actions.

In his sermons and pamphlets, Wesley warned his adherents that they could not indulge in the popular vices of the day and be true Methodists. No sincere believer could gamble, he said, since it was immoral to attempt to get something for nothing. He not only condemned drunkenness, but forbade Methodists to traffic in liquor, pointing out that it was against their principles to profit by hurting others. He also spoke out against smuggling and political bribery at a time when these practices were common. In fact, few forms of private or public vice escaped his strong censure.[46]

But, ruling on manners as well as morals, Wesley extended his prohibitions to include dancing, card-playing, and love of finery or luxuries of any sort. He himself abstained from tea for twelve years, and he urged his followers to stop using it, because he considered the beverage a luxury and, in addition, bad for the nerves.[47] He wrote a pamphlet called *The Duty and Advantage of Early Rising*, in which he said that six hours of sleep is sufficient for most people. According to Wesley, too much time spent in bed produced various ill effects: it caused nervous disorders, weakness of sight, flabby flesh, and a tendency toward sundry forms of intemperance.

In censoring practices which did not come directly within the sphere of morals, Wesley had in mind two principles of

[46] J. W. Bready, *England: before and after Wesley*, London, 1938, pp. 242 ff., 313–14.

[47] Tyerman, *op. cit.*, I, 522.

Methodism. He considered almost any form of self-indulgence bad—first, because it acted as a deterrent to godliness, and secondly, because it might require money which otherwise could be expended upon the poor. He was also interested in promoting good manners for their own sake and, since he drew his followers from the barbarous multitude, he found it necessary to teach them certain elementary principles of courtesy. This he did by republishing, in several issues of the *Arminian Magazine,* extracts from an old etiquette book called *The Refined Courtier,* which advised against such coarse practices as voiding in public, blowing one's nose vociferously, and breathing into another's face.[48]

Above all Wesley preached industry, sobriety, and devotion to duty, and because his followers practiced these virtues and added others to them, their moral standards did improve. Methodists were seldom seen at cockfights or bear-baiting sessions. Few of them indulged in luxuries of any sort, but their frugality was matched by their generosity to the indigent. If their views were narrow, they had, nevertheless, definite convictions and fixed standards which rescued them from the moral anarchy of their time. If their attitude toward pleasure was puritanical, they were helping, nonetheless, to form the modern Englishman's hatred of grossness and brutality. And for these better standards John Wesley was largely responsible. To a surprising degree his followers accepted his opinions not only in matters of faith, but in the realm of manners and conduct. Methodism, therefore, was more than a sect. It was a culture and a way of life.

By 1780, however, there were only 43,830 Arminian Methodists—too small a group to effect any noticeable change in national character.[49] Perhaps the revival would have proceeded more rapidly if the Methodists had remained a united sect, but the ranks were split when George Whitefield, who had been one of Wesley's first associates, withdrew from the main body of believers. Taking some members with him, Whitefield became the leader of the Calvinistic Methodists. For several years there-

[48] *Arminian Magazine,* Vol. XI (1788).
[49] Tyerman, *op. cit.,* III, 330.

after the two groups constantly assailed each other in pamphlets, and their quarrels undoubtedly furthered the common impression that both cliques were composed of half-mad fanatics.

The chief bone of contention was the question of predestination. Upon most other points the two Methodist sects, despite their mutual animosity, were in agreement. Both believed in justification by faith alone and in conversion by a process of illumination. As far as manners were concerned, both groups exerted about the same kind of influence, for Whitefield, like Wesley, exhorted his followers to practice strict self-discipline and to abstain from worldly pleasures. But the Calvinistic Methodists in Britain were to remain a relatively small body. By 1831, when the Arminians had 2,818 congregations, the Calvinistic Methodists had only 427 congregations, of which 300 were in Wales. The Wesleyans, therefore, being much more numerous, were to have a greater influence upon manners.[50]

A third Evangelical group was slowly forming within the Church of England. Though influenced considerably by Wesleyanism, the revival within the Establishment had its distinctive features. For one thing, the leading figures were usually Calvinists. The most prominent among them was the Reverend John Newton, ex-captain of a slave ship and friend of the poet Cowper. Newton, who was really the leader of the first generation of church Evangelicals, had been influenced by Whitefield, and he in turn became the mentor of many serious persons who were troubled by doubts. After consulting with him they frequently adopted his views upon election and predestination. Several other Evangelical clergymen of the Establishment, notably Henry Venn, William Romaine, and John Berridge, had belonged to a Calvinistic clique of which Lady Huntingdon, the friend of Whitefield, was patroness. Inasmuch as these men converted many to their beliefs, it followed that there was a revival not just of religion, but of the doctrines of Geneva.[51]

[50] J. R. McCulloch, *A Statistical Account of the British Empire*, London, 1839, II, 286.

[51] *A New History of Methodism*, I, 270; James Stephen, *Essays in Ecclesiastical Biography*, "The Evangelical Succession," London, 1849, Vol. II.

In various other respects the church Evangelicals differed from both the Wesleyans and the Whitefieldians. The clergy, instead of becoming itinerant preachers, usually remained in their parishes. Though their religious beliefs were similar to those of the Methodists, they did nothing to break with the Establishment. Their followers, for the most part, belonged to a higher social class than the adherents of Wesley. Because there were no religious societies, bands, or class-meetings to unite the converts scattered in different parishes, the church Evangelicals were not organized as a distinct body of believers. That is, they were not so organized at first. Later on they were to overcome this deficiency by instituting dozens of societies, and with meetings to attend, with errands and missions to perform, the faithful were to have little time for rest or contemplation. In fact, once they had formed a solid phalanx of believers, the church Evangelicals were to become the most aggressive group in the country and the one which would influence manners most.

These days of glory had not yet come, but the middle years of the eighteenth century yielded a few prophetic signs of the future. There was, for instance, a growing interest in religious books, old ones that had gathered dust since the seventeenth century, and new works inspired by the zeal of recent converts. The authors of the latter were often church Evangelicals. James Hervey, one of the first writers to be influenced by the revival, had produced his *Meditations among the Tombstones* shortly before Fielding published *Tom Jones*. The two works had nothing in common except their popularity. Hervey's theme, and he treated it at great length, was the brevity of life and the imminence of death. Despite its lugubrious tone, this work, by 1788, had had twenty-five London printings. Not so successful was Henry Venn's *Complete Duty of Man* (1763), though this book, with its dull and ponderous exposition, appeared in a ninth London edition in 1807. William Romaine's *Life of Faith* (1763), *Walk of Faith* (1771), and *Triumph of Faith* (1795) were also widely read.[52]

[52] *British Museum Catalogue.*

More readable than any of these is Thomas Scott's *The Force of Truth* (1779). "In this narrative," said Scott, "little more is contained than a history of the workings of my heart, that forge of iniquity; and of my conscience, that friendly monitor." [53] Writing with considerable candor, the author traced the steps in his conversion, carefully analyzing the changes in his intellectual and spiritual views. He had become a clergyman, he confessed, because he wished to be free from laborious duties and to have time to read. He had been a rather apathetic divine until he came under the influence of John Newton, the turning point in his life. Developing a serious interest in religion, he went through a slow process of enlightenment while reading Locke's *Reasonableness of Christianity,* Burnet's *Pastoral Care,* William Law's *Serious Call,* the works of Hervey and of several other writers on religious subjects. Finally, after much meditation, Scott became a convinced Evangelical and Calvinist.

The Serious Call, however, was the religious work which most frequently inspired eighteenth-century readers. Although Law was not an Evangelical, his book probably did more to further the revival than any other written in this period. Samuel Johnson found its message so compelling that he changed his convictions after reading it. John Wesley, who published his own version of Law's text, described it as "a treatise that will hardly be excelled if it be equalled, in the English tongue, either for beauty of expression, or for justness or depth of thought." [54] Whitefield, Scott, Venn, Newton, and several other leading Evangelicals developed strong convictions upon reading this book, and several of them confessed that *The Serious Call* first awakened their interest in the religious revival. [55]

Books of this kind were helping to kindle enthusiasm, and the time was not far distant when religious and moral literature would be the steady diet of the general reading public. But no one realized how near that day was. In fact, in 1782, when John

---

[53] *The Force of Truth,* London, 1779, "Preface."
[54] Green, *op. cit.,* p. 29.
[55] *Dictionary of National Biography,* "William Law."

Wesley published his "Estimate of Manners at the Present Time," he took an almost pessimistic view of conditions. After a lifetime spent in crusading against irreligion, he observed,

Ungodliness is our universal, our constant, our peculiar character . . . a total ignorance of God is almost universal among us. The exceptions are exceedingly few, whether among the learned or the unlearned. High and low, cobblers, tinkers, hackney coachmen, men and maid servants, soldiers, tradesmen of all ranks, lawyers, physicians, gentlemen, Lords, are as ignorant of the Creator of the world as Mohametans or Pagans.[56]

No one, perhaps, was better able to take the pulse of the nation than John Wesley, but his diagnosis was incomplete. To be sure, there was on the surface little evidence of improved manners or morals. The upper classes appeared to be as skeptical and dissipated as ever. Most clergymen continued to be somewhat lax about the performance of their duties. The masses, as shown by the Gordon riots, seemed to be no less lawless than heretofore. Nevertheless, conditions were different from those existing fifty years earlier. Those among the lower ranks who had become Methodists had so improved their conduct that they could not be classed with the barbarous multitude. If orthodox clergymen, in the main, continued to be uninterested in the revival of religion, that attitude worked to the advantage of the Evangelicals, for there was no other group competing with them in making proselytes. And the new converts gained each year were making the nucleus of Evangelical believers ever larger. Furthermore, as the penultimate decade was to show, the spirit of the age was beginning to change.

[56] *Works,* London, 1856, XI, 152.

CHAPTER TWO

A DECADE OF INNOVATIONS
1780-1790

IN 1783 the magistrates decided that henceforth criminals condemned to die should be executed in the prison yards instead of being carted to Tyburn. There were to be no more processions to the gallows, with morbidly curious spectators lining the route. To some people, especially to those who believed that the exhibition of culprits served as a deterrent to crime, the abandonment of the old system seemed unwise. When he heard of the new ruling, Dr. Johnson, his work now over and with but one more year to live, flew into a passion. "The age is running mad after innovation," he exclaimed, "all the business of the world is to be done by innovation; men are to be hanged in a new way; Tyburn itself is not free from the fury of innovation." [1]

The old order was indeed changing. All over the civilized world, in the decade of 1780–1790, there were signs and portents of a new era. In America, where three million people had just secured their independence, a government such as men had hitherto only dreamed of was taking shape. From France came rumblings of discontent, prophesying the end of an old regime. In England the agrarian system which had been in effect for centuries was crumbling, the industrial revolution had started, and new discoveries had brought the nation to the threshold of a great scientific age. These changes were bound to influence

[1] J. Boswell, *The Life of Samuel Johnson, L.L.D.*, ed. by G. B. Hill, Oxford, 1887, IV, 188.

manners. Though the political innovations abroad were not to have their repercussion upon English society until the next decade, the new economic order was already affecting the habits and standards of many people.

Perhaps conditions had to become worse before they could get better. At any rate the first effect of both the new agrarian system and the rise of industrialism was to depress the standards of a large section of the population. Under the old agricultural system rural workers had possessed a degree of economic self-sufficiency. Many of them had been freeholders, secure in their right to a cot and a few acres of land. With the development of more scientific methods of cultivation, however, the plots of many freeholders were reclaimed by wealthy landlords to become part of large estates. The new system, while profitable to the owners, brought hardship to the dispossessed rural workers. Although some of them were employed as day laborers, their income was usually reduced, and when it fell below the subsistence level, they were forced to make demands upon the parish rates. As a result these local taxes, which since Elizabethan times had been the principal means of supporting the indigent, rose from approximately two shillings per head of population in 1750 to five shillings in 1785.[2]

In despair, some of the agricultural workers left their own districts, hoping to find employment elsewhere. It was difficult for them to enter towns where work might be obtained, however, for the Settlement Act of 1662 had fixed the responsibility of supporting the poor upon the communities to which they belonged and, at the same time, empowered the overseers of a parish to evict any strangers who might become a charge to the ratepayers. Consequently, many migratory workers and their families, failing to find employment, were forced to become vagrants.[3] There was no John Steinbeck to dramatize the plight of these outcast victims of the economic order, but one of the justices described their condition as follows:

[2] Gilbert Slater, *Poverty and the State,* London, 1930, p. 77.
[3] *Ibid.,* pp. 54 ff.

Idle and disorderly persons of both sexes and of all descriptions are everywhere to be met with, living many of them in a state of perpetual vagrancy, profligate, diseased, and miserable in the extreme; a nuisance and expense to the community, and a standing reproach to the government under which they live.[4]

The growth of the manufacturing industry was also creating grave social problems. Although factory workers generally received higher wages than rural laborers, crowded tenements, the absence of health provisions, and the exploitation of child labor made for miserable conditions of life. Furthermore, the proletariat of the new industrial towns, which were rapidly springing up, especially in the northern counties, were less tractable than artisans and laborers in small communities, and the police were sometimes hard pressed to maintain law and order.[5]

These various problems eventually became a matter of grave concern to the authorities and other members of the upper classes. One thing appeared certain to them: conditions were getting progressively worse. But many people, failing or refusing to see that economic maladjustments were largely responsible for the social ills of the nation, attributed high taxes, vagrancy, and lawlessness to what they considered the degraded and vicious nature of the lower orders. The search for some way to cope with conditions, therefore, led to a renewed interest in a reformation of manners and morals. This approach to the problem of poverty failed, of course, to solve the nation's economic difficulties and, as time went on, distress increased and parish rates continued to rise. Nevertheless, the reform measures that were adopted in the period 1780–1790 were to have an important effect upon manners.

One of the abuses which reformers hoped to correct was drunkenness. In the eighteenth century people of all ranks were accustomed to drinking to excess. Gouty port drinkers, who boasted of being three or four bottle men, usually disturbed no more than the domestic scene, but besotted members of the

---

[4] H. Zouch, *Hints Respecting the Public Police*, London, 1786, p. 2.
[5] Witt Bowden, *Industrial Society in England*, New York, 1925, pp. 211 ff.

lower classes were constantly disrupting the king's peace by their tavern quarrels and lawless depredations. Their favorite beverage was gin. In the old days the common people had been ale drinkers, but since the end of the seventeenth century, when the right to manufacture liquor had ceased to be a monopoly of the Distillers' Company, spirits had become so cheap that vendors guaranteed that a penny's worth would produce intoxication. Consequently, gin became the favored anodyne for all the miseries that plagued the ignorant and poverty-stricken masses:

Not only were there in London and Westminster six or seven thousand regular dram-shops, but cheap gin was given by masters to their work-people instead of wages, sold by barbers and tobacconists, hawked about the streets on barrows by men and women, openly exposed for sale on every market stall, forced on maidservants and other purchasers at the chandler's shop, distributed by watermen on the Thames, vended by pedlars in the suburban lanes, and freely offered at every house of ill-fame.[6]

Although Parliament had attempted earlier in the century to regulate by taxation the consumption of liquor, this method had proved ineffectual. Sterner measures were adopted in the 1780's. The drive began in the industrial districts of the north, where constables and justices of the peace, with the support of leading citizens, closed a number of licensed houses. The newspapers carried accounts of these activities, and the local authorities in other places rapidly adopted similar measures. Soon virtually every county was participating in this temperance movement. Several parishes passed resolutions, warning publicans that they would lose their licenses if they sheltered vagrants or allowed cockfights on their premises. Other towns established the rule that no new licenses should be issued except at the pleasure of the chief taxpayers. At Gloucester, where the rates had risen sharply since the opening of two additional public houses, the principal inhabitants petitioned the authorities to suppress these establishments, and the justices granted their request. A par-

[6] Sidney Webb and Beatrice Webb, *The History of Liquor Licensing in England*, London, 1903, p. 22.

ticular effort was made throughout the country to restrict the hours for selling liquor, and except in London Sunday closing became a regular practice.[7] The most surprising feature of this temperance drive was the whole-hearted favor accorded it by the upper classes. After its long spree, the eighteenth century seemed curiously sobered.

The reformers managed to achieve some of their immediate objectives. Certain communities reduced the number of their taverns by half. In the nation as a whole the total number of licensed houses fell from 37,172 in the year 1779 to approximately 30,000 in 1799.[8] This represented a significant reduction, especially since the population during this time was fast increasing. These statistics do not necessarily prove that the masses were becoming more temperate, but there is other evidence, yet to come, which clearly shows that from this time drunkenness was less prevalent not only among the poor but in all ranks of society.

Various other schemes were employed to discipline the lower classes, but aside from the temperance movement only one of these measures, the introduction of a new system of popular education, was to have an important influence upon manners. Since the establishment of charity schools, almost nothing further had been done to educate the masses. In a few places, to be sure, the authorities had established free schools, supporting them by the local rates. There were also various types of private institutions, but the fees charged made them prohibitive for the poor, most of whom never learned so much as to read simple English. Conditions were very different in Scotland, where almost every town made some provision for educating the common people. Calling attention to this fact, Adam Smith, in *The Wealth of Nations,* had observed that England or any country would benefit from an educated populace:

The more they are instructed, the less liable they are to the delusions of enthusiasm and superstition, which, among ignorant nations, frequently occasion the most dreadful disorders. An instructed and

---

[7] *Ibid.,* pp. 51 ff.   [8] *Ibid.,* p. 80.

intelligent people besides are always more decent and orderly than an ignorant and stupid one. They feel themselves, each individually, more respectable, and more likely to obtain the respect of their lawful superiors, and they are therefore more disposed to respect their superiors.[9]

At a time when the masses appeared to be growing more unruly, the practical advantages of popular education, which the great economist had so well described, particularly impressed the reformers. All that was needed to arouse enthusiasm was a new system which would catch public interest, and Robert Raikes of Gloucester had discovered what he believed to be a novel plan of education. Raikes, who was the owner of the successful *Gloucester Journal,* had for some time been interested in prison reform. After interviewing a good many prison inmates, he had come to the conclusion that the chief cause of crime was ignorance. One Sunday, while entertaining this thought, he happened to see a group of ragged urchins playing in the streets. He inquired about them and learned that the children worked in the pin factories of Gloucester six days a week, and celebrated the seventh by robbing orchards and creating such a din that it was impossible for a respectable citizen to take a Sunday nap. Believing that they must eventually become criminals unless something was done to correct their habits, Raikes decided to round up these ragamuffins and to give them some form of instruction on the Sabbath. For this purpose he instituted what he called Sunday schools.[10]

Raikes's experiment was an important one because it led to the nation-wide establishment of Sunday schools. The idea was not original with him, for these schools had existed in Italy as early as the sixteenth century, and a few English parishes had instituted them shortly before Raikes adopted the plan.[11] The earlier Protestant Sunday schools had no more than a local influence, but those established at Gloucester gave rise to an im-

[9] *The Wealth of Nations,* ed. by E. Cannan, London, 1920, II, 272–73.
[10] J. C. Power, *Rise and Progress of Sunday Schools,* New York, 1871, pp. 33 ff.
[11] W. H. Watson, *The First Fifty Years of the Sunday School,* London [1866], p. 4.

portant movement in education. In his newspaper Raikes advertised the schools intensively, and it was not long before interested persons in other parts of the country learned of them through notices printed in the *Gentleman's Magazine* and other periodicals.

One of those to whom the Sunday school system most appealed was William Fox, a philanthropist who liked to drive about the country distributing free copies of the Bible to the poor. On these journeys he was disheartened to discover hamlets and villages where not one in twenty could read. Hoping to find some way to educate the masses, he had already consulted various persons about forming a society for this purpose when he heard of the Gloucester plan. It seemed to answer requirements, and Fox and his associates decided to found a nonsectarian association to encourage its adoption. The Sunday School Society, thus organized in 1785, within the next ten years helped to establish more than a thousand schools.[12]

It should be remembered that the chief function of Sunday schools during the first fifty years of their existence was to teach children to read. Ordinarily the pupils did not attend any other school, and without these institutions most of them would have remained illiterate. Although Bible reading constituted the main part of the curriculum, as it did in charity schools, the Sunday schools did not at first teach catechism. Needless to say, the children, meeting only one day a week for classes, received but a meager training. After four years, however, they were at least able to read. Raikes described the Gloucester system as follows:

I endeavor to assemble the children as early as it is consistent with their perfect cleanliness—an indispensable rule; the hour prescribed in our rules is eight o'clock, but it is usually half after eight before our flock is collected. . . . After the sermon in the morning they return home to dinner, and meet at the schools at half after one, and are dismissed at five, with strict injunctions to observe a good behavior, free from all noise and clamor.[13]

---

12 Power, *op. cit.*, pp. 60 ff.　　　13 *Ibid.*, pp. 171 ff.

Sometimes the teachers met their classes on other days of the week, giving the brighter pupils a chance to learn writing and arithmetic. These subjects were usually not taught on Sunday, however, and the rules of the Sunday School Society specifically stated that instruction on the Sabbath "should be restricted to reading in the Old and New Testament and to spelling as a preparation for it." [14] This provision expressed the pious belief of many people that to teach any other subject would violate the sanctity of the Lord's Day. But there were expedient as well as pious reasons for limiting instruction. The purpose of Sunday schools was to reclaim the poor from their deplorable habits, not to erase the traditional barriers between classes. There was always the fear that, if they were given very much education, the humble would exalt themselves above the station to which they were born. Even the religious leaders and humanitarians, while strongly in favor of popular education, seldom expressed any interest in the democratic ideal of equality of opportunity. It was clear that the enthusiasm of Sunday school patrons sprang chiefly from a desire to police the poor. That was the purpose Raikes had in mind, and when he described the benefits produced by the schools, he emphasized their disciplinary value, saying:

The good effects of the Sunday schools established in this city are instanced in the account given by the principal persons in the pin and sack manufactories, wherein great reform has taken place among the multitudes whom they employ. From being idle, ungovernable, profligate, and filthy in the extreme, they say the boys and girls are become not only cleanly and decent in appearance, but are greatly humanised in their manners—more orderly, tractable and attentive to business, and of course, more serviceable than they were expected to find them.[15]

Philanthropists like William Fox were equally inclined to stress the prudential reason for founding Sunday schools. They

[14] *A plan of a Society . . . for the Support and Encouragement of Sunday Schools*, London, 1810, p. 14.
[15] J. H. Harris, *Robert Raikes*, New York, 1899, p. 304.

would serve to educate children in religious principles, said Fox, but they would also help "to prevent vice, to encourage industry and virtue . . . and to bring men cheerfully to submit to their station." [16] The same note occurs in the appeal which the Sunday School Society made to secure funds:

This institution may be considered a political as well as a religious one, claiming the attention of those even who, if not particularly zealous in the cause of Christianity, cannot be insensible to the advantages that would accrue to society from the preservation of good order and the security of persons and property.[17]

Even Wesley was apparently inclined to regard Sunday schools chiefly as a means to cope with delinquency. After visiting a Methodist institution at Bingley, he wrote, "I find these schools springing up wherever I go. Perhaps God may have a deeper end therein than men are aware of. Who knows but some of these schools may become nurseries for Christians." [18] Wesley appears to have perceived only vaguely the opportunity that the schools afforded to promote the religious revival. It was not long, however, before other Evangelicals realized that these institutions could indeed serve as nurseries for teaching the younger generation their beliefs.

One of the pioneers in the Sunday school movement was Mrs. Sarah Trimmer, the mother of a large family and a staunch though non-Evangelical churchwoman. She was also the author of various moral tales, educational works, and guides to etiquette, and her tightly laced opinions, as it will appear, helped to shape the standards of the early Victorians. The Sunday schools which Mrs. Trimmer instituted at Brentford probably differed little from such schools elsewhere, but she set herself up as an authority and won such a reputation as an educator that even George III paid a visit to her classes. According to Mrs. Trimmer, some of her pupils who had not known a letter upon entering school were able, in less than a year, to read the Bible proficiently. She was equally proud of the neat appearance the children made. Because many had nothing but rags to cover them, the school

[16] Power, *op. cit.*, p. 78.   [17] *Ibid.*, p. 92.   [18] *Journal*, VII, 3.

provided them with decent apparel to wear on Sundays. But Mrs. Trimmer established the rule that Sunday garments should be issued Saturday night and returned on Monday morning.[19] During the rest of the week it was apparently left to God to temper the wind to the shorn lamb.

The Evangelicals were particularly zealous in the founding of Sunday schools. Rowland Hill, a Calvinistic Methodist, first introduced these institutions in London, and the Wesleyans organized their own society to encourage the movement. The most famous of all Evangelical Sunday schools, however, were those under the direction of Hannah More, the friend of Samuel Johnson and a successful writer of the times. One of her best-liked works was a play called *Percy,* which was first produced in 1777. A decade later, when this drama was revived, Mrs. More refused to attend the performance, for the Evangelicals banned theater-going, and the author of *Percy* had recently been converted. Instead of Dr. Johnson, the Reverend John Newton was now her counselor. She retired from London and its gay society and with her three less celebrated but equally celibate sisters she went to live at Cowslip Green near Bristol. Her withdrawal from the fashionable literary circles of London merely marked the beginning of a new career. Throwing herself into the Evangelical cause, Hannah More was to become its most artful and persuasive writer. Indeed, it is no exaggeration to say that her books and pamphlets, more than any others, paved the highroad to Victorianism.

Hannah More and her sisters, all of whom shared her Evangelical views, established their first Sunday school at Cheddar in 1789. This venture proved so successful that within the next ten years they founded additional schools in twelve different parishes in this region. The Misses More, concentrating upon the moral training of their charges, kept tab upon their conduct even after they left school. But, for the girl graduates at least, virtue had its reward. Provided she could produce a testimonial of good character, each girl who attended Sunday school received on her

[19] Sarah Trimmer, *The Oeconomy of Charity,* London, 1801, I, 315 and *passim.*

wedding day a present of five shillings, a pair of white stockings, and a new Bible. Even an insurance plan introduced by the More sisters was administered with regard to morality. In different parishes Female Benefit Clubs were formed. Members paid a shilling to join and one and a halfpence weekly. Benefits were paid at death, sickness, and childbirth, but as a discouragement to imprudence, a woman was entitled to receive the lying-in award only if she had been married for nine months. Another distinctive feature of the Cheddar plan of education was the meetings held on Sunday evenings for older people of the parish. At these sessions they sang hymns, listened to a sermon, or heard a chapter read from the Bible. Only a few people, drawn by piety, curiosity, or both, had at first attended the gatherings, but eventually a good share of the inhabitants came to them. According to the More sisters a great change was effected in the whole religious tone of this section. Before they instituted their Sunday schools at Cheddar, only about twenty persons normally attended the Sunday services; ten years later the town had eight hundred regular churchgoers.[20]

As a result of these sociological experiments, the inhabitants of the district were said to be much improved in manners and morals. Not all the Sunday school patrons supervised the conduct of the poor so carefully as did Hannah More and her sisters, but wherever schools were established similar claims were made. Although some of these reports should be discounted, there can be no doubt that the Sunday schools did better the standards of the lower classes. It was unfortunate, of course, that this plan of social amelioration was accompanied by an over-paternalistic spirit, and that the founders were so frequently dominated by merely prudential motives. Nevertheless, something was better than nothing. Before this time the chief influence upon poor children had been their home environment, and, because their parents were often ignorant and depraved, it was difficult for the younger generation to escape falling into

[20] Martha More, *Mendip Annals*, ed. by Arthur Roberts, London, 1859, p. 24 and *passim*.

bad habits. But now, coming under the care of a Sunday school teacher, many children learned new standards of conduct. The Sunday School Society stipulated in its rules that pupils must come to class washed and with their hair combed, and directed the teachers to discipline their charges for lying, pilfering, using indecent language, or otherwise misbehaving.[21] Elementary though these lessons were, many children did not learn them at home. Consequently, Sunday school pupils were by comparison almost models of decorum.

Sunday school children were further distinguished by their ability to read. The few books made available to them opened the eyes of many to a new way of life, different by far from the Caliban existence they had known. As early as 1787 Raikes estimated that 250,000 pupils were enrolled in Sunday schools.[22] Eventually the number was to be much larger, but on the eve of the French Revolution more children were being educated than at any previous time, and the fact that the masses were becoming literate was to contribute greatly to the change in the character of English society,

NEW EVANGELICAL ACTIVITIES

The interest which Evangelicals like Hannah More evinced in the Sunday school movement was characteristic of their eagerness to participate in any plan to promote a reformation of manners and a revival of religion. But it was becoming increasingly apparent that the Evangelicals would never be satisfied simply to improve public morality. Like their Puritan ancestors, they censured most types of amusement, distrusting gaiety, suspecting that levity was a brand of impiety, and associating mirth with sinfulness. Sticklers for form, they had a large number of precepts to guide the righteous through the snares of the workaday world and still more rigorous rules for proper conduct on the Sabbath. In short, the Evangelicals, especially those belonging to

21 *A Plan of a Society . . . for the Support and Encouragement of Sunday Schools,* p. 14.
22 Harris, *op. cit.,* p. 215.

the church party, were endeavoring to change the character of
society from one extreme to another, to go from the England
of Hogarth to the England of Victoria.

As strict Sabbatarians, the Evangelicals were particularly
pleased when, in 1781, Bishop Porteus, the only member of the
hierarchy who favored the principles of the revival, introduced
a bill in Parliament to prohibit Sunday evening amusements.
The measure was especially intended to put a stop to gatherings
at Carlisle House, where, for three shillings, patrons could take
refreshment, walk about, and converse with one another. Because he believed that unsupervised discussions of religion led
to skepticism, Porteus further proposed that Sunday evening de-
bating societies be suppressed. Both measures had the support
of Richard Hill, a Calvinistic Evangelical, who delivered his
maiden speech before Commons in favor of them. Although
several non-Evangelical members of Parliament strongly objected to the proposals as intolerant, Porteus finally succeeded
in getting his bill enacted.[23]

There were other signs that the Evangelicals were preparing
the way for their future dominance. In 1783 several of them,
realizing the advantage of a central organization, formed the
Eclectic Society. The members included the Reverend John
Newton; Thomas Scott, author of *The Force of Truth;* John
Clayton, an Independent clergyman of strong Calvinistic convictions; Richard Cecil, a famous Evangelical preacher; and the
wealthy Methodist layman, John Bacon. The Eclectic Society
was typical of many later Evangelical organizations, for while the
church group dominated it, representatives of other sects co-
operated with them. Serving principally as an advisory council,
the Eclectic Society never became very large, but it had an important part in determining Evangelical policies and was responsible for creating some of the great religious and charitable
associations of the early nineteenth century.[24]

The Evangelical cause was further assisted by two popular

[23] *The Parliamentary Debates,* London, 1814, XXII, 262 ff.
[24] *Eclectic Notes,* ed. by John H. Pratt, London, 1856.

authors who knew how to season didacticism with entertain-ment. One of these was Hannah More; the other was the poet, William Cowper. Though more gentle than most Evangelical writers, Cowper frequently scolded the clergy for scanting their duties, denounced Sabbath-breaking, and condemned the pre-vailing freedom of manners. In addition to censuring morals, he helped to spread Evangelical religious doctrines by mingling comments upon the natural evil of man and upon salvation by faith with amusing accounts of life at Olney. He was the one important poet associated with the revival, and, because all sorts of people read his works, Evangelical principles got a hearing among many who otherwise would not have listened to them. The poet himself confessed that his chief purpose in writing was to reform and evangelize readers: "My sole drift is to be useful —a point which, however, I should in vain aim at, unless I could likewise be entertaining. I have therefore fixed two strings to my bow; and by the help of both, have done my best to send my arrow to its mark." [25]

Aside from Cowper, the most distinguished layman to join the Evangelical party was William Wilberforce. Born in 1759, the scion of a wealthy Yorkshire family, Wilberforce, shortly after his twenty-first birthday, was elected to Parliament from Hull. In London, while Parliament was in session, he found time to join in the fashionable pastimes of the day. He gambled, danced, attended Mrs. Siddons's parties, and sometimes, the Evangelicals whispered, stayed up half the night over a bowl of punch. This course of life continued for only a few years. Af-ter a summer spent upon the Continent with Isaac Milner, a Cambridge don and an Evangelical clergyman, Wilberforce de-veloped a more sober disposition. Upon his return to England he made the Reverend John Newton his confidant and, under the influence of this fiery Calvinist, like many others who con-sulted him, the youthful Wilberforce became an Evangelical. Once converted, he had neither the time nor the inclination for wine parties. He renounced the company of Mrs. Siddons and

[25] Thos. Taylor, *Life of William Cowper*, Philadelphia, 1834, p. 96.

began to consort with such serious-minded folk as Bishop Porteus and Hannah More. While he was visiting the pious mistress
of Cowslip Green the plan for her Sunday schools had been
evolved. Wilberforce, after a ride over to see the Cheddar gorge,
had returned to the Misses More and told them that something
must be done to improve the morals of that district. When the
sisters suggested establishing Sunday schools, their wealthy young
guest had immediately offered to finance the plan.[26]

From the time of his conversion Wilberforce, both in Parliament and in private life, was a strenuous worker on behalf of
the revival. In 1787, while brooding upon the corrupt conditions of the age, he came across some accounts of the old Societies for the Reformation of Manners. Much impressed by the
activities of these vigilance organizations, he sounded out several people upon the subject of instituting a new watch and
ward society. His friends encouraged the idea, promising their
support. Then, to prepare public opinion, the king was asked
to issue a special proclamation against vice. Nothing loath,
George III obliged with the following edict:

We do hereby strictly enjoin and prohibit all our loving subjects,
of what degree or quality soever, from playing on the Lord's Day
at dice, cards, or any other game whatsoever, either in public or
private houses. . . . Our further pleasure is, and we do strictly
charge and command all our judges, mayors, sheriffs, justices of the
peace, and all other our officers and ministers, both ecclesiastical and
civil, and all other subjects, to be very diligent and strict in the discovery and effectual prosecution and punishment of all persons who
shall be guilty of excessive drinking, blasphemy, profane swearing
and cursing, lewdness, profanation of the Lord's Day, or other dissolute, immoral, or disorderly practices; and that they take care also
effectually to suppress all public gaming houses, and also all un-
licensed public shows, interludes, and places of entertainment, using
the utmost caution in licensing the same; also to suppress all loose
and licentious prints, books, and publications, dispersing poison to
the minds of the young and unwary, and to punish the publishers
and vendors thereof.[27]

---

[26] R. Coupland, *Wilberforce*, Oxford, 1923.
[27] *Part the First of an Address to the Public from the Society for the Suppression of Vice*, London, 1803, pp. 22–24.

The Proclamation Society which Wilberforce formed to carry out these injunctions was, in many respects, similar to the old Societies for the Reformation of Manners, but it differed from them in that it included several illustrious members who felt no compulsion to keep their identity secret. The Duke of Montagu became the first president, and several other people of noble rank lent their names to the society. The Archbishops of Canterbury and York and seventeen other bishops were also enrolled.[28] Never before did a reform organization have the support of so many distinguished representatives of the hierarchy and nobility. Not since the beginning of the century had there been such a manifestation of reforming zeal.

Still, many members of the Proclamation Society were not Evangelicals, and it would appear that the enthusiasm for this association sprang partly from the hope that it would help to solve the economic difficulties of the nation. Shortly before Wilberforce inaugurated his society, several justices of the peace, meeting at the General Quarter Sessions at Pontefract, Yorkshire, had passed a resolution deploring the fact that "the commission of crimes and offenses hath increased to an alarming degree." [29] To cope with this problem they urged private citizens to form voluntary groups for the purpose of detecting culprits and bringing them to trial. Acting upon this suggestion, several towns in Yorkshire did form vigilance associations. Meanwhile the authorities in other parts of the country, having heard, perhaps, of the Pontefract resolutions, began to stir themselves. In Middlesex the Grand Jury drew up a statement, warning the magistrates to deal harshly with all vagrants, prostitutes, and Sabbath-breakers. A similar statement emanated from the Grand Jury of the City of London, though in this instance the authorities appear to have been principally concerned about the profanation of the Lord's Day.[30]

[28] R. I. Wilberforce and Sam. Wilberforce, *The Life of William Wilberforce,* I, 129–38.
[29] [Samuel Glasse], *A Narrative of Proceeding towards a National Reformation,* London, 1787, p. 17.
[30] *Ibid.,* pp. 23 ff.

Although Wilberforce had planned his society without any knowledge of these measures, he heard about them before the king issued his proclamation and apparently decided that it would be good strategy to have his organization press economic as well as Evangelical reforms.[31] At any rate the society for the first few years of its existence seems to have been equally concerned with problems of vagrancy and with the enforcement of vice laws. Some of the authorities, in fact, assumed that the sole purpose of the king's decree was to discipline the poor. According to William Godschall, a justice of the peace, "The licentiousness designed to be obviated by the Proclamation hath its source in a want of attention to the conduct of the lower degree of people, a want of discipline and employment for the adult, and of instruction of the infant poor." [32] Nevertheless, when the king forbade card-playing on Sunday and ordered his officers to suppress gaming houses and other places of entertainment, he must have intended these injunctions to curb the pleasures of the upper classes.

What Wilberforce and his Evangelical friends wanted, of course, was a reformation of manners in all ranks. Although it does not appear that his society prosecuted anyone belonging to the upper classes, the proclamation gave the Evangelicals an opportunity to condemn corruption in high life. Wesley's *Arminian Magazine,* calling attention to "the deluge of depravity which has been pouring in upon us," blamed "the great and opulent" for having contaminated the manners and morals of the nation. Because the wealthy generally despised religion and neglected to observe the Sabbath, said the writer, servants and other members of the lower classes had lost respect for Christian principles.[33] From a very different source came a similar admonition. Its author was the Duke of Grafton, a notorious rake who had recently been converted. The duke's pamphlet, written specifically to encourage the aims of the Proclamation Society, af-

[31] Wilberforce and Wilberforce, *op. cit.,* pp. 129–38.
[32] *A General Plan of Parochial and Provincial Police,* London, 1787, p. 101.
[33] *Arminian Magazine,* XII (Sept., 1789), 496 ff.

firmed that vice had greatly increased of late years, chiefly because the upper ranks set such a bad example. Inasmuch as "they
were guilty of every excess for which the proclamation called
upon them to punish their inferiors," said Grafton, there could
be no improvement in manners or morals until the superior
classes mended their ways.[34]

Regarding the vices of the upper ranks, few could speak with
greater authority than the aging duke, but for some reason people seemed to be more interested in what Hannah More had to
say upon the subject. In *Thoughts upon the Importance of the
Manners of the Great* she, too, accused the rich of teaching bad
habits to the poor. As an example she cited the practice of instructing servants to tell callers whom one did not wish to receive that the master or mistress was "not at home." A true
Evangelical, Mrs. More denounced all forms of Sunday amusements, even objecting to a stroll in the public gardens and
attendance at concerts, including those devoted to sacred music.[35]

Having reproached the "great" for their bad habits, Hannah
More next assailed them in a book called *An Estimate of the
Religion of the Fashionable World* (1790). Most members of the
upper classes, she wrote, possessed no more than a nominal kind
of Christianity, for they failed to promote piety among their
servants, neglected family worship, and brought their children
up without teaching them proper moral restraints. Furthermore,
many people held the prejudiced view that religion was opposed to politeness, wit, and urbanity. Not even the philanthropic impulse, which the eighteenth century prided itself upon,
escaped the criticism of Hannah More. Every day one read in the
newspapers of munificent subscriptions to hospitals and other
charitable institutions, and one often heard that benevolence
was the reigning virtue of the age, she said, but to be a real virtue, benevolence must spring from religious convictions. In
stressing this point the author was underlining the Evangelical
belief that good works, unaccompanied by faith, could not effect

---

[34] A. H. Fitzroy, Duke of Grafton, *Hints*, London, 1789, p. 9 and *passim*.
[35] *Works*, New York, 1855, V, 181 ff.

salvation. Indeed, the chief purpose of this volume was to interest readers in the principles of the revival.[36]

These books marked the beginning of Hannah More's long series of works devoted to furthering the Evangelical cause. The author had found a new reading public. Or were the same people who had delighted in her plays merely adopting new interests? Certainly they could find little entertainment in either of her denunciations of high society. Yet both books sold extremely well, *Thoughts* reaching an eighth edition in 1792, and *An Estimate* a fifth in 1793.[37] From this it might be inferred that the upper classes were becoming more serious-minded and that some at least were genuinely concerned about reforming their ways. Even outside Evangelical circles there was a new trend, a growing interest in decorum and a slight tendency toward prudery.

NEW MIDDLE-CLASS CONVENTIONS

It is interesting to note that the proclamation of 1787 enjoined the police to suppress "all loose and licentious prints, books, and publications dispersing poison to the minds of the young and unwary." From an examination of earlier proclamations against vice, it would appear that this was the first to forbid the circulation of indecent literature. If this is true, what explains the unprecedented concern for this type of censorship? Very probably, as the wording of the proclamation seems to indicate, the purpose was to protect newly literate readers. Nevertheless, there was evidence that public opinion was becoming somewhat more censorious. Certain speech taboos had been introduced, and many writers had adopted a more circumspect tone than had been customary among authors earlier in the century.

In some quarters manners showed a genuine improvement. This was due not so much to the religious revival as to changing

[36] *Ibid.*, pp. 220 ff.
[37] *Dictionary of National Biography* (hereafter cited as *DNB*), "Hannah More."

social conditions. A period of peace, preceding the American Revolution, had aided commerce, and as business conditions became prosperous, there had emerged a new middle class, which had its own standards. Leslie Stephen described this new stratum of society as follows:

Johnson's Club was to some extent a continuation of the clubs of Queen Anne's time. But the wits of the earlier period who had met at taverns to drink with their patrons were a much smaller and more dependent body. What had since happened had been the growth of a great comfortable middle-class—meaning by middle-class the upper stratum, the professional men, the lawyers, clergymen, physicians, and merchants who had been enriched by the growth of commerce and manufactures; the country gentlemen whose rents had risen, and who could come to London and rub off their old rusticity. The aristocracy is still in possession of great wealth and political power, but beneath it has grown up an independent society which is already beginning to be the most important social stratum and the chief factor in political and social development.[38]

If conduct showed some improvement, the example and influence of men belonging to this newly arisen class merit some credit for the change. Certainly the members of Johnson's circle were, without being priggish, less coarse, more self-respecting, and generally better-mannered than the Queen Anne wits. Johnson, himself, acting as a moral arbiter, exercised a chastening influence upon a large group of acquaintances. At times, of course, he was extremely censorious. Even Hannah More in her pre-Evangelical period had received a wilting blast from him when she mentioned, innocently enough, that she had read *Tom Jones*.[39] But Johnson was no prude. He spoke in candid terms, sometimes using words that would have shocked the euphemistic Victorians. Upon one occasion, when Boswell tried to defend a woman who was, in Johnson's opinion, an adulteress, the great moralist had exclaimed, "My dear Sir, never accustom your mind

[38] *English Literature and Society in the Eighteenth Century*, London, 1904, pp. 192–93.

[39] Wm. Roberts, *Memoirs of the Life and Correspondence of Hannah More*, London, 1834, I, 168–69.

to mingle virtue and vice. The woman's a whore, and there's an end on't." [40]

Joshua Reynolds, another member of Johnson's group, also had the reputation of being an arbiter of conduct, and, according to Joseph Farington, he and a small circle of his artist friends had an important influence upon manners. Perhaps Farington overestimated the contribution of this set when he wrote about it fifty years later. Nevertheless, it is interesting to note his general observation upon the changing standards of the period about 1770:

At this time a change in the manners and the habits of the people of this country was beginning to take place. Public taste was improving. The coarse familiarity so common in personal intercourse was laid aside, and respectful attention and civility in address gradually gave a new and better aspect to society. The profane habit of using oaths in conversation no longer offended the ear, and bacchanalian intemperance at the dinner-table was succeeded by rational cheerful ness and sober forbearance.[41]

These changes must have been confined to the social stratum which Leslie Stephen describes, and even in this class manners had probably not been altered as much as Farington would lead one to believe. To be sure, cultivated people highly esteemed courtesy and civility, and Johnson would not have tolerated irreverent language. But Boswell and other members of the group who were fond of the bottle sometimes appeared at polite gatherings in a bacchanalian humor. On the other hand, drinking habits had apparently improved somewhat since the previous generation, for Dr. Johnson remarked that people drank less than their ancestors, explaining that it was due "to the change from ale to wine." Whether or not this was the cause,

[40] Boswell, *Life of Johnson*, II, 247. It now appears that Johnson used such expressions much more frequently than the reader of Boswell's *Life* might infer. Writing about 1790, the famous biographer apparently felt compelled to "Bowdlerize his hero," in order that certain frank expressions of Johnson would not offend the more prudish tastes of late eighteenth-century readers. See *Private Papers of James Boswell from Malahide Castle*, ed. by Geoffrey Scott and Frederick Pottle, privately printed, 1928–34, VI, 191 ff.

[41] *Memoirs of the Life of Sir Joshua Reynolds*, London, 1819, p. 55.

conditions differed from those of his youth, "when all the *decent* people in Litchfield got drunk every night, and were not the worse thought of." [42]

In this statement Johnson implies that public opinion had grown somewhat more censorious. No doubt it had, but it was still very tolerant. Writers commonly expressed themselves in frank terms without shocking any large group of people. Fielding and Smollett, though quite as outspoken as the Queen Anne wits, were popular authors, and the typical eighteenth-century reader found nothing offensive in their novels. Even works that were definitely bawdy circulated freely. To mention only a few, there was in the 1780's an annual publication called *Harris's List of Covent Garden Ladies*. This work, which "was sold openly in booksellers' shops," contained erotic descriptions of various whores. Apparently it served as an advertising medium for those who were seeking a larger clientele. Another publication of this type, called the *Ranger's Magazine,* was introduced as late as 1795. In it, besides a directory of high-priced prostitutes, were to be found ribald stories under such provocative captions as: "The Annals of Gallantry—Essence of Trials for Adultery—Crim Con—Seduction—Choice Anecdotes—Warm Narratives —Curious Fragments—Amatory Histories of Tête à tête—and Wanton Frolics." [43]

The fact that such works were allowed to circulate shows that neither the law nor public opinion exercised much censorship. Nevertheless, if Victorian standards had not yet arrived, the transition in taste had begun. This was nowhere more apparent than in the sentimental literature of the time. Ever since Richard Steele had introduced audiences to sentimental comedy, this type of drama had been popular, and eventually many novelists and essay writers had adopted a sentimental tone. There was even a *Sentimental Magazine,* which, upon its introduction in 1773, had made an appeal for subscribers with the following unctuous statement:

[42] J. Boswell, "Journal of a Tour to the Hebrides," *Life of Johnson,* V, 59–60.
[43] Francis Place, B.M., Add. MSS 27,825, section 17.

What was caviare to the last century will promote disgust in this. As we have increased in politeness, we have likewise increased in the chastity of our literary productions. . . . Our ancestors placed their amusement in laughter, we place ours in chastity of sentiment. If they were more witty, they were less modest than us.

This assertion, so solemn, and so full of cant, to say nothing of its bad grammar, was nonetheless indicative of a new trend in literature. Many authors of the late eighteenth century had adopted a similar tone. As a literary genre, sentimentalism had little to recommend it, but its popularity might be taken as evidence that many readers, while not very critical of style, really wanted a literature that avoided coarse expressions and blatantly vulgar themes. These requirements the sentimental writers fulfilled. They took pains to pay an eloquent if somewhat tawdry tribute to virtue, and their language, though florid, was generally most circumspect. No lady, no matter how delicate her sensibilities, had cause to blush when seeing a sentimental comedy or reading a sentimental novel. And the fact that there were now a large number of women readers helps to explain the new trend in literature and manners.

The number of women readers had apparently started to increase toward the end of the seventeenth century, and the frequent jibes at learned ladies made by writers in the Queen Anne period show that women were, more and more, cultivating intellectual interests.[44] From this time, too, there were more women authors, most of whom, whether they wrote novels, plays, or poetry, generally eschewed vulgar themes and ribald language. More important, however, so far as the ultimate change in the tone of literature and manners was concerned, was the growing army of women readers.

"All our ladies read now," said Samuel Johnson in 1778.[45] To older people, who could remember the time when needlework was the chief sedentary occupation of many women, this fact seemed almost phenomenal. But it was not difficult to explain.

[44] Marjorie Nicolson, "The Microscope and English Imagination," *Smith College Studies in Modern Languages*, XVI, 37 ff.
[45] Boswell, *Life of Johnson*, III, 333.

Boarding schools, which had become extremely popular after the middle of the eighteenth century, were educating thousands of young women. These institutions were particularly favored by the socially ambitious daughters of the newly wealthy middle class. But even a comparatively poor tradesman could afford to educate his daughters, for there were several inexpensive boarding schools which offered a curriculum closely modeled after that of the more exclusive seminaries. Calling attention to this fact, a grumpy contributor to the *Sentimental Magazine* observed:

Every village in the neighborhood of London has one or two little boarding-schools, with an inscription over the door: "Young Ladies Boarded and Educated." The expense is small and hither the blacksmith, the ale-house keeper, the shoemaker, etc. sends his daughter, who from the moment she enters these walls becomes a young lady. . . . Surely the plan of these schools ought to differ as much from that of the great schools intended for the daughters of the nobility and gentry as the stations in life of the scholars differ fron one another. This is, however, so far from being the case that, the article of expense excepted, the plan is the same; and the daughter of one of the lowest shopkeepers at one of these schools is as much miss and young lady as the daughter of the first viscount at the other.[46]

In boarding schools young ladies learned to do simple sums, to write a fair hand, and to read the more elegant English authors. French was also a favorite subject, though most of the pupils probably acquired no more than a smattering of this language. A great deal of attention was given to etiquette and refined accomplishments, and until she had learned dancing, deportment, and proper carriage, no young lady could consider her education complete. It was to the teaching of these niceties to girls of the lower middle class that the writer in the *Sentimental Magazine* objected. Arguing that it was a poor way to train girls to become "frugal housewives to honest tradesmen," he remarked, "It would be of much more consequence they should be well instructed in how to wash the floor than to dance upon it." [47] How many floors went unwashed or how many honest husbands were neglected

[46] *Sentimental Magazine*, I (July, 1773), 209–10.   [47] *Ibid.*

while boarding-school wives languished over novels is not on record, but the fact that thousands of young women had become readers was to be of great consequence.

Relatively few writers in the first part of the eighteenth century had addressed their thoughts exclusively to women. To be sure, there had been various periodicals for ladies, but most of these were extremely short-lived.[48] Even the occasional publication that was designed for female readers might not differ very much from works intended for masculine interest. Consider, for instance, the *Ladies' Magazine,* or the *Universal Entertainer,* which was introduced as late as 1749. A typical eighteenth-century miscellany, it makes no presumption that the taste of women differs in any way from that of men. Nor did it attempt to engage the interest of women by even such obvious appeals as printing recipes, articles on dress, or items of domestic economy. It introduced itself as "a most innocent, diverting and profitable entertainment for young masters and mistresses by giving them an early view of the polite world." But the polite world of the mid-eighteenth century was not very circumspect, and the magazine contained various ribald allusions. Commenting upon this fact, Francis Place observed that the magazine was printed on a good grade of paper, showing that it was intended for readers of the upper ranks. From this he concluded, very justly, that "the examples of grossness, therefore, are not the result of wit, as caused by going out of the way to pander to the appetite of the vulgar, but are such as respectable people admitted without complaint and consequently were to them not exceptional." [49]

When, with the development of boarding schools, the number of women readers greatly increased, publishers were quick to take account of the fact that they had a new and what might prove a very profitable market for literature. There was a distinctly different tone to the *Ladies' Magazine,* or *Entertaining Companion for the Fair Sex,* which appeared in 1770. Making a pro-

[48] Bertha M. Stearns, "Early English Periodicals for Ladies," *Publications of the Modern Language Association* (hereafter cited as *PMLA*), XLVIII (March, 1933).

[49] B.M., Add. MSS 27,825, p. 90.

found bow to feminine readers, the editors introduced the periodical with the following remarks:

As your sex is in this age more employed in reading than it was in the last, it is something surprising that no periodical production should at present exist calculated for your particular amusement, and designed to improve as well as to delight.

There is a kind of elegance appropriated to the fair sex which is overlooked in compositions intended for men, but it is necessary to fix your attention or gain your applause. . . . It is intended in this collection to present the sex with most elegant patterns for the tambour, embroidery, or every kind of needlework. . . . Interesting stories, novels, tales, romances, intended to confirm chastity and recommend virtue will be displayed to the inspection of reason; and the housewife as well as the peeress shall meet with something suitable to their different walk in life.[50]

As the style of the foregoing passage shows, the periodical was marked by the sentimental tone then at its height. Sometimes it contains a coyly salacious note, as when it warns ladies that May is the month when the passions are most easily excited and they must, at this time of year, put a double guard upon their chastity. But it has none of the coarseness of the earlier ladies' magazine and, with its instructions in needlework and domestic economy, it is as feminine as the *Ladies' Home Journal* or *Woman and Home*. Apparently it was a great success, for it lasted nearly fifty years.

Writers were equally aware that women readers were now very numerous, and, because the boarding-school miss particularly enjoyed fiction, a great many novels were produced for her entertainment. In these novels women were almost invariably portrayed in a flattering light. The hero might be a scamp whose reformation occurred only in the final chapter. But the heroine, however beset by adversity, was a pattern young lady. Her virtue was impregnable; her delicacy never failed. Indeed, as the authors of *Pamela's Daughters* have shown, the prudish Victorian heroine figured just as frequently in novels of the eighteenth century as she did in those of the following period.[51]

[50] *Ladies' Magazine*, I, 3-4.
[51] See R. P. Utter and G. B. Needham, *Pamela's Daughters*, New York, 1936.

How much the familiar heroine of fiction influenced the conduct of women, it is impossible to say. But no doubt young ladies of the late eighteenth century endeavored to fashion themselves after Pamela and Evelina with as much devotion as today's adolescents give to their favorite actress of the films. Readers of Jane Austen will recall that both *Northanger Abbey* and *Love and Freindship* poke fun at girls who try to be heroines. Another novel, Eaton S. Barrett's *The Heroine,* exploits the situation at even greater length, for the whole plot is concerned with a young woman who, after a surfeit of novels, goes into the world and tries to live according to the following formula:

A heroine is a young lady, rather taller than usual, and often an orphan; at all events possessed of the finest eyes in the world. Though her frame is so fragile that a breath might scatter it like chaff, it is sometimes stouter than a statue cast of iron. She blushes to the tips of her fingers, and when other girls would laugh, she faints. Besides, she has tears, sighs, and half sighs at command, lives a month on a mouthful, and is addicted to pale consumption.[52]

One thing seems certain. If novel-reading served no other purpose, it increased the vocabulary of its fair addicts and made them more discriminating in speech. In 1791 Miss Anna Seward, the Lichfield poetess, observed that in the company of some ladies of Burton she had heard several words like "hilarity," "stipulate," "contemporary," and "phenomenon" used with easy familiarity. "Twenty years ago," she added, "scarce any of these words would have been understood, much less used, by the generality of private gentlewomen." [53]

If women were using new and longer words, they were also dropping certain old expressions. In the same year that Miss Seward made her observation, a writer in the *Gentleman's Magazine* remarked:

All our mothers and grandmothers used in due course of time to become *with-child,* or as Shakespeare has it, *round-wombed* . . . but it is very well known that no female, above the degree of a chamber

---

[52] *The Heroine*, London, 1909, p. 39.
[53] E. M. Symonds, *Side-Lights on the Georgian Period*, London, 1902, p. 89.

maid or laundress, has been *with-child* these ten years past; every decent married woman now becomes *pregnant;* nor is she ever *brought-to-bed,* or *delivered,* but merely at the end of nine months, has an *accouchement;* antecedent to which she informs her friends that at a certain time she will be *confined.*[54]

According to this writer neither men nor women, except of the very lowest class, used the word "sweat." For some time it had been noticeable that a person with any degree of refinement "merely perspires." There were "a thousand other instances" of similar changes in speech, said this observer. These he does not list, but he concludes, "We are every day growing more delicate, and, without doubt, at the same time more virtuous; and shall, I am confident, become the most refined and polite people in the world." [55]

In making this prediction the contributor to the *Gentleman's Magazine* uses a somewhat bantering tone and throughout the article he speaks half in jest. But jesters oft prove prophets. Although the changes in customs and habits, like the political and economic innovations of the decade 1780–1790, were as yet tentative and experimental, the day was not far distant when euphemisms would be substituted for many terms which had hitherto been used unblushingly, when the Evangelicals would dictate the moral standards of the middle class, and when, through the influence of Sunday schools and similar institutions, even the poor would become respectable. All that was needed in this time of flux was some shock to set the nation firmly upon a new course, and that was to come with the French Revolution.

[54] *Gentleman's Magazine,* LXI (Dec., 1791), 1100.   [55] *Ibid.*

CHAPTER THREE

REFORM OR RUIN

THE WHOLE COURSE of English history was profoundly affected by the French Revolution. Indeed, it is almost impossible to exaggerate the influence of that event upon English thought and its consequent effect upon English policies and customs. During the decade 1790–1800, as the Revolution increased in violence, people in authority became progressively more alarmed, fearing that England might suffer the contagion of democratic principles. Ordinarily the ruling classes might have been inclined to make some concessions to the liberals, with the hope of averting a popular uprising. But those in power had seen the Revolution start in France with the introduction of relatively mild political reforms, only to proceed to the most drastic and cruel measures. Fearing that any compromise with the demands of English liberals might set Britain upon a similar course, the authorities were driven to adopt an extremely reactionary stand. As a result, changes which might otherwise have been introduced at this time—a reform of the rotten borough system, the extension of the franchise, and restoration of rights to Catholics—were put off for another generation. Liberal opinion was stifled, and a powerful opposition to theories of political reform became the basis of a new and inflexible conservatism.

But this conservatism was not limited to the sphere of economic and political life. It penetrated the whole social fabric of the country, modifying old customs and altering standards of behavior. To be sure, other circumstances had an important share in causing manners to change—the reforms undertaken in the previous decades of the eighteenth century, the development of popular education, and the flourishing of Evangelicalism. But these movements were themselves affected in one way or another as the reverberations from across the channel grew louder.

To a large degree, conservative opinion was consciously created by those in power. Using propaganda with great effectiveness, they produced a mass of doctrinaire literature to convince their countrymen that it would be folly to adopt democratic ideas of government or to part with traditional British institutions. The propaganda was no less concerned with urging social conservatism.. Like Burke, the great spokesman of all who were strongly opposed to the principles of the French Revolution, the ruling classes considered that event a great moral disaster. Seeing in France what they believed to be the collapse of a civilization, they were impressed by the idea that the stability of a nation depended not only upon the maintenance of law and order, but upon the character of its manners. This was Burke's view when he wrote:

Manners are of more importance than laws. Upon them in a great measure the laws depend. The law touches us but here and there and now and then. Manners are what vex or soothe, corrupt or purify, exalt or debase, barbarize or refine us, by a constant, steady, uniform and insensible operation, like that of the air we breathe in.[1]

In France, said Burke, a licentious system of manners was born of the French Revolution. In England a conservative system of manners was to be fathered by the reaction to that revolution. Although it would require a few more decades for Victorianism to become general, the period 1790–1800 marked a turning point in English social history. By the beginning of the nineteenth century many customs that had long prevailed were disappearing, and new standards of conduct were taking their place. From this time nothing was to impede the development of Victorianism, for propaganda, aided by certain attendant cir-

[1] Edmund Burke, "Letters on a Regicide Peace," *Works,* London, 1803, VIII, 172.

cumstances, was rapidly forming strict public opinion upon questions of manners and morals. To understand the changes which occurred in English social life, therefore, one must examine various forms of propaganda issued in the last decade of the eighteenth century.

ANTI-JACOBIN PROPAGANDA

Even among the propertied classes there had been considerable sympathy for the French Revolution when it first began. Then, late in 1790, Burke had published his *Reflections on the French Revolution,* condemning the Jacobins for so completely razing the basic structure of society and pointing to some of the more frightening consequences of their drastic measures. With the publication of this book, sympathy for the Jacobins began to give way to distrust, and when Paine answered Burke in *The Rights of Man* distrust yielded to alarm, for Paine not only defended the principles of revolution, but attacked many British institutions and urged the necessity of radical reforms in the English system of government. What most disturbed people of the ruling class was the fact that *The Rights of Man,* published in a cheap pamphlet edition, was finding numerous readers among the factory proletariat, miners, and those generally who constituted the barely literate fringe of the population. Within a year after it was published, this strongly persuasive work was estimated to have sold 200,000 copies.[2]

The report that the lower classes were avidly reading *The Rights of Man* particularly alarmed the ministry, who recalled the author's contribution to the American Revolution. Still more vivid in their minds was the example of France, where popular sentiment, aroused by republican writers, had flared into revolt against the established system of government. Determined to avert a similar course of events in England, Pitt's ministry decided to outlaw the works of Paine and any other writings that appeared to menace the existing order. The English reign of terror began when the king issued a proclamation instructing his

[2] M. D. Conway, *The Life of Thomas Paine,* London, 1892, I, 346–47.

officers to apprehend printers and writers of seditious books and pamphlets. Paine escaped to France just in time to avoid arrest, but his publishers were seized and sentenced to prison. Other authors who had expressed sympathy for Jacobin principles were tried and convicted. It became dangerous even to utter a casual remark in criticism of the government, for spies were posted widely, and more than one person received a harsh sentence for having spoken indiscreetly in a tavern or on the street. Under these conditions, free speech and freedom of the press ceased to be rights of Englishmen.[3]

At the same time, in order to counteract any influence liberals might have had, a group of loyalists founded the Association for Preserving Liberty and Property against Republicans and Levellers. While this organization professed that it had no connection with the government, liberals believed, and with excellent reason, that its members were tools of the ministry. Its founder appears to have been John Reeves, a lawyer who had recently returned from an appointment as chief justice in Newfoundland. At any rate Reeves was chiefly responsible for shaping the policies of the association, which had its first meeting in November, 1792, at the Crown and Anchor Tavern. At this gathering the members passed a resolution, declaring that the purpose of their society was to oppose "the circulation of mischievous opinions . . . conveyed in the terms 'the rights of man,' 'no king,' 'no parliament,' and others of like import." To accomplish this aim it was proposed, first, to organize loyalist groups throughout the country; secondly, to suppress seditious publications; and thirdly, to publish and circulate propaganda in defense of the established system of government.[4] In pursuing these objectives during the next two years, the members of the association showed a surprising knowledge of the technique of propaganda.

Everywhere loyalists were eager to join the crusade against Jacobinism, and within a short time, under the direction of

[3] *Ibid.*, II, 127 ff.

[4] *Association Papers*, London, 1795, "Proceedings"; *Gentleman's Magazine*, XCIX (Nov., 1829), 468–69.

Reeves and his London associates, they formed a network of
branch societies throughout the country. Almost every town and
many small villages must have had one, for in less than a year
there were 2,000 of these local organizations.[5] Acting as vigilanti,
the members assiduously searched the shelves of bookshops for
copies of *The Rights of Man* and eavesdropped in the tavern and
in the market place for any expression of sympathy with republican ideas. Many of them, believing that they had discovered
dangerous and seditious plots, sent reports to the central London
association. Their correspondence, which is preserved at the
British Museum, is an amazing record of public sentiment. A
resident of Bristol notified Reeves that a local bookseller named
Samuel Johnson was selling the works of Paine; a Liverpool
loyalist wrote that in his town a group of schoolmasters and dissenting ministers had just formed a Jacobin society; from a London correspondent came word that a bookseller opposite Covent
Garden had "for sail **Payn** books and treasonable songs"; more
literate but equally alarmed, a member of the association at
Swansea announced that some leveler had recently chalked up
"NO KING" upon several houses.[6]

To accomplish its second objective, the suppression of seditious works, the London association employed professional spies
to visit bookshops and to report anyone selling Jacobin books or
pamphlets. When, by this means, Reeves and his associates had
secured evidence against a bookseller, they turned their information over to the government or themselves instituted a prosecution. As a result, several publishers were found guilty of selling *The Rights of Man* and similar works, and some of them were
sentenced to as much as three or four years in prison.

The chief business of Reeves's association, however, was to
print and circulate anti-Jacobin propaganda. It was quickly realized that short pamphlets, which could be turned out at small
cost and in large quantities, were the most effective type of publication. There was no dearth of writers, for patriots and aspir-

5 *Association Papers*, p. v.
6 B.M., Add. MSS 16,919, f. 19; 16,920, ff. 14 and 49.

ants to authorship were eager to enlist in the pamphlet war, and anti-Jacobin essays, ballads, and sermons poured into the headquarters of the London association. Several of these were selected for publication in pamphlets that sold for a penny.[7]

The association had several ingenious schemes for distributing these pamphlets. It sent consignments of them to the branch societies, which served as convenient depots of supply for local areas. It mailed bundles of tracts to the country clergy and magistrates, knowing that they could be relied upon to circulate them. Coffeehouses, taverns, and barber shops received allotments for their patrons. Some of the more industrious members of the association even stitched anti-Jacobin pamphlets into copies of periodicals before they were sent to their subscribers. Moreover, patriots who lived in fear of revolution ordered large lots of the cheap tracts to give away. Employers frequently passed them out among their workers, and other loyalists thrust them into the hands of pedestrians on the streets. Widely distributed by such methods, the anti-Jacobin pamphlets inevitably reached a large number of readers—more, certainly, than ever read Paine.[8]

The pamphlet writers made a special attempt to convince the lower classes of the folly of equalitarian doctrines. To compete with the popular style of *The Rights of Man*, they frequently tried writing in a colloquial vein. One of them, for instance, composed a series of letters in which two rustics exchange views upon the newfangled notions of republicans and levelers and heartily condemn them. But the propaganda was not intended for the poor alone. Pamphleteers did their best to convince Englishmen of all classes that Paine was a scoundrel and that his republican ideas were false. Britons already possessed liberty, they maintained, and equality was a foolish dream, quite unnatural to the laws of society. Playing upon ancient prejudices, the writers denounced the French as traditional enemies who had tried to outwit John Bull at every crisis in history. Appealing to na-

[7] B.M., Add. MSS 16,919–16,928.
[8] *Ibid.*, particularly "Hints on Proceedings," MS 16,926, f. 37.

tionalism with hearty bluffness, they asked Englishmen if they wished to follow the example of French knaves and rascals. In some of the pamphlets rebellion was made to appear as typical of the French as hand-kissing or foppery. What, it was asked, had a nation of beefeaters to do with any of these Gallic affectations? [9]

Several writers of established reputation engaged in the pamphlet war upon Jacobinism. Arthur Young, the famous agricultural economist, sent the association his essay called *The Example of France, a Warning to Britons.* William Paley, the theologian, contributed a sedative called *Reasons for Contentment.* The poor, he argued, really had an enviable position, for they had none of the cares of the wealthy and governing classes and their only responsibility was to accept their lot without grumbling.

The most successful of all the pamphleteers was Hannah More, who became an anti-Jacobin writer at the instigation of Dr. Beilby Porteus, Bishop of London. Alarmed at the prospect of a revolution in England, Porteus had asked her to write something in a popular vein which would appeal to the lower orders. This she did, publishing *Village Politics* under the pseudonym of Will Chip. It was immediately popular among all ranks of society. Even the royal family read it with pleasure. Delighted with the success of the work which he had himself suggested, Bishop Porteus wrote to its author:

Village Politics is universally extolled; it has been read and greatly admired at Windsor and its fame is spreading over all parts of the kingdom. I gave one to the Attorney-General, who has recommended it to the Association at the Crown and Anchor, which will disperse it throughout the country.[10]

And so it happened that *Village Politics* soon afterwards appeared among the publications of Reeves's anti-Jacobin society. According to the biographer of Hannah More, the government thought so highly of her effort that it purchased several thousand copies to distribute among its subjects. It was easily the most popular of all the anti-Jacobin pamphlets. Indeed, no other

[9] *Association Papers.*

[10] William Roberts, *Memoirs of the Life and Correspondence of Hannah More,* London, 1834, II, 348.

work of any sort seems to have been so widely read at the time.[11]

Inasmuch as *Village Politics* advanced the typical loyalist arguments against republicanism, its popularity must have been due to the novelty of having such sentiments cast in the form of dialogue. The work, to be sure, was skillfully contrived to interest even the uneducated reader. No one could fail to understand the discussion which took place in *Village Politics* between Jack Anvil, the blacksmith, and Tom Hod, the mason. And no one could escape seeing that Tom, who had been reading the works of Paine, was badly worsted in his attempt to uphold the cause of equality and the rights of man. In the end, even Tom had to agree with loyal Jack that it was fitter to be a free Englishman than to aspire to equality with one's betters or to embrace other wrong-headed notions of the French.

Another form of propaganda issued by the association is of particular interest. Ballads, aggressively anti-Jacobin in tone, were often included in its pamphlets. The verses to these songs had been contributed by some of the more lyrical loyalists, but only the words were new, for they were to be accompanied by the music of old favorites like "Hearts of Oak" and "Derry Down." It was an adroit method of spreading anti-Jacobin sentiment, since even the illiterate could learn the verses when they were sung to familiar tunes. Typical of these political ballads was one called "A Word to the Wise":

> Come hither, dear countrymen, listen to me.
> I'll cure your diseases without bribe or a fee,
> And expose the vile tricks of those scoundrel French quacks.
> Whose nostrums would make us their porters and hacks.
> > Derry down, *etc.*
>
> · · ·
>
> Tom Paine told them once how to ruin our fleet,
> 'Tis this which makes him and Monsieur so sweet.
> But they and their cronies in malice and sin,
> Had best catch the beast e'er they dare sell his skin.
>
> · · ·

---

[11] H. Thompson, *Life of Hannah More*, London, 1837, p. 136.

Our tars are true-hearted, our soldiers are brave,
And who that is British will e'er be a slave,
Assisted by heaven in so righteous a cause,
We'll die for our king, our freedom, and laws.[12]

To popularize the loyalist songs, members of the association distributed them among the itinerant ballad singers of London. Those street musicians who were so indiscreet as to sing anything else were hauled up before a magistrate for a reprimand. Then they would be given some of the patriotic ballads, with the promise that the police would not molest them so long as they sang songs in praise of king and country. Although the association was not trying to effect a moral reformation, it helped, incidentally, to drive out of existence the old ditties which celebrated bawdry and thieving. When street singers were forced to adopt loyalist songs, people forgot the old ballads, and the new generation never learned them. Consequently, said Francis Place, the picaresque and lewd songs which had delighted the eighteenth-century populace were no longer heard by 1820.[13]

At every turn the association found the agents of the government eager to coöperate with them in this manner. But just what was the connection between Reeves and the ministry? At the time, it was believed that the members of the association were hirelings of Pitt, but that was not exactly the situation. Although Reeves anticipated political favors from the government, it had not employed him to start the Association for Preserving Liberty and Property. He was a place-seeker rather than a pensioner. But the ministry was grateful for his assistance, and Reeves eventually secured the appointment of printer to the king, a lucrative office which he had himself named as the reward due him for his services as unofficial minister of propaganda.[14]

Reeves's associations continued in existence for only a few years, for they soon accomplished their purpose. So well had they succeeded in creating anti-Jacobin sentiment that in some

[12] *Association Papers,* section 4.
[13] B.M., Add. MSS 27,825, pp. 144–45.
[14] "Windham Papers," B.M., Add. MSS 37,825, pp. 32 ff.

places the common people, who had most to gain by the introduction of liberal reforms, burned Tom Paine in effigy. If *The
Rights of Man* had made a few converts in England, the masses
were definitely not in favor of its democratic theories of government. Ardent loyalists for the most part, they showed no inclination to rebel against the government. In fact, as a result of
anti-Jacobin propaganda, the only popular disturbances were,
ironically, the riots that occurred when mobs entered the premises of alleged republicans and destroyed their property.[15]

Nevertheless, the country did not regain its calm. On the
contrary, England was entering upon one of the most critical
periods in its history. Pitt's government had gone to war with
France, and, except for brief intermissions, the war was to continue until the final defeat of Napoleon. Internally conditions
remained unsettled, for crop failures, the high price of grain,
and unemployment added to the distress of the masses. Yet the
Tories did nothing to improve the situation. Instead, by capi-
talizing upon untoward events, they kept the country in a perpetual state of alarm, in order to defeat any liberal movement,
and so successful was their propaganda that people became
afraid of any form of liberalism, including freedom of manners.

ALARMS AND EXCURSIONS

As the French Revolution reached its more violent stage,
many Englishmen were convinced that the rise of republicanism
meant the end of all traditional institutions. Jacobinism was a
system, said Burke, and he voiced the fear of conservative think-
ers when he wrote, "If that system is not destroyed in France,
it will infallibly destroy the present order of things from one
end of Europe to the other." [16] Certainly the revolutionists in
France were making a clean sweep. They had abolished royalty,
executed the king and queen, and sent thousands of others to
the guillotine. Not content with destroying every vestige of the

[15] M. D. Conway, *The Life of Thomas Paine*, I, 370 ff.
[16] *Correspondence of Edmund Burke*, London, 1844, III, 219.

old political order, they had struck equally hard at organized religion, seizing church property and forcing hundreds of priests to seek refuge in England.

These circumstances particularly impressed the English clergy with the horror of revolution, so much so that many of them abused the rights of their office to give the established system of government a religious sanction and to make any attempt to alter it seem heretical. The Reverend Robert Nares, for instance, preaching a sermon against republicans and levelers, said, "Contempt of authority, overthrow of laws, turbulence and insurrection, these are rights which are not found within the Christian code." [17] Other members of the clergy flocked to Reeves's associations, offered their anti-Jacobin sermons for publication, and used the pulpit to warn their congregations against the diabolical schemes of political reformers. As ardent Tories, they undoubtedly helped to maintain the established order, and the government was grateful for their assistance. Liberals, on the other hand, were disgusted with the part played by the clergy. Expressing his resentment in "A Letter to the Bishop of Llandaff," which he was discreet enough not to publish, the youthful Wordsworth remarked, "With a servility which has prejudiced many people against religion itself, the ministers of the Church of England have appeared as writers upon public measures only to be advocates of slavery civil and religious."

The publication of Paine's *Age of Reason,* a few years after the appearance of *The Rights of Man,* served to further the belief that Jacobinism was the sworn foe of the church, for when the most notable advocate of republicanism openly declared himself a proponent of deism, many people were convinced that democracy and religious skepticism went hand in hand. *The Age of Reason,* like Paine's earlier work, caused a furor of alarm. Not that a treatise upon deism was anything new to the eighteenth century, for numerous books had appeared upon the subject earlier in the period, and every educated person had heard discussions of natural religion. But Paine was more openly blas-

[17] "Man's Best Right," London, 1793, p. 17.

phemous than his predecessors. Careful readers of *The Age of Reason* saw that it denied both the validity of Scripture and the Atonement of Christ, and they were naturally shocked by its grossly heterodox views. It was also clear that Paine, writing with characteristic vigor, intended his book to be read not merely by the learned, but by all ranks and degrees of people. Thus, at the end of the eighteenth century, when Chubb and Tindall, Collins and Morgan, and the other early advocates of deism were dead and forgotten, "a new species of infidel writing" had appeared, which, to orthodox Englishmen like Bishop Porteus, was the more vicious in that it was "addressed to the masses" and "most dexterously brought down to the level of their understanding." [18]

Paine's attack upon organized religion affected both church and state, for these two institutions were bound together in what Warburton had called "a political league and alliance for mutual support." [19] In this alliance reciprocal advantages existed. The church received a public endowment to support its clergy, its bishops sat in the House of Lords, and it had further privileges not possessed by other denominations. On the other hand, the hereditary monarch of the nation, and not the Archbishop of Canterbury, acted as head of the church. There was, moreover, a tacit agreement that the clergy would support the established political order and its personnel.[20] The alliance between church and state thus served as a mutual assistance pact. When Jacobin theories had threatened the established form of government, the clergy came to its defense. Now, with the publication of Paine's deistical work, the civil authorities came to the assistance of organized religion.

Shortly after the appearance of *The Age of Reason* an impoverished bookseller named Thomas Williams was arrested for selling it. The Proclamation Society, now headed by Bishop Porteus, brought the indictment and retained Thomas Erskine

[18] Beilby Porteus, *Works*, London, 1833, VI, 277.
[19] Quoted in Norman Sykes, *Church and State in England in the Eighteenth Century*, Cambridge, 1934, p. 320.
[20] *Ibid.*, pp. 320 ff.

to prosecute the case. At the trial, though the bookseller was charged with vending a blasphemous work, the chief emphasis was placed upon the seditious character of Paine's book, for in England, where religion was considered the basis of civil society, an attack upon orthodox belief was equivalent to an attack upon the state. Justice Ashhurst, who presided at the trial of Williams, stated the case clearly when he said of the publication of *The Age of Reason:*

All offenses of this kind are not only offenses to God, but crimes against the law of the land, and are punishable as such, inasmuch as they tend to destroy those obligations whereby civil society is bound together, and it is upon this ground that the Christian religion constitutes part of the law of England.[21]

To some people, indeed, *The Age of Reason* appeared to be a more subversive work even than *The Rights of Man.* Erskine, the prosecutor for the government at the trial of Williams, had been the defense attorney for the publishers of Paine's political work. Although a liberal, he felt he was not deserting his principles in taking an active part in suppressing a deistical book. To him the free circulation of *The Rights of Man* seemed a lawful attempt to effect a change in government, but *The Age of Reason,* by attacking organized religion, struck at the basis of government. Thus, in his view, the book seemed to promote anarchy.[22] When the court found Williams guilty, Erskine, however, urged the members of the Proclamation Society to let the defendant off with a light sentence, for the man, who had never been more than a scapegoat, now confessed himself truly repentant. But Porteus and his friends refused to show any mercy toward their victim, and, after pleading with them in vain, Erskine threw up his brief. It was due to the clemency of the judge, finally, that Williams received a sentence of only one instead of three years in prison.[23]

The trial of Williams was but the first of a series of prosecutions for circulating *The Age of Reason.* Before the period of the

[21] *State Trials,* XXVI, 715.   [22] *Ibid.,* pp. 668 ff.
[23] M. D. Conway, *The Writings of Thomas Paine,* New York, 1894, IV, 17 ff.

French Revolution, despite the fact that a number of deistical works had been published, it would appear that only two of their authors, Thomas Woolston and Peter Annet, had been tried for their freethinking views.[24] Beginning with the conviction of Williams, however, proceedings were frequently instituted against writers and publishers of unorthodox works. In fact, no time in English history has been so much characterized by suppression and repression as the period from the French Revolution to about 1830. Determined to prevent the expression of any view that might threaten the established order, the government regularly prosecuted what it considered seditious and blasphemous publications. It also attempted to ban allegedly obscene works, for, according to the law, anything which was detrimental to morality might, by its effect upon society, become harmful to the nation. As will later appear, however, state censorship was to prove largely ineffectual. Public opinion, and not the law, was to be the principal force in creating Victorian reticence.[25]

Long after the trial of Williams the upper classes continued to be disturbed by reports that the common people were, with great avidity, reading *The Age of Reason*. Actually, although copies of this book were still circulated, rumor probably exaggerated the interest of the masses in the deistical views of Paine. In this time of nervous excitement, however, one was inclined to credit statements like the following, especially when they appeared in reputable magazines under the signature of dignitaries like Bishop Porteus:

Publications of the most impious and indecent nature have, I know, been distributed with infinite activity and industry, not only in the metropolis and its neighborhood, and in large manufacturing towns, but in little obscure villages in remote parts of the kingdom; nay they have even found their way into the very bowels of the earth, among the miners of Cornwall, and the Colliers of Newcastle, some of whom are said to have sold their Bibles in order to purchase *The Age of Reason*.[26]

---

[24] J. B. Bury, *A History of Freedom of Thought*, New York [1913], p. 172.
[25] See below, chap. ix.   [26] *British Critic*, XIV (Sept., 1799), 243.

Many persons were particularly shocked to hear that the poor who had learned to read the Bible in Sunday school were now absorbed in Tom Paine. To the respectable classes there was bitter irony in this outcome of their philanthropy. They had promoted Sunday schools, believing them to be the best means to keep the poor orderly and submissive. Now, according to reports, the lower ranks were reading a radical writer, who taught them contempt for authority. There had always been some objection to educating the masses, and now the opponents of the Sunday school system renewed their attacks. One writer, for instance, maintaining that the illiteracy of the rank and file was the best guarantee of domestic peace, said that those who had been educated, "having imbibed the doctrines of seditious writers, will be the first to excite rebellions." He suspected, even, that the supporters of political reform had plotted to extend the Sunday school system "for the purpose of illuminating the common people." [27]

Under attack, various founders of Sunday schools felt called upon to defend themselves. Mrs. Trimmer, for one, stoutly asserted that the children educated in her schools were not reading objectionable books. But for the introduction of Sunday schools, she said, England might have had some genuinely pernicious system of education, since the "philosophers" had for some time been talking about "enlightening the people." [28] The best practical answer to the opponents of the Sunday schools, however, came from Hannah More, Mrs. Trimmer's Evangelical rival. These two philanthropists had met each other upon several occasions—once when the Bishop of Salisbury was present. He had complimented them as two singular women, "one who undertook to reform all the poor, the other all the great." [29] This had occurred before Hannah More had established her Sunday schools and before she had written *Village Politics*. Mrs. Trimmer had been ahead of her in several projects, but in the end it was Mrs. More who carried off the laurels.

[27] *Gentleman's Magazine*, LXVII (Oct., 1797), 919 ff.
[28] *The Oeconomy of Charity*, pp. 151 ff.   [29] Wm. Roberts, *op. cit.*, II, 101.

Hannah More answered the critics of the Sunday school system by demonstrating that the literacy of the masses, far from acting as a threat to established institutions, might serve to bolster them. All that was necessary was to provide the poor with literature of the right sort. Although various learned authors had written works to confute Paine's deistical teachings, the masses were not likely to read expensive and abstruse treatises. Aware of this fact, Bishop Porteus wrote to Hannah More, as he had written after the publication of *The Rights of Man*, asking her to write something in the manner of *Village Politics* to counteract the influence of *The Age of Reason*.[30] At first she had not felt equal to the task, but apparently the reports that the poor were reading Paine and the frequent attacks upon the Sunday school system convinced her that she ought to act upon the bishop's request, for in 1795, aided by her sister Sarah, she began her *Cheap Repository* tales. Some years later Hannah More explained her motive as follows: "To teach the poor to read without providing them with safe books has always appeared to me as a dangerous measure. This induced me to the laborious undertaking of the *Cheap Repository* tracts, which had such great success that above two millions were sold in one year." [31]

Inasmuch as the *Cheap Repository* appeared in monthly installments, Hannah More probably meant that the twelve issues that appeared in the course of one year sold two million copies. It seems hardly possible that a single installment could have sold that number, at a time when the population was less than nine million, and when probably not more than a third of the nation was literate. Even so, the success of the *Cheap Repository* was truly phenomenal. Never before, certainly, had any periodical attained a circulation of two million copies a year. Indeed, with the exception of the Bible, probably no publication of any sort had ever been so widely read. Although the *Cheap Repository* was introduced to supply reading matter for those who had been educated in Sunday schools, the tracts proved so entertaining that they were read not merely by the poor, but by people of

[30] *Ibid.*, II, 366.   [31] *Mendip Annals*, p. 6.

all ranks. But Hannah More's periodical was not intended solely for entertainment. Published during the critical period 1795–1798, it had a definitely propagandist purpose, and its influence upon public opinion was undoubtedly great.

When Hannah More started the *Cheap Repository,* religious and moral tracts were by no means a novelty. Throughout the eighteenth century the S.P.C.K. and other organizations had constantly circulated a literature consisting of sober exhortations to holy living and expositions of doctrine. The writers of these pamphlets, however, had depended upon the importance of their message to interest readers. They had not tried to entertain them. Shortly after the founding of Sunday schools a more informal type of cheap literature had appeared. It also had a moral purpose, but it attempted to interest and even to entertain its readers. Of this sort Mrs. Trimmer's *Family Magazine* was a noteworthy example. No one—not even Hannah More—was so thoroughly convinced that the reading habits of the poor should be carefully supervised. Describing the noxious influence of reading what she termed immoral books, Mrs. Trimmer had traced the progress of error to its fatal conclusion. Said she:

Many thousands of thoughtless young creatures of both sexes are betrayed into vice by putting themselves into the power of the enemy. At first they read these infamous publications under the notion of amusement, and by degrees lose all sense of virtue until they can take pleasure in nothing but riot, intemperance, obscenity, and profaneness—which too frequently end in an *ignominious death!* [32]

To save readers from this end, Mrs. Trimmer had started her *Family Magazine* in 1788. Each monthly installment was composed of an article for Sunday reading, which was really a sermon, a few stories exemplifying the triumph of virtue over vice, and some songs and ballads highly flavored with morality. After publishing only eighteen issues of this periodical, Mrs. Trimmer had abandoned her subscribers to the fate of reading less instructive works.

[32] *Family Magazine,* I, "Preface."

In several respects the *Cheap Repository* used the *Family Magazine* for its model. It, too, contained Sunday readings, moral tales, and ballads; and its heroine, Mrs. Jones, was copied from the character of Mrs. Andrews, who appeared in the stories of Mrs. Trimmer. But while the author of the *Family Magazine* had been the first to reject the expository style of older tracts in favor of narrative and verse, it was Hannah More who really exploited the idea. Neglecting to credit Mrs. Trimmer, her friends hailed her as a genius who had made moral writing popular by seasoning it with entertainment. Though far from a genius, Hannah More was a skillful writer, and her tracts appealed to a wide variety of readers. They pleased the upper classes by defending the established order, and they entertained the newly literate because they employed a simple style and sugar-coated their doses of morality.

The popularity of the *Cheap Repository*, however, was achieved in part by the organized efforts to circulate it widely. The Association for Preserving Liberty and Property had established a technique for disseminating propaganda, and several Evangelicals, following the example of Reeves, formed a similar society. Henry Thornton, one of the leading Evangelicals, served as secretary of the Cheap Repository Association, and among its subscribers were the Proclamation Society, Wilberforce, Richard Hill, and Thomas Bowdler, later notorious as the expurgator of Shakespeare. Like Reeves's organization, the Cheap Repository Association founded branch societies to circulate its tracts, and through them it secured thousands of readers. The following is a description of the methods employed:

These societies have not only exerted their influence by circulating the tracts in their own families, in their schools and among their dependents, but also by encouraging booksellers to supply themselves with them; by inspecting retailers and hawkers; giving them a few in the first instance, and directing them to their purchase; also by recommending the tracts to the occupiers of a stall at a fair, and by sending them to hospitals, workhouses, and prisons.[33]

---

[33] *Cheap Repository Tracts* for the year 1795, London, J. Marshall, "Appendix."

The *Cheap Repository*, though started to counteract the influence of *The Age of Reason*, developed much more extensive aims. It became, in fact, a manual of conduct. If the lower classes could be taught to regulate their lives according to a strict code, it was assumed that they would be immune to infidel writers, free from rebellious tendencies, and submissive to their lot. The *Cheap Repository* was timely, too, for 1795 was a particularly lean year in England. Because of crop failures and the resulting high price of grain, there were grave fears that a hungry populace might rebel. In some places minor riots did occur. That there were not more disturbances of this kind may very well have been due to the propagandist influence of the *Cheap Repository*. According to the biographer of Hannah More, one ballad in particular was directly responsible for quelling two riots —one at Bath and the other at Hull.[34] In this ballad, entitled "The Riot, or Half a Loaf Is Better than No Bread," two representatives of the lower classes discuss affairs. One of them, who is suffering from hunger, proposes to raid the flour mills and meat shops. The other overrules this suggestion by assuring his companion that conditions in England are not so grievous as elsewhere:

> For though in old England the times are but sad,
> In others I'm told they are ten times as bad;
> In the land of the Pope there is scarce any grain,
> And 'tis still worse, they say, both in Holland and Spain.

To deal with the problem of want, Mrs. More also wrote for her periodical a story called "The Way to Plenty." Her purpose, she said, was "to convince the common people that their extreme poverty is caused still more by their total want of economy than by the badness of the times." [35] "The Way to Plenty" shows the exemplary cheerfulness of Tom White and his spouse in the face of strained economic circumstances. Instead of complaining, the Whites help those who are worse off than themselves. At parish meetings Mrs. White and the minister recommend ways of preparing soups, stews, and other dishes at a

---

[34] Thompson, *op. cit.*, p. 158.   [35] Roberts, *op. cit.*, II, 472–73.

nominal cost. It was, of course, Hannah More's artful method of teaching the poor to use cheap recipes. Perhaps her instructions did some good. At any rate she may well have been better qualified to advise in matters of domestic than political economy.

It was no accident, of course, that the conduct recommended in the *Cheap Repository* would greatly accommodate the sense of security of the upper classes. Nor was it surprising, with Mrs. More as lawgiver, that the principles extolled were those associated with the religious revival. The *Cheap Repository*, in fact, became one of the best advertisements for Evangelical teachings. In the activities of Mrs. Jones, a benevolent busybody who figures in several of the tales, one gets some idea of their range. The reader is introduced to Mrs. Jones just after she has heard a sermon on the Good Samaritan. A little later, when her clergyman stops at her cottage for a visit, he finds her weeping bitterly. He inquires the cause of her grief, and she explains that his sermon has driven her to despair because, being poor, she is not able to help the unfortunate. The minister assures her that wealth is not necessary to perform deeds of philanthropy, and with his encouragement Mrs. Jones embarks upon various projects. She compels shopkeepers who have kept their establishments open on the Sabbath to refrain from this practice. Through her influence with the gentry she eliminates two of the three alehouses in the town. Discovering that the local baker sells bread underweight, she persuades the blacksmith to inform on him. Mrs. Jones next starts a Sunday school. Some of the farmers object to this enlightenment of the peasantry, but she soon convinces them that it is a wise plan to instruct the poor. There is already a charity school in the town, but, finding that it is badly managed, Mrs. Jones introduces several reforms. Among other things, she teaches the charity girls to use the recipes found in the *Cheap Repository* in order that they may prepare themselves to be frugal housewives. Indeed, one might almost suspect that the prototype for Mrs. Jones was none other than Hannah More herself.[36]

[36] *Cheap Repository*, "A Cure for Melancholy" and "The Sunday School."

At first, because the *Cheap Repository* was intended to supply a doctrinaire literature for the poor, it was published in the
form of penny pamphlets and printed on an inferior grade of
paper. Eventually, however, Mrs. More had to bring out a de
luxe edition of the tracts, for, as she explained, "the gentry,
among whom they are quite as much read as by the common
people, wish to have them in a better form for their children, for
schools, etc." [37] Today the popularity of the *Cheap Repository*
seems baffling, for it antagonizes the modern reader, with its con-
descending attitude toward the poor, its convenient and narrow
morality, and its frequent use of cant phrases. But the tone of the
tracts apparently did not annoy readers at the time of the French
Revolution. Sobered by conditions, the upper classes felt that
this type of literature deserved to be widely read, since it might
save England from the chaos ruling in France. Moreover, there
was a demand for fiction, and in the absence of pulp magazines
readers turned to the short stories of the *Cheap Repository*.

As propaganda, especially for various Evangelical reforms, the
tracts were undoubtedly effective. In the "History of Mr. Fan-
tom," the reader learned that evil befell those who followed the
teachings of *The Age of Reason*. In one of the favorite stories,
"The Shepherd of Salisbury Plain," the reader discovered that
submitting to one's lot was a virtue which sometimes gained an
earthly reward. In "The Two Wealthy Farmers," he was presented with a ready-made attack upon card-playing, fine dressing, and reading romances. If he chose to read "The History of
Tom White," he could not escape a sermon upon inebriety and
neglect of duty.

The ballads contained in the *Cheap Repository* were equally
moralistic. "Robert and Richard" tells the story of a young man
who, against the advice of his sober friend, adopts a *carpe diem*
philosophy. Richard gets a young woman with child. When she
drowns herself in the mill pond, her ghost returns to haunt her
seducer, and Richard finally dies from complications resulting
from horror and excessive drinking. "The Roguish Miller," on

[37] Roberts, *op. cit.*, II, 457.

the other hand, is a warning against dishonesty, describing how a miller who had cheated his customers finally lands in prison. Invariably the ballads taught the lesson that vice never pays, and that one false step may lead to ruin. Error sometimes pursued a strange course, however. In "The Story of Sinful Sally" the heroine first stooped to folly when she became a kept mistress. Then she acquired the further vicious habit of reading novels. After that her complete moral collapse quickly followed. To readers not familiar with the Evangelical code, this must have seemed a curious kind of morality. When associated with the loyalist cause and introduced under the guise of fiction or verse, however, strict Evangelical doctrines did not seem so objectionable as they might have sounded in the sermon of an Evangelical minister. Henceforth, English readers would have the opportunity of becoming extremely familiar with Evangelical principles.

The patriotic services of Hannah More and other Evangelicals of the church party undoubtedly served to increase their prestige. No group was more active in defending the established order while the country was passing through the crisis caused by the French Revolution, and their intense loyalty and ardent anti-Jacobinism allowed them to appear in a more favorable light than heretofore. Like most members of the upper classes, the well-to-do Evangelicals genuinely abhorred the philosophy of republicans, but in their efforts to suppress democratic ideas they never forgot that their real mission was to further the teachings of the revival. Nor did they hesitate upon occasion to associate their moral reforms and religious views with the popular principles of political conservatism. Furthermore, conditions were now favorable to a revival. Worried by the new philosophies and the disturbing course of events, people of the upper classes in particular were showing more interest in religion than they had shown for generations. All English churches gained adherents during the period of the French Revolution, but because Evangelicalism was the strongly proselyting creed of the time, it attracted probably the greatest number of converts. It would be unjust to say that these new adherents were necessarily hypocritical, for the doctrines of the revival profoundly stirred the emotions of thousands. Nevertheless, in adopting Evangelical belief, the wealthy found nothing to conflict with their economic or political views and, if they joined the church party, they attached themselves to a group which, by its militant efforts to maintain the established order, was helping to protect their material interests.

One thing was certain—the revival was losing its early purity of character. It no longer had the sincerity and singleness of purpose with which Wesley had endowed it. As he had feared, spiritual values began to suffer when the Evangelicals became a more wealthy group. To be sure, they continued to seek the salvation of mankind, but sometimes they made it appear that one's redemption depended upon following Tory principles. Not that the adoption of expedient interests hindered the growth of Evangelicalism, for in this last decade of the eighteenth century it was just entering upon its most flourishing period. But from this time it became more worldly in its aims, until eventually Evangelicalism was less a creed than a code, more a formula than a faith.

THE CONSPIRACY

As the eighteenth century waned, new alarms terrorized the country. Paine's *Age of Reason* had frightened people who regarded it as a threat to established religion, but now something yet more sinister than deism appeared. According to certain writers, an international plot was afoot, aimed at the destruction of organized religions and governments throughout the world. The belief in the existence of such a conspiracy was one of the most curious popular fallacies in history. Not only in England but on the Continent and in the new American Republic, the myth was widely credited. Because the conspirators, supposedly, planned to overthrow religion throughout Christendom, people of all nations shared the alarm. But in England, where something almost like a panic psychosis had existed for years, the news of this conspiracy climaxed earlier alarms.

Two books were chiefly responsible for spreading the delusion. One was John Robison's *Proofs of a Conspiracy against All Religions and Governments of Europe;* the other, the Abbé Barruel's *Mémoires pour servir à l'histoire du Jacobinisme*. Both appeared in 1797, and the fact that two men who had never heard of each other had reached substantially the same conclusion lent startling credence to the idea. According to Barruel three different groups had for some years been plotting against Christianity. These were the Order of Illuminati, members of Masonic lodges on the Continent, and the French Encyclopedists. Through their mutual conniving, Barruel maintained, the French Revolution had been brought about, but that uprising, supposedly, was only the first act of an international plot. Robison, although he did not stress the influence of the Encyclopedists, otherwise agreed with the main contentions of Barruel. Each of these writers assured his readers that the plotters were engaged in further machinations. According to Robison there were in England several societies of the association "formed for the express purpose of rooting out all religious institutions and overthrowing all the existing governments of Europe." [38]

However mistaken, both these writers were probably sincere. Robison was a reputable Scotchman, distinguished for his scholarship in other fields. Barruel was an émigré French priest of extensive knowledge. Their books were documented, and they had some authentic sources upon which to base their contentions. There was, in fact, enough truth in some of the circumstances to establish a foundation for the fantastic superstructure they erected upon it.

In 1776 Adam Weishaupt had started a secret society in Bavaria called the Order of Illuminati. Repudiating existing religious and political institutions, the members hoped to establish a rule of reason among men and thereby to develop a higher civilization. Apparently the Illuminati in the beginning were a species of perfectibilitarian dreamers, though later on they showed definitely anarchistic tendencies. When Baron Franz

[38] *Proofs of a Conspiracy*, London, 1798, 4th ed., pp. 10–11.

Friederick Knigge joined the order in 1780, he expanded the organization by enrolling members of Masonic lodges in it and by founding societies in other parts of Germany, as well as in Switzerland and Austria. Dissension arose within the ranks, however, and after quarreling with Weishaupt, Knigge left the order.[39]

In the meantime, Carl Theodore, ruler of Bavaria, started a campaign to abolish the societies in his country. From papers seized in 1786, it would appear that the Illuminati had then become truly vicious, for their documents showed that they were "an organization devoted to the overthrow of religion and the state, a band of poisoners and forgers, an association of men of disgusting morals and depraved tastes." [40] Carl Theodore issued several edicts, decreeing that anyone joining the societies should be banished and have his property confiscated. These stern measures succeeded in destroying the order in Bavaria, and soon afterwards the organizations in other countries collapsed. By 1787 the system of Illuminati, this curious, half-cinematic product of the age of reason, had ceased to exist.[41]

The legend of the Illuminati, however, had just begun. Ten years later it provided the basis for the chimera of conspiracy. Far from believing that the societies were dead, Robison and Barruel were convinced that they still operated secretly and that, in association with Masons, Jacobins, and freethinkers, they were planning to destroy existing governments and religions throughout the world, and especially in England. Their best evidence, these writers thought, was the example of what had occurred in France, and to many people it seemed conclusive. Confronted by perplexing circumstances, they were prone to seize upon any simple explanation. The political and economic conditions that had caused the French Revolution and the successive phases through which it passed were difficult to comprehend. So, too, was the sudden demand by the masses elsewhere for a share in

[39] Vernon Stauffer, *New England and the Bavarian Illuminati*, New York, 1918. Chap. iii appears to be the best scholarly source of information upon the European Order of Illuminati.

[40] *Ibid.*, p. 182.   [41] *Ibid.*, chap. iii.

government. Consequently, many people were readily convinced that a conspiracy existed, for it seemed to explain not only the French Revolution, but many other disturbing aspects of the age.

The report of the conspiracy spread throughout all England. Robison's book, which was first published in Scotland, appeared in three London editions within the year. Extracts from Robison and Barruel were printed in some of the periodicals, and the substance of their works was given in brief form in various pamphlets. Relatively few readers, apparently, questioned the evidence presented by the authors. When their books were discussed in the *British Critic,* the reviewer praised the accuracy and scholarship of both writers, and suggested that anyone who expressed doubt about the authenticity of their "proofs" was probably in sympathy with the conspirators.[42] Although the members of the Eclectic Society were educated men, not one so much as hinted, in discussing this subject, that the conspiracy might be a myth. The only concern of this group was to find some means to thwart the designs of organized infidelity. The best plan, they believed, would be to exercise more control over literature.[43]

In his *Proofs of a Conspiracy* Robison had contended that the suppression of the Illuminati by the Bavarian government was only formal and that the members, in order to avoid suspicion, were now organized in "reading societies." [44] Perhaps it was this statement which made current literature suspect. At any rate it was commonly rumored that the conspirators planned to "illuminate" the masses by encouraging popular education and by providing them with propaganda. Inasmuch as the plotters were thought to be extremely adroit, it was believed that they often inserted their doctrines in books which at first glance might appear to be innocent. Any book, therefore, might have a baneful effect, and reading became a dangerous occupation. It seemed easy now to explain the publication of *The Age of Reason,* for this treatise was apparently one of the products of the conspiracy.

[42] *British Critic,* X, 407 ff.   [43] *Eclectic Notes.*   [44] Stauffer, *op. cit.,* p. 210.

To guard against further works designed to overthrow established institutions, many readers and even some critics felt that it was necessary carefully to examine every new book and to be particularly wary of any which criticized organized government or religion.

For several years writers who believed in the existence of a conspiracy helped to sustain the idea that reading was a dangerous occupation. Mrs. Jane West, a satellite of Mrs. Trimmer and the author of numerous books, took great pains in her *Letters Addressed to a Young Man* to explain that a "widely-extended plot" was the chief cause of the French Revolution. As a warning against further schemes of the conspirators, she told her readers that several periodicals of the day were suspiciously hostile to established government and religion. Many critics and authors were not to be trusted, according to Mrs. West, who longed for the good old days when parents could safely encourage their children to develop a taste for books. "Deistical tenets were then enveloped in the thick pages of some metaphysical treatise," she said; "they were not insinuated into novels and pamphlets, and lowered to every capacity, or degree of leisure and information." [45]

Mrs. Trimmer, who was equally alarmed at the news of a conspiracy, started a periodical to shield readers from its contaminating principles. The *Guardian of Education* specialized in reviews of juvenile literature and educational works, for Mrs. Trimmer believed that the Illuminati and others were endeavoring to "infect the mind of the rising generation through the medium of children's books." [46] Her magazine, which appeared in monthly installments between 1802 and 1806, was unusual in one respect. Mrs. Trimmer announced that she would judge books, not on their literary merit, but solely upon their moral and religious views. This she did, and because her judgments were extremely severe, she sometimes condemned the most innocuous fairy tales. On the other hand, if a book contained

[45] *Letters Addressed to a Young Man*, London, 1801, III, 160 ff.
[46] *Guardian of Education*, Vol. I, "Introduction."

enough moral and religious cant, no matter how poor it might be, it inevitably received the cordial approval of the lady.

It would be ridiculous to say that critical canons were generally altered by the belief in a conspiracy, for the better-informed reviewers of the early nineteenth century were unaffected by it. Nevertheless, a good many middle-class readers were getting their opinions, not from the *Quarterly Review* or *Blackwood's*, but from writers like Mrs. West and Mrs. Trimmer, who gave them the impression that, though books have their purpose, one must exercise the most rigid discrimination in reading them. Both these ladies were inclined to believe that literature, like liquor, had a certain medicinal value, but that books and bottles had better remain in the cabinet except upon those occasions when a wise doctor or a judicious reviewer prescribed that they should be opened. Eventually, of course, people forgot about the conspiracy, but as later events will show, the rumor lasted for several years. Furthermore, in some quarters at least, an extreme wariness with regard to literature survived well into the nineteenth century, contributing to the distrust which many Victorians had for unconventional views and to their taste for safe and unsound writers like Mrs. Trimmer.

Although a good many people genuinely believed that a conspiracy existed, others who were less gullible probably encouraged the notion, hoping thereby to discredit any criticism of government or religion. To what extent professional propagandists used this device it is impossible to say, but John Reeves, the former leader of the now defunct Association for Preserving Liberty and Property, strongly favored this plan to defeat liberal opinion. In a letter to Lord Liverpool, Reeves recommended that the government should encourage the sale of the books written by Barruel and Robison. Though he laughed at the idea of a conspiracy, Reeves regretted that Barruel's work on this subject had not sold better and suggested that it should be subsidized. "The pen militant," he concluded, "might save the expense of many regiments." [47]

[47] B.M., Add. MSS 28,231, f. 305.

Perhaps nothing came of this particular suggestion, but from other instances it is obvious that the government, or those at least who were most interested in maintaining its *status quo*, had learned that the pen was indeed mightier than the sword. Although the French Revolution was itself sufficiently terrifying to make most Englishmen resist the idea of any radical change, those in power further instilled fear among the people in order to oppose any economic or political reforms. They could deny liberals the right to express their views, they had the best writers on their own side, and they employed every artifice to maintain the old order. Never before, perhaps, had men used propaganda so effectively. A generation later James Mill, who saw what had happened, said of these measures to thwart liberal opinion, "No such monstrous case of gulling, no such inordinate swallow of delusion, we verily believe, is to be found in the history of civilized man." [48]

Rumor and propaganda, and the real and imaginary fears they provoked, were creating a state of mind favorable to all forms of conservatism. Gone was the aplomb of the eighteenth century. Gone, too, was much of the cynicism that had characterized that period. Even without the concurrence of the religious revival, more conservative social standards, greater sobriety of manners, and a higher degree of moral earnestness would probably have developed following the French Revolution. But the country was not allowed to drift along upon the tide of events, for the Evangelicals at last had an opportunity to foist their strict views upon society.

In the closing years of the eighteenth century, with the nation frightened by the delusion of a conspiracy, and at a time of general apprehension that national calamity threatened the survival of traditional institutions, the Evangelicals vigorously renewed their demands for a thorough reformation of morals and manners. Formerly, it had been customary to consider the vices of the poor the cause of their wretchedness; now, several writers

[48] *Westminster Review*, VI (Oct., 1826), 252.

blamed the wickedness of all classes for the dangerous state of the nation.

In his *Practical View of the Prevailing Religious Systems,* which he published in 1797, Wilberforce wrote, "To the decline of religion and morality our national difficulties must, both directly and indirectly be chiefly ascribed." All classes must reform, said Wilberforce, for it was a false view which held that only the grossly criminal practices of the poor were truly vicious, excusing corruption in high life by saying that vice lost half its evil by losing all its grossness. Lasciviousness, drunkenness, and revelry—these sins the wealthy must renounce. But to have any thorough reformation of morals, urged Wilberforce, it was necessary to forswear other pastimes as well—to shun the theater, to abandon, if not wholly at least as a regular practice, the habit of reading novels, and to deny oneself the pleasure of playing cards and making journeys on the Sabbath. Within six months after it was published, the *Practical View* had sold 7,500 copies.[49]

Another voice raised in the wilderness of despair was that of John Bowdler, a member of a prominent Evangelical family. His book was appropriately entitled *Reform or Ruin,* for he offered his readers an unequivocal choice of these two courses. By reform he meant, not a change in the system of government or the amelioration of economic conditions: "The only reform which can save us, if adopted in time," wrote Bowdler, "is a thorough reform of principles and practices." Instead of blaming the state of the nation upon the prolonged war with France, mismanagement of government, or poor harvests, he attributed it to corruption in private life. Vicious habits prevailed among all ranks, he said. The clergy were so much engrossed in trifling amusements that they neglected their duties; the nobility and gentry were given to gaming, adultery, and luxurious living; the middle classes were absorbed in worldly pursuits; the lower ranks indulged too much in drunkenness, idleness, and complaining. No one, no matter what his rank, escaped castigation

[49] Wm. Wilberforce, *Practical View,* New York, 1851, p. 454 and *passim.*

in *Reform or Ruin*. Yet the readers who bought up eight editions of this book within a year apparently valued it for the simple explanation it offered of all difficulties.[50]

Arthur Young also sounded a warning to his countrymen. Earlier he had proved himself a clear thinker and an extremely capable writer upon economic problems. Like many others, however, he had apparently become frightened by the course of the French Revolution. Now, in 1798, shortly after his conversion to Evangelicalism, he published a book in which he appeared to be more the zealot than the scholar. In *An Enquiry into the State of the Public Mind among the Lower Classes,* Young argued that the poor were better off in England than elsewhere and that the country had "the freest government that ever blessed mankind." The clergy had neglected their duties, however, and "the new lights" and "French philosophy" had taught the middle and lower classes infidelity and discontent. To wrest them from their mistaken notions it was imperative for the upper ranks to set a good example. This they could best do by showing more interest in religion and by paying strict regard to their moral conduct:

The true Christian will never be a leveller; will never listen to French politics, or to French philosophy. He who worships God in spirit and in truth will love the government and laws which protect him without asking by whom they are administered. But let it not be imagined that such characters will abound among the lower classes while the higher by their Sunday parties, excursions, and amusements, and vanities; by their neglect of public worship and their families show that they feel not themselves, what perhaps they talk of, or recommend for the poor.[51]

Still another writer to ascribe public grievances to private immorality was John Bowles. In his *View of the Moral State of Society,* he averred that atheism, coming from France, had infected England. According to Bowles society was rotten to the core. The only hope of improvement was to have women reform

[50] *DNB*, "John Bowdler"; *Reform or Ruin*, London, 1798.

[51] *An Enquiry into the State of the Public Mind*, London, 1798, p. 25 and *passim*.

their unchaste conduct and to have the upper classes abandon luxury and riotous living. Unlike the others who wrote in this vein, Bowles was not an Evangelical, but he too maintained that "the present calamitous and perilous situation of the world is chiefly owing to its moral depravity." [52]

In making such an issue of moral reform, these various writers had mixed motives. Wilberforce and Bowdler were perhaps chiefly interested in promoting the religious revival. Possibly Arthur Young was too, though he had been accused of deserting the liberal cause to become a hireling of the ministry when, shortly after appearing as a loyalist writer, he was appointed to the Board of Agriculture. There can be no doubt that Bowles was a professional propagandist. He had written pamphlets for Reeves's association, and when the nation went to war with France, he had published various works in which he defended the policy of the ministry. Pitt had rewarded his services by appointing him to a commission to dispose of Dutch contraband, but, as Parliament later proved, Bowles and the other commissioners grossly cheated the government.[53] With him certainly, and perhaps in a lesser degree with other writers, the cry for moral reform was propagandist strategy to drown out the demands of those seeking political and economic reforms.

Whatever their motives, these authors were widely read, and no doubt they influenced the thinking of a large number of readers. Wilberforce's *Practical View,* in particular, was credited with making numerous converts to Evangelicalism. Others who read these books, while not converted, developed the conviction that an investment in virtuous conduct, or at least the appearance of it, seemed wise when brokers offered it as the only

[52] *A View of the Moral State of Society at the Close of the Eighteenth Century,* London, 1804, p. 72 and *passim.* An earlier edition appeared in 1800.

[53] The infamous character of John Bowles was exposed in a discussion which took place in Parliament when a vote of censure was passed upon the Dutch commissioners for their peculations. As one of the commissioners, Bowles was particularly condemned, since he had patronized morality so much in his writings. Yet, as one member of Parliament remarked, he was typical of those who raised the loudest cries of alarm during the period of the French Revolution. See *The Parliamentary Debates,* XIV, 291 ff. (May 1, 1809).

security. Certainly manners were changing, not just because of the influence of writers like Wilberforce, Young, and Bowdler, but as the result of all the forces which were put into operation by the reaction to the French Revolution. As one writer observed, "The French Revolution illustrated the connection between good morals and the order and peace of society more than all the eloquence of the pulpit and the disquisitions of moral philosophers had done for many centuries." [54]

By the end of the eighteenth century the curtain had been rung down on the old sophisticated comedy of manners, and the stage was being set for the Victorian scene. In 1798 it was announced that the Lord Chancellor had refused to hold any more public dinners on the Sabbath. Ranelagh, the once fashionable resort, famous for its gardens and concert hall, was so little patronized that in 1803 the management finally closed it. Gambling had ceased to be reputable. Of course people continued to enjoy the pastime in private, but if they were discreet they drew their blinds, for the justices of late had severely penalized offenders who had been caught playing for stakes.[55] Observers noted with approval that the clergy were paying more attention to their duties. Some of them had introduced weekday sermons in addition to Sunday services. More surprising, large congregations turned out to listen to them. "It was a wonder to the lower orders throughout all parts of England to see the avenues to the churches filled with carriages. This novel appearance prompted the simple country people to inquire what was happening." [56] Well they might ask, for this unusual display of piety was a sign of something truly momentous. The whole pattern of English social life had begun to change.

[54] *Annual Register* for 1798, p. 229.
[55] *Social England,* ed. by H. D. Traill, London, 1896, V, 498.
[56] *Annual Register* for 1798, p. 229.

PART TWO: 1800-1830

CHAPTER FOUR

TOWARD A NEW OPINION

AT THE BEGINNING of the nineteenth century many Englishmen were aware that manners were rapidly changing, but no one, not even the reformers, could have foreseen how profound the transformation was to be. For Victorianism was the product not alone of the zeal of reformers. Its development depended, in the final analysis, upon a corresponding growth of public opinion, a phenomenon without which the exhortations of a hundred Hannah Mores would have availed little.

Many factors contributed to the creation of Victorian opinion, and no one of them, considered separately, adequately accounts for it. The religious revival was obviously of prime importance, but Evangelicalism reached its zenith shortly before the accession of Victoria, and thereafter its influence waned. Strict standards of conduct, on the other hand, survived until the twentieth century, when circumstances once more altered public opinion. During the Victorian era a rigorous code was maintained, not by any one religious group, but by public fiat. In the end the people, or that stratum which controlled public opinion, ruled upon manners. To account for the rise of Victorianism it is necessary, therefore, to consider the circumstances which altered eighteenth-century points of view and favored the development of a different set of opinions.

It should be remembered that during the eighteenth century public opinion was not so strong a force as it was later to become. To be sure, mass opinion of a sort existed. Most Englishmen, for example, distrusted the French and believed them to be rascals. Catholics were generally known as "papists," and the use of this term reflected a national prejudice toward the Roman religion. But slow methods of communication restricted the dissemination of opinion throughout the country, and, because books and newspapers, the chief vehicles of expression, could never reach more than the comparatively small literate section of the population, the opportunity to develop collective beliefs was necessarily limited.

Insofar as opinion ruled the nation, it was the opinion of the upper classes. But their views, while they might determine the political and economic policies of the country, had little effect otherwise upon the mass of people. Moreover, their own standards were so lax as to render ineffective any attempt they themselves might make to improve manners. At other times the clergy had helped to maintain certain standards of manners and morals, but in the eighteenth century church attendance was decreasing and clerical influence waned. Religion was no longer so important a determinant of conduct. Indeed, the lax manners of the eighteenth century were owing in large measure to the absence of *any* force strong enough to formulate and to maintain the unwritten laws which normally govern society.

Toward the close of the eighteenth century, as we have seen, these conditions began to change. Amid the alarms of the French Revolution the nation became more receptive to moral reform. The Evangelicals pressed the importance of this reform and pointed its course, and propaganda, becoming more effective as literacy increased, served to indoctrinate the people with Evangelical teachings. Within a few decades public opinion not only expressed itself more forcibly than heretofore, but as it developed it crystallized upon questions of manners and morals. Such, in simple outline, is the explanation of the beginnings of Victorianism. But the full story is much more detailed. Public opinion could never have been formed so rapidly nor have become so strict an arbiter, had it not been for certain attendant favorable circumstances.

For one thing, large numbers of people were changing their

social status. An expanding population, the advent of the industrial system, and the consequent increase in national wealth afforded opportunities for many enterprising individuals to improve their economic condition. Those who did so frequently bettered their social position as well. As Leslie Stephen remarked, "There is probably no period in history at which a greater number of people have risen to distinction." [1] This did not mean that the class system was disappearing. The old barriers remained, but more people were hurdling them.

Something more was in progress than a mere shifting of population from one class to another. An influx of new members created distinct groups within the traditional social ranks. There was now a new entrepreneur middle class which differed from the older merchant bourgeoisie. Its members had amassed their fortunes in cotton, steel, and other new industries, and their wealth, serving as a passport, frequently enabled them to enter Parliament and to marry into older families. [2] There was even a new aristocracy of a sort, totally unlike the old one, with its ancient titles and landed estates. This "new aristocracy," as Shelley acidly remarked, consisted of "attorneys and excisemen, and directors and government pensioners, usurers, stockjobbers, country bankers, with their dependents and descendants." [3]

Farther down the social ladder equally significant changes were occurring. Many who had been born to that large class known as the poor were able to improve their social situation. It was an interesting coincidence that popular education had been extended just at a time when there was a greater demand for people with some schooling. And this was coincidence, for the founders of Sunday schools intended these institutions to be moral seminaries which would serve at the same time to content their pupils with a humble station in life. Actually the Sunday schools trained many members of the lower classes to do the socially preferable clerical work for which the new era

[1] *The English Utilitarians*, London, 1900, I, 112–13.
[2] W. Cunningham, *The Growth of English Industry and Commerce*, Cambridge, 1903, II, 617 ff.
[3] P. B. Shelley, "A Philosophical View of Reform," London, 1920, p. 45.

brought an increasing demand. Of the Sunday school product, one writer observed, "His clerkly skill exempted him from manual labor, and as a shopman, bookkeeper, or town's officer—perchance in the higher dignity of parish clerk or school master—he rose a step above his original situation in life." [4]

Other opportunities to better one's position were afforded by the growing industrialization of the country. With the introduction of machinery, the demand for skilled mechanical workers naturally increased. Indeed skilled factory workers, differing from the old artisan class and the indiscriminate group of unskilled workers, constituted virtually a new stratum in the ranks of labor. The new factories also required men to act as superintendents, managers, and overseers. The number of such positions was, of course, limited, but they went almost invariably to persons who had received some schooling.

Because clerks, skilled workers, and factory supervisors received better wages, they were able to improve their conditions of living. Not infrequently they became substantial members of middle-class circles. But even if they remained in the lowest order of society, they served to bolster its standards of conduct, for they were more cleanly, more orderly, and better informed than the masses in general. According to Francis Place, the educated workers formed a distinct group and many of them refused to associate with others of their rank. Nevertheless, he added, even the most ignorant and most despised among the poor of London improved their habits somewhat, owing to a greater consciousness that there were approved types of conduct.[5] Symbolically, the term used to designate the class changed. In the eighteenth century the masses were commonly called "the poor." Poor they remained, but later they were referred to as "the lower orders" or "the working classes." Nor were these mere euphemisms of the Victorian age. The self-esteem of the masses had increased, and their improved standards appear to have won them a degree of respect from those higher in rank.

[4] R. Guest, *A Compendious History of the Cotton Manufacture*, Manchester, 1823, pp. 37–38.
[5] See below, chap. vii.

These changes in social and economic status had an important effect upon the opinions of those concerned. In the first place, as the masses grew more literate and more articulate, public opinion became much more truly the expression of the great body of people. They were no longer the brutish and ignorant pariah class of the eighteenth century. Though still without the franchise, they were capable of legislating upon manners, for they had formed opinions from their reading and were better able to express their beliefs. Inasmuch as their own standards had been improved, it followed, moreover, that their opinion was upon the side of stricter public morality.

Newcomers to the higher brackets of society were also prone to change their opinions. Without the traditional views of the class in which they found themselves, they were open to conviction and, living in a troubled world, they were particularly receptive to religious conviction. Consequently, it frequently happened that people who altered their social position changed their religious beliefs as well. Some, like Tom Paine and Francis Place, became deists or skeptics, but the great majority became Evangelicals.

One of the most interesting conversions of the time was that of James Lackington, a self-made man who alternately turned Evangelical, atheist, and finally Evangelical again. Lackington was the son of a journeyman shoemaker. After working at his father's trade for several years, he went to London, where he opened a combined shoemaker's shop and bookstall. Dealing in secondhand books, he prospered and was able to give up the shoemaking trade. His book business continued to thrive and eventually, he said, it yielded him an income of £4,000 a year.[6]

At one time in his youth Lackington had joined the Methodists, but upon reading Amory's *John Buncle* he had become an atheist. This and other experiences of his early life he detailed in his *Memoirs*, published in 1791. Adopting a worldly, eighteenth-century attitude toward the events of his life, he bragged

[6] *Memoirs of the First Forty-Five Years of the Life of James Lackington*, London, 1791.

about getting women with child, ridiculed Methodism, and sneered at his temporary conversion. Shortly after publishing this work, however, Lackington once more became a convert to Evangelical belief, and this time there was no backsliding. In his *Confessions,* published in 1804 as a recantation of the earlier work, he apologized for his thrusts at Methodism and confessed his change of heart. Henceforth he proved to be a vigorous apostle of the revival. Part of his fortune went for the construction of Methodist chapels, and in the closing years of his life he became an Evangelical preacher.[7]

People like Lackington, who had risen from the lowest order of society, were particularly inclined to become Evangelicals. Without a cultural heritage, they had no objection to the unintellectual character of the revival. Many, perhaps, had never belonged to any church, but when they attained a respectable position in society, they were disposed to join some religious organization. Under the circumstances, it was natural for them to become converts to the most vigorous, the most actively proselyting religion of the time. But Evangelicalism was more than a religious creed. For those who genuinely accepted its teachings it was a way of life. With its taboos and proscriptions, its pronouncements upon the minutest acts of the individual, Evangelicalism provided believers with a set of rules to guide them in almost every social situation. And that sort of instruction, no doubt, was welcomed by those who felt uncertain of the manners appropriate to their new rank. The code was extremely strict, but it was the code of an increasingly powerful social clique, and, according to Evangelical teaching, the only one that offered a surety of salvation.

Because the moral code of the Evangelicals was an integral part of their religion, each convert added to the number of those who favored moral reform. And Evangelicalism was thriving. By the first decade of the nineteenth century it had, scattered among the different Protestant denominations, perhaps a million adherents. The Methodists now constituted a significant section

---

[7] *The Confessions of James Lackington,* London, 1804.

of the population; the older dissenting sects, influenced by the revival, had attracted many new believers; and each year the Evangelicals in the church became more numerous.

The Methodists were growing both in numbers and in wealth. Before he died in 1791, John Wesley had observed, with disapproval, that many of his followers were amassing modest fortunes. Nevertheless, he realized that this was partly the result of their practicing the frugality and industry which he had preached, and he exhorted them to increase their generosity in proportion to their wealth.[8] The Methodists, welcoming newcomers of all kinds to their fold, also gained many adherents among the newly rich. In the Establishment a man who had risen from the ranks might be snubbed; among the Methodists he found a democratic and fraternal spirit. Hence factory owners and business men frequently became converts.[9]

Meanwhile the Methodists continued to proselyte among the poor. The rise of industrial communities gave them new opportunities to win converts, and Methodist preachers often gained a foothold in the rapidly growing factory towns before the more unwieldy Establishment could build churches or provide clergymen. By 1800 the Arminians alone had 940 chapels in the United Kingdom. Their members numbered 109,961, and adherents of all kinds probably totaled over 500,000.[10] From this time Methodism continued to flourish and to increase that proportion of the population which held strictly defined views upon questions of religion and morals.

Methodism also served as a tonic for the older dissenting sects. Like all religious bodies, Baptists, Congregationalists, and Presbyterians had fared poorly in the unspiritual milieu of the early eighteenth century. Their numbers had diminished and, had it not been for the revival, their congregations might have dwindled to insignificant groups or perhaps have disappeared altogether. But Methodism, by reviving the evangelical spirit, fired the older dissenting sects with new zeal, and, instead of losing

[8] L. Tyerman, *The Life and Times of the Reverend John Wesley*, III, 594–95.
[9] *A New History of Methodism*, I, 341.   [10] *Annual Review*, 1803, p. 209.

adherents, they began to gain new members. This tendency was reflected in the greater number of chapels. In 1760 the three Nonconformist groups had a total of only 1,252 congregations; by 1808 they had increased the number to 2,002. In the following years they won still more adherents, and under the impulse of the times Nonconformity regained much of its early puritanical spirit.[11]

Within the Established Church the Evangelicals were strongly entrenched, and here were to be found the most wealthy and influential converts. Particularly powerful were a group of laymen who had taken up their residence at Clapham Common, just outside London. Though not openly schismatic, they were so independent—so disdainful at times—of church authority that they were called the "Clapham Sect."

The prominence of the Clapham Sect dates from about 1792, the year in which John Venn was appointed to the living at Clapham Common, and Henry Thornton established his home there. Both were second-generation Evangelicals. (Venn's father was one of the first Evangelical clergymen in the Establishment, and the elder Thornton was a wealthy and philanthropic merchant whom Cowper had celebrated for his probity.) Not many members of the Clapham Sect belonged to the old families of English nobility. They represented, rather, the new upper-middle class, which had already begun to figure prominently in public life. In addition to Wilberforce, who was their leader, other Claphamites who served in Parliament were Charles Grant, James Stephen, and Henry Thornton.[12]

The Claphamites were still more distinguished, however, as promoters of sundry philanthropic, religious, and moral enterprises. Their names appeared upon the rosters of numerous societies as presidents, vice-presidents, secretaries, and committeemen, or as founders. Possessed of considerable wealth, they drew upon their private resources to support the different Evangelical associations and, having a genius for organization,

---

[11] H. W. Clark, *History of English Nonconformity*, London, 1913, II, 245, 313.
[12] *DNB.*

they made them powerful agencies of the revival. Most humanitarian movements of the time had their support. They were bitter foes of slavery, and perhaps their best claim to distinction rests upon the valiant fight they waged against slave-trafficking. They also helped to reform prison conditions, and they were extremely generous in their benefactions to the poor. Henry Thornton himself never gave less than £2,000 a year to charity, and the other Claphamites made large donations to aid the indigent and ill, orphans and reformed prostitutes.[13]

Here was proof—if proof were needed—that the Evangelical emphasis upon salvation by faith did not exclude good works. Nevertheless, the duty to which the Claphamites most ardently devoted themselves was conversion. Their missionary societies sent representatives to Africa and the South Seas to convert pagans, and their other organizations made every effort at home to spread Evangelical belief by providing the nation with an endless supply of moral and religious works. Even their charity associations were used chiefly as proselyting agencies, for what Sydney Smith said of the Evangelicals generally was particularly applicable to the Clapham Sect: "One thing must be taken for granted respecting these people,—that wherever they gain a foothold, or whatever be the institutions to which they give birth, *proselytism will be their main object."* [14]

The members of the Clapham Sect were neither strongly Arminian nor strongly Calvinistic. If they leaned toward either side, they favored mildly Calvinistic views. In general that was the disposition of most church Evangelicals. But some, like John Newton, were deep-grained Calvinists; others were firm Arminians.

It was natural that belief should differ from individual to individual as it did from sect to sect, inasmuch as the Evangelicals had no authoritative body to define and interpret specific doc-

---

[13] James Stephen, "The Clapham Sect," *Essays in Ecclesiastical Biography,* II, 292. For other works on the Clapham Sect, see: John Stoughton, *Religion in England from 1800 to 1850,* London, 1884, Vol. I. John Telford, *A Sect That Moved the World,* London, 1907.

[14] *Edinburgh Review,* XI (Jan., 1808), 355.

trines. The church Evangelicals rejected the authority of the bishops. The older dissenting sects had from the beginning stood for autonomous rather than centralized authority. The Methodists, to be sure, had had in John Wesley a strong leader and lawgiver, but after his death even the Arminian Methodists fell into disagreement and split into separate groups. Among the different Evangelicals, the only basic tenets held in common were a belief in the natural depravity of man and a belief in salvation by faith. Nevertheless, the emphasis placed upon these doctrines sharply distinguished the Evangelicals of all denominations from other Christians; and despite the differences existing among themselves, they showed great willingness to coöperate with one another.

One bond they had in common—the desire to make England a religious nation. Because this seemed more important to them than points of dogma, the Evangelicals were usually more friendly to converts of other sects than to the unregenerate of their own church. This was particularly true of the Evangelicals belonging to the Establishment. Often they turned their backs upon the church societies and joined with Methodists and dissenters to establish rival organizations. By doing so, of course, they gained the enmity of orthodox churchmen, but this did not deter them. Holding strong religious convictions, they repudiated the apathetic spirit so commonly found within the Establishment and considered themselves the only true churchmen.

No matter what their sect, the Evangelicals were distinguished from the non-Evangelicals by their outward show of piety and their greater seriousness. They all held strict views upon manners and morals, abstained from certain pleasures, and were inclined to censure those who indulged in them. In other words, they all subscribed to the same rigorous opinions upon conduct, and this agreement gave them the appearance of being cut from the same pattern.

To their enemies, it seemed that Evangelicals almost arbitrarily imposed restrictions upon normal pleasures. This was not entirely true. Their strict opinions upon conduct were derived in part from their religious beliefs. Nevertheless, their moral code was not always well articulated with their religious dogmas, especially since the Evangelicals eagerly seized upon any argument to vanquish what they considered popular vices. One of these vices was the theater, and when, at a meeting of the Eclectic Society, Evangelicals of different denominations discussed the evils of the stage, they showed their willingness to lay hands upon any stick to beat a dog. All agreed that the theater was vicious, but for a variety of reasons. On the stage, they said, evil characters often prospered, wicked people by practicing benevolence were made to appear in an agreeable light, and God's name was taken in vain. Comedies promoted gallantry, and tragedies were rife with blasphemy. The theater corrupted servants who attended it, supported a profligate society, and was a meeting place for bad company. It endangered the state, too, for everyone knew that the French theater had nursed the revolution. Finally, and with utter seriousness, the Reverend Josiah Pratt added this objection: "A sermon is the essence of dullness after a play; this shows the evil of the playhouse." [15]

From this discussion it would appear that logic was not a strong point of the Evangelicals. Nevertheless, certain features inherent in Evangelicalism help to explain, if not logically at least psychologically, the careful guard they placed upon their own actions and the watchful concern they had for the conduct of others. Perhaps the emphasis upon sudden conversion induced this attitude, for a person "saved" either by election or by the new birth supposedly changed his whole course of living. If he was really saved, his exemplary conduct distinguished him from the unregenerate. Thus conduct became a test which proved whether one belonged to God's chosen people. Those who favored Calvinistic belief, moreover, had to guard against the appearance of antinomianism, the belief that the elect were freed from the restraint of all moral laws. Few Calvinists actually became antinomian, but their enemies insisted that it was the logical step for those who had an unalterable conviction that they

[15] *Eclectic Notes*, pp. 157–62.

were predestined to salvation. The Calvinists, therefore, had to be doubly watchful of their conduct.

More important and, indeed, the chief reason for Evangelical insistence upon a strict code of conduct was the belief that worldliness of any sort made salvation difficult. Holding this view and emphasizing it as they did, the Evangelicals formulated rules to govern the most minute acts of the individual. Practices that normally come within the scope of manners they placed within the sphere of morals. Matters of etiquette became problems of ethics. Restrictions and taboos were multiplied and made binding upon the faithful. Most Evangelicals, for instance, would have subscribed to the interdictions placed upon conduct by the "Spiritual Barometer." This guide, which appeared in one of their magazines, is reproduced on the opposite page.[16]

From a study of the barometer, it is apparent that the upper half consists of religious precepts, in most of which ardent Christians at all times have believed. The lower half, on the other hand, lists many taboos particularly associated with Evangelicalism. Some of these were familiar in Puritan times, but otherwise had never formed part of the Christian code. Yet the Evangelicals apparently ranked them with the Ten Commandments. According to the barometer, it was a heinous sin to visit the theater, to delight in novels, or to attend a Sunday party. In showing the degree of evil attached to particular practices, moreover, the barometer ranks masquerades with adultery, and a love of novels with skepticism.

While not all Evangelicals would have graded these practices in just this way, strict professors of every denomination believed that attendance at the theater, a Sunday stroll in the public gardens, or any kind of levity on the Sabbath were offenses of an egregious nature. To delight in pleasure revealed a worldly disposition, and, according to the Evangelicals, no Christian should engage in unnecessary worldly pastimes. Granted even that an occasional indulgence did not corrupt him, there was always the possibility that he would set a bad example to weaker individuals.

16 *Evangelical Magazine,* VIII (Dec., 1800), 26.

THE SPIRITUAL BAROMETER

70 — Glory; dismission from the body.

60 — Desiring to depart to be with Christ; patience in tribulations; glorying in the cross.

50 — Ardent love to the souls of men; following hard after God; Deadness to the world by the cross of Christ.

40 — Love of God, shed abroad in the heart; frequent approach to the Lord's Table; meeting for prayer and experience.

30 — Delight in the people of God; looking to Jesus.

20 — Love of God's house and word; daily perusal of the Bible with prayer; vain company wholly dropped.

10 — Evangelical light; retirement for prayer and meditation; concern for the soul; alarm.

0 — Indifference; family worship only on Sunday evenings; private prayer frequently omitted; family religion wholly declined.

10 — Levity in conversations; fashions, however expensive or indecent, adopted.

20 — Luxurious entertainments; free association with carnal company.

30 — The theater; Vauxhall; Ranelagh, etc.; frequent parties of pleasure; home of God forsaken; much wine, spirits, etc.

40 — Love of novels, etc.; scepticism; private prayer totally neglected; deistical company prized.

50 — Parties of pleasure on the Lord's day; masquerades; drunkenness; adultery; profaneness; lewd songs.

60 — Infidelity; jesting at religion; sitting down in the chair of the scoffer.

70 — Death; perdition.

Consequently, the attitude of the participant did not matter, and a large number of practices were tabooed without qualification. Sydney Smith thus summed up this attitude of the Evangelicals:

It is not the abuse of pleasure which they attack, but the interspersion of pleasure, however much it is guarded by good sense or moderation;—and it is not only wicked to hear the licentious plays of Congreve, but wicked to hear *Henry V* or *The School for Scandal;*—it is not only wicked to run about to all the parties in London and Edinburgh, but dancing is not fit for a person preparing himself for eternity.[17]

Holding these opinions, the Evangelicals gave them currency by adding to their numbers in the period 1800–1830. More than that, they instilled many of their beliefs in those who never became Evangelicals. What happened was well described by Lucy Aikin, who said that the Evangelical party "at length became great enough to give the tone to society at large." [18] Without imposing all its religious and moral teachings upon the nation, it swayed public opinion to support a rigorous code of conduct. And when public opinion became a strict arbiter of manners, Victorianism had arrived.

It is doubtful, however, if the Evangelicals could have so thoroughly altered public opinion without the occurrence of a counter-reformation within the church. Yet they were indirectly responsible for this also, for the counter-reformation was, at least partly, the result of the revival. At the beginning of the nineteenth century orthodox churchmen awoke to find that the Evangelicals were no longer a small band of zealots. They had become a powerful body of believers, too numerous to be ignored. During the revolutionary decade, alarmists had feared that skepticism would destroy orthodox belief, but now it appeared that the real threat to the Establishment was Methodism and Nonconformity. For the vigorous proselyting of the dissenting sects was attracting members away from the church, and the fact that some Evangelicals remained within the fold gave no

[17] *Edinburgh Review,* XI (Jan., 1808), 357.
[18] *Correspondence of William Ellery Channing, D.D., and Lucy Aikin,* London, 1847, p. 396.

assurance, because it was believed that they were boring from within. Once again, therefore, the cry became, "The Church in danger!"

Determined to check the progress of Nonconformity, church-men began by renewing their attacks upon Methodists and Evangelicals generally. Some, in order to end the missionary ac-tivities of itinerant preachers, proposed that Methodist clergy-men be required to attach themselves to a particular locality. Others attacked the Evangelicals in pamphlets, contending that they were political radicals and that their doctrines would lead to infidelity. It was even alleged that their emphasis upon salva-tion by faith led to a neglect of moral duties and explained the immorality of the times.[19] But these charges were too patently absurd to have much effect, and orthodox churchmen, having failed with satire and abuse, turned now to other measures.

The new plan was to fight fire with fire. Orthodox members of the church determined, about 1810, to adopt some of the Evan-gelical tactics. The first measure was to revive the older church societies and to establish new ones patterned after the Evangelical organizations. Then, to compete with Nonconformist programs of popular education, the church created, under its own super-vision, a national system of elementary schools. At the same time it began to publish and circulate great quantities of tracts and religious books. Before long, indeed, the church was imitating virtually all the Evangelical practices. This policy, while it failed to check the progress of dissent, had its effect upon the orthodox group. Although the orthodox had adopted it largely in self-defense, their somewhat artificially induced enthusiasm soon de-veloped into a type of seriousness closely akin to that of the Evangelicals themselves.

At the same time a more genuinely motivated revival was go-ing on in the church. This had been started toward the close of the eighteenth century by a small group of high churchmen who

19 See, for instance, Robt. Fellows, *The Anti-Calvinist*, London, 1801; [James Sedgwick], *Hints to the Public*, London, 1808; Richard Yates, *The Church in Danger*, London, 1815.

believed in practicing a greater degree of piety than was common outside Evangelical circles. During the early part of the nineteenth century the leader of this group was Joshua Watson, a wealthy merchant. His associates, clergymen, for the most part, included his brother, the Reverend John Watson, a brother-in-law, the Reverend Henry Norris, and the Reverend Christopher Wordsworth, brother of the poet.[20]

This little band of zealots, several of whom lived at Clapton, bore such a notable resemblance to the Clapham Sect that it was similarly nicknamed. The "Clapton Sect," though not so influential as the other group, performed much the same services for orthodoxy as Wilberforce and his friends did for Evangelicalism. Its members served upon various committees, helped to revive the S.P.C.K., and were instrumental in founding several new church societies. When the Establishment introduced its program to educate the poor, Joshua Watson was one of the originators of the plan; and when a society was formed to build additional churches, he was one of the directors. The other Claptonites also lent their assistance to these efforts to keep up with the Evangelicals, and, by setting an example for other churchmen, the Clapton Sect contributed to a spiritual awakening within the Establishment.[21]

For various reasons, then, the church experienced a counter-reformation which roused it from its long slumber. As a result the body of orthodox members became more zealous, certainly —and more genuinely religious, perhaps—than at any time since the seventeenth century. In fact, by 1825 it was difficult to distinguish between an ardent churchman and an Evangelical. One was about as pious as the other. Neither would tolerate the manners that had prevailed in the previous century. Both had rigidly defined opinions upon questions of morals and conduct. The number of people, among the different sects and in all religious groups, who favored strict standards was consequently very great

20 J. H. Overton, *The English Church in the Nineteenth Century*, London, 1894, chap. ii.
21 *Ibid.*

—great enough, indeed, to make public opinion an enforcing agency.

Victorian standards had been developing for several decades and, once they had the support of public opinion, they quickly set the prevailing tone of manners. This did not mean the complete adoption of Evangelical rules or religious beliefs. The earnest Victorian might be of any religious persuasion; he might be of none. His code of conduct was often not so rigorous as that of the Evangelicals. He did not necessarily abjure the theater or novels, but he did insist that they conform to certain standards of propriety. He did not forswear pleasure, but he regarded life with a type of seriousness unknown to his eighteenth-century ancestors. Secretly he might object to the social conservatism of his age, but, fearing the strict tribunal of public opinion, he usually conformed to the approved modes of conduct. To be sure, his deference to them was sometimes mere lip service. But even hypocrisy was less culpable than flouting public opinion. Commenting upon the improvement in manners during the first quarter of the nineteenth century, the *Morning Chronicle* (October 1, 1827) remarked, "Our men of rank may occasionally *assume* a virtue which they have not, they may sometimes be greater hypocrites than their forefathers were, but hypocrisy is, at all events, an homage offered to public opinion, and supposes the existence of a fear of the people."

The expression of this view as early as 1827 indicates that by this time public opinion had become a stern arbiter of conduct. As noted in this chapter, certain conditions had made the English peculiarly receptive to reform and had created a distinctly different attitude of mind. But the development of strict public opinion, although aided by attendant circumstances, was not entirely, nor even chiefly, adventitious. Victorianism was, in large measure, the product of conscious efforts to alter popular views upon the subject of manners and morals. The measures which were specifically adopted to foster rigorous public opinion well deserve detailed consideration.

CHAPTER FIVE

THE SOCIETIES

DURING THE eighteenth century a philanthropic impulse had led to the establishment of numerous charitable institutions to succor the poor, the ill, and the unfortunate. Many of these foundations were secular in character, for benevolence was the reigning virtue of the age, existing alike in the hearts of believers and unbelievers. There were, of course, in addition to the nonsectarian establishments, various denominational organizations like the S.P.C.K. and the Methodist tract and Bible societies, which specialized in publishing and distributing literature. But the different religious sects, although given to works of mercy, had not yet introduced their large and highly organized philanthropic associations. A feeling existed that charity should be more a matter of individual giving than of organized benevolence. The Methodists particularly emphasized this idea. Though extremely generous to the poor, they believed in avoiding ostentation and consequently endeavored to cultivate a disposition for private rather than public philanthropy.

In the nineteenth century the philanthropic impulse continued to be strong, but the spirit of benevolence was increasingly adulterated by other interests. A desire to keep the poor subservient, though manifest even in the eighteenth century, became, after the French Revolution, a dominating motive of philanthropists. Charitable and religious aims were intermingled as the Evangelicals gained a stronger hold, and most of the large societies founded by them were equally concerned with providing relief for the poor and converting them to the teachings of the revival. By engaging believers in some sort of volunteer work, moreover, these organizations were intended to promote zeal among converts. A great deal of importance was attached to performing charitable work and eventually, because the Evangelicals set the fashion, participation in one of the societies became almost a social requisite. Philanthropy was already a fad by 1813, when Mrs. Barbauld wrote, "There is certainly at present a great deal of zeal in almost every persuasion. . . . Bible societies, missionary schemes, lectures, schools for the poor are set afoot and spread, not so much from a sense of duty as being the real taste of the times." [1]

The number of societies founded in the first few decades of the nineteenth century was very great. Some of them were well endowed, for there were now many wealthy Evangelicals whose contributions made it possible to support large national foundations. The members of the Clapham Sect were particularly generous with their money and time, and their names could be found upon the rosters of almost every philanthropic agency. Very often they were the leaders in forming a new society, but the other Evangelicals and even the non-Evangelicals were soon imitating them, for in this time of watchful religious rivalry each sect was eager to have its own organizations. Frequently, to be sure, the Evangelicals of different denominations coöperated, allowing one large association to serve their common interests. More often they insisted upon having their own societies.

A further reason for the multiplication of societies was the great degree of specialization in their activities. There were separate and distinct associations to aid infants, beggars, prostitutes, chimney sweeps, the aged, the indigent and homeless, indigent mechanics, and the indigent families of deceased clergymen. Sundry missionary societies were formed to work in different areas and with different groups. Some devoted their efforts to the conversion of savages in Africa and the South Seas, some to that of foreigners on the Continent, of Catholics in Ireland, or of sinners at home. Various associations were founded to distribute Bibles and tracts to soldiers and sailors, to prisoners of

[1] *The Works of Anna Laetitia Barbauld,* London, 1825, II, 107.

war, to incarcerated criminals, and to the poor. Still other societies were concerned with the promotion of education, specializing in the supervision of Sunday, day, infant, or adult schools.
Finally, there were innumerable miscellaneous societies concerned with such problems as the enforcement of Sabbath laws,
the building of churches, and the suppression of objectionable
literature.

It is impossible to discuss all these societies in a work of this
kind. Nor is that necessary. Little need be said about the foreign
missionary societies; and certain other organizations may better
await discussion until later in this volume. Here it will suffice to
trace the rise of some of the more important groups, to show
the scope of their activities, and to consider their influence.

THE RELIGIOUS TRACT SOCIETY

In 1798, three years after she introduced the *Cheap Repository,* Hannah More had discontinued her series of monthly tracts.
Apparently she had found the writing of these moral tales a
wearisome business. Certainly she had not lost favor with readers, for her tracts continued to circulate for several decades, making their author a formidable rival of hack writers who lived by
publishing chapbooks and halfpenny ballads. The popularity of
the *Cheap Repository* particularly pleased the Evangelicals, and
they determined to keep the reading public supplied with moral
and religious tracts. A year after Hannah More discontinued her
series, therefore, a group founded the Religious Tract Society.

The members of this organization explained that their intention was to provide the poor with a safe literature:

The universal diffusion of education has augmented beyond cal-
culation the number of individuals who are able to read, and it is
hardly necessary to observe that they require to be supplied with
publications not too expensive for them to purchase, the contents
of which are intelligible to minds not highly cultivated. Unhappily
the advocates of infidelity have availed themselves of this opportunity, and are diffusing much poison far and wide.[2]

---

[2] *Proceedings of the First Twenty Years of the Religious Tract Society,* London,
1820, p. vi.

No doubt, since their organization was founded just at a time when reports of a conspiracy were rife, the members of the tract society genuinely believed that skeptics were plotting to pervert the religious views of the newly literate section of the population. It soon became apparent, however, that the chief purpose of the association was to promote the doctrines of the revival. This was only natural, inasmuch as the founders were ardent Evangelicals. They were drawn from the various Protestant denominations, for the Religious Tract Society was a coöperative venture.

For the first few years the society reverted to the policy of the older tract associations. Instead of the lively stories and ballads of the *Cheap Repository,* it produced a series of sober admonitions similar to those published by the S.P.C.K. *Friendly Hints to Servants* advised the humble to be content in the station to which it had pleased God to call them. *The Unfortunate Female* was addressed to prostitutes and reminded them that it was never too late to repent. *Advice to a Young Man on Entering the World* counseled youth to observe the Sabbath and to read the Bible. Tracts of this description were not so popular as the *Cheap Repository* publications, however, and within a few years the society adopted a different policy. In order to make its works more interesting, it formulated the following rules for the guidance of tract-writers. Without indulging in levity, tract-writers should endeavor "to whet the appetite of the reader." Each tract should contain an account of a sinner's salvation, to impress the reader that to be saved "one must be born of the spirit and justified by faith." A tract should be simply written, it should be forceful, and, despite its brevity, it should contain a number of religious ideas. Finally, tracts should make an appeal to all sorts of readers—to young and old, to the wealthy and the poor, to "careless and awakened sinners." [3]

Growing more aggressive, the society determined in 1805 to secure a monopoly for religious tracts. So far it had had to compete with secular works which hawkers sold in the streets of

[3] Samuel Green, *The Story of the Religious Tract Society*, London, 1899, pp. 6-7.

London. These tracts the society considered "vicious and profane," and in order to keep them from circulating it agreed to
sell its own tracts to the hawkers at less than the cost of printing
them. Thus assured of a larger profit from religious tracts, the
hawkers sold them in preference to the others. At the same time
the society endeavored to make its own works more interesting
by publishing them in the form of narratives and dialogues and
illustrating them with cuts. These measures helped to destroy
the competition of secular tracts and greatly increased the sale
of the society's publications.[4]

Certain tracts, notably those of Legh Richmond, were particularly popular with readers. An Evangelical clergyman, Richmond was best known as the author of *The Dairyman's Daughter, The Young Cottagers,* and *The Negro Servant.* By the middle of the nineteenth century the society had published 1,354,616
copies of these three stories.[5] Its other works, while not quite so
popular, were nevertheless widely read, with the result that the
Religious Tract Society became one of the chief sources of literature for nineteenth-century readers. The following figures show
the total number of tracts which it produced in different years: [6]

Year	Copies of Tracts Published
1804	314,613
1814	3,100,000
1824	10,012,760
1834	14,339,197
1844	15,367,676

This amazing circulation was possible largely because Evangelical zeal made tract distribution a favorite occupation. A contributor to the *Evangelical Magazine* wrote that he distributed
tracts wherever he went and suggested that every godly person
making a business or pleasure trip carry a supply to pass out on
the journey.[7] The Reverend Samuel Kilpin said that when he

[4] *Ibid.,* pp. 11–12. *Proceedings,* pp. 74–75.
[5] Wm. Jones, *The Jubilee Memorial of the Religious Tract Society,* London,
1850, p. 150.
[6] Sam. Green, *op. cit.,* pp. 24, 28, 45.
[7] *Evangelical Magazine,* VIII (Oct., 1800), 410.

traveled he dispersed about a hundred tracts every five miles. His record was exceeded by another person, however, who purchased from the society over a period of years no fewer than 741,000 handbills and tracts.[8] The members of the Religious Tract Society not only scattered their pamphlets along the highway, but distributed them in hospitals, prisons, and army encampments. Some of the more ardent Evangelicals even boarded ships in port and gave the tracts to sailors, who, according to their captains, read them with interest and were as a result better behaved.[9]

The society further increased the circulation of tracts by selling them to the auxiliary associations which it established in all the principal towns. By 1815 there were 124 of these distributing agencies. Each of them had its own corps of volunteer workers, whose task was to peddle the tracts from house to house. Thousands of people were thus employed, especially after the institution of the loan system in 1818. When a local chapter of the society adopted this plan, it divided a town into districts and appointed one of its members to visit every house in a particular neighborhood. Making a call every week or fortnight, the visitor collected the tract left on his last visit, lent the subscriber a new one, and received a small payment. With this system in force, several families were able to read the same copy of a tract, and the circulation of the society's publications was therefore much larger even than its statistics indicate.[10]

The introduction of various other projects gave the society a still more eminent position in the publishing field. To encourage their use in school, it bound the tracts in volumes and sold them to educational institutions at cost. In 1811 it began to issue a series of tracts especially designed for children, and in 1824 it started publishing a periodical called the *Child's Companion*. The society also introduced a magazine for adults, which sold 260,000 copies the first year it appeared. After 1823 it published religious books as well as tracts. Eventually it established branches on the Continent from which it distributed its works

---

[8] Wm. Jones, *op. cit.*, pp. 160, 173.
[9] *Proceedings*, pp. 424 ff.   [10] Wm. Jones, *op. cit.*, pp. 214 ff.

in translations. To assist the illiterate folk across the channel to read tracts written for them, the society even issued a French spelling book.[11]

By the middle of the nineteenth century the Religious Tract Society was circulating its works in 110 different languages and dialects, and a total of 4,363 different titles appeared upon its lists.[12] Yet, although it was easily the most important tract society, it was only one of many agencies engaged in publishing moral and religious works during the first part of the nineteenth century. There was also the venerable S.P.C.K., the Society for Promoting Religious Knowledge among the Poor, the Endeavour Society, which members of the Establishment had founded in 1794, and various other groups under the supervision of the Methodists, the Unitarians, and the older dissenting sects.

Through their combined efforts nineteenth-century readers were constantly supplied with tracts. What is more, the tracts, priced at a penny, were within the reach of all. They were brief, and even a sluggish reader could get through them. Written in simple English, they could be understood by anyone who was literate. The tracts were therefore admirably suited to that large section of the public which was just learning to read. But both rich and poor read these works, for the public had developed a great interest in moral and religious literature of all kinds. Many read virtually nothing else. With the exception of the Bible, the tracts held the foremost place.

THE BIBLE SOCIETIES

At the opening of the nineteenth century the principal agency for publishing and distributing the Bible was the S.P.C.K. For over a hundred years it had been engaged in this work, but having suffered from the unspiritual milieu of the eighteenth century, it was no longer the vigorous evangelizing agency that it had been in the Queen Anne period. Even the religious revival had so far failed to reanimate it. Because of the revival and the

[11] Sam. Green, *op. cit.*, pp. 13, 30 ff.
[12] Wm. Jones, *op. cit.*, p. 150 and Appendix III.

growing literacy of the masses, however, there was a much greater demand for the Bible than heretofore. In Wales, where Calvinistic Methodism was flourishing, the clergy could not secure enough Welsh Bibles to supply their congregations. Although the S.P.C.K. had printed a translation of the Bible in Welsh in 1799, the issue was soon exhausted, and, despite requests for another edition, the society showed no interest in providing one. In fact, when a clergyman from Wales, the Reverend Thomas Charles, went to the S.P.C.K. to ask for more Welsh Bibles, he was told that the society had no intention of publishing another edition for some time.[13]

This refusal resulted in the organization of a competing Bible society. When the S.P.C.K. denied his request, Charles went to the Religious Tract Society, of which he was a member, and asked the committee of that organization for assistance in printing a cheap Welsh Bible. The Evangelical members of this group seized the request as an opportunity to found another society to publish Bibles, not for Wales alone, but for the whole kingdom. Thus, in 1804, the British and Foreign Bible Society came into existence.[14]

Like the parent organization, the new society was nonsectarian. Of the thirty-six members who served as a committee, fifteen belonged to the Church of England, fifteen to other denominations, and six were foreigners resident in England. But the direction of the association fell chiefly to members of the Clapham Sect. The first president was Lord Teignmouth, and the first treasurer, Henry Thornton—both prominent Claphamites. Other members of the Clapham Sect, including William Wilberforce, Granville Sharp, Charles Grant, and Zachary Macaulay, served on the committee of the society, and the fact that it became one of the wealthiest organizations of the nineteenth century was due largely to the patronage of this group.[15]

Because Bible reading was an important part of the revival,

[13] William Canton, *History of the British and Foreign Bible Society*, London, 1904, I, 6 ff.
[14] *Ibid.*   [15] *Ibid.*, p. 15.

the Evangelicals were eager to circulate the text as widely as possible. At times, when discussing the beneficent influence of Scripture, they became almost mystical, as in the following passage
from one of their periodicals: "It would seem that the very touch
of the inspired volume had power to communicate new feelings,
and to kindle new desires; to elevate the standards of principle,
and to raise the tone of morals; to purify the springs of domestic
happiness, to tame the fierceness of the passions, and to civilize
manners." [16]

There were other reasons, however, for forming an organization to circulate the Bible. It had become almost a formula at
this time to ascribe the origin of a society to a desire to combat
infidelity. Hence, with the bogey of conspiracy evidently in
mind, the founders of the Bible association said that their purpose was to defeat "the recent attempts which have been made
upon the part of infidelity to discredit the evidence, vilify the
character, and destroy the influence of Christianity." [17] But it
was not simply a matter of defending the faith. The Bible, like
the tracts, was to help destroy Jacobinism and keep the poor submissive. This is apparent from statements appearing in the
Christian Observer, and since this periodical was published by
the Clapham Sect, its views may be considered to represent those
of upper-crust Evangelicals generally. Appealing for funds to
support the Bible society, the editors said:

To the rich and middle ranks it may be urged: you have a deep
interest in the welfare of the poor. If the security of the state depend
upon the loyalty and morals of its people, by what other means can
you contribute so essentially to the preservation of order, to authority
of the law, and the stability of government? . . . is it not, then, a
matter of policy as well as of duty, to create an interest among the
lower classes for the possession and perusal of the sacred records
from which benefits so great and various are acknowledged to flow? [18]

It is impossible to deduce how much weight this argument
had with subscribers, but the British and Foreign Bible Society
received large donations and became one of the wealthiest re-

[16] *Christian Observer,* XI (July, 1812), 464 ff.
[17] Canton, *op. cit.,* I, 21.   [18] *Christian Observer,* XI (July, 1812), 464 ff.

ligious organizations of the nineteenth century. By 1821 it had an annual income of £89,154 and its resources enabled it to produce numerous editions of the Bible each year. The following figures, showing the annual production of the Bible and the Testaments, give some idea of the development of this organization: [19]

Year Ending March	Bibles and Testaments
1810	64,468
1815	249,932
1820	256,883
1824	290,495
1829	365,424

By 1854, when the society celebrated its fiftieth anniversary, it had published a total of more than 20,000,000 Bibles and Testaments in England. Even these figures do not indicate the full scope of the organization. Like the Religious Tract Society, it entered the foreign field and, in addition to publishing Bibles in London, it issued several thousands from its depositories on the Continent. By its fiftieth anniversary it had affiliated associations all over Europe. Directly or indirectly, it was responsible for the printing of the Bible in 152 languages and dialects.[20]

At home every division of the country had a branch Bible society, for the London headquarters developed an extensive network of subsidiaries. Decentralizing its system even further than the Religious Tract Society, the British and Foreign Bible Society had three different types of local agencies. There were the auxiliaries which reported to the London unit, the branches which in turn reported to the auxiliaries, and the associations which operated in small sections and reported to either the auxiliaries or the branches. By 1830 a total of 2,349 such subsidiaries formed the links of an extensive chain of Bible dispensaries.[21]

The most ingenious plan for circulating the Bible was by the

[19] George Brown, *The History of the British and Foreign Bible Society*, London, 1850, II, Appendix III.
[20] *Ibid.*, p. 540.   [21] Canton, *op. cit.*, I, 354.

system of house-to-house canvassing which the society introduced in 1812. The purpose of this scheme was to sell the Bible on the installment plan. An appointed representative of the society visited each house in a particular neighborhood and collected a penny a week from every subscriber. This contribution entitled a person to be enrolled in one of the associations, and when he had made payments in full he received a copy of the Bible. Sometimes, to be sure, the Bible was bestowed as a gift, but the general practice was to sell it at cost price. It was best for the poor to buy it on the weekly savings plan, the Evangelicals argued, since it encouraged frugality and made them cherish the Bible the more when they finally received it. This method of selling the Bible became extremely popular with the upper classes, especially with the ladies, and thousands of them, with their subscription pads, made weekly invasions into the homes of the poor. Using the installment purchase plan, the society also organized juvenile associations to which children gave a penny a week, and ship associations to which sailors contributed their mite.[22]

Although the Evangelicals were extremely enthusiastic about the plan, others were strongly opposed to it. Even the payment of a penny a week meant a sacrifice for indigent families. Yet the social pressure exerted by a visit from one higher in rank made it difficult to refuse a subscription. To some honest observers, it seemed the final indignity heaped upon the poor. The society, however, defended its practice through its spokesman, C. S. Dudley. Arguing that it was futile to relieve poverty by direct aid and that one could help the lower classes only by teaching them "the correct principles of action" found in the Bible, Dudley averred that, as a result of these visits, the poor showed great improvement in their conduct. Gratified by the condescension of their superiors, they endeavored to make their homes and persons neat in order to win approval. Drunkenness and swearing had noticeably decreased among them and, since

[22] *Ibid.*, I, 53 ff. C. S. Dudley, *An Analysis of the System of The Bible Society*, London, 1821.

they had taken to reading the Bible, they were more content with their lot and consequently less inclined to sedition. The visitors, too, said Dudley, had received great benefits from their work, for they now read the Bible more frequently and had become more virtuous.[23] These assertions, supported by testimonials, overrode criticism, for visiting appeared to promote moral reform, and each year public opinion was growing more determined that England should be a moral nation.

The British and Foreign Bible Society had many critics, but it throve on opposition and, willingly or unwillingly, fathered several other organizations. For the purpose of circulating Holy Writ in Ireland, it formed the Hibernian Bible Society. Another offspring was the Prayer Book and Homily Society, which was founded to silence critics who objected to circulating the Bible without The Book of Common Prayer. Still another society was born when a certain clique tried to oust the Unitarian members from the British and Foreign Bible Society. Finding most members opposed to this, the malcontents themselves resigned and formed the Trinitarian Bible Society. But neither this nor any of the other associations became a serious rival of the original organization.[24]

The most bitter opponents of the British and Foreign Bible Society were found among orthodox churchmen. Because they viewed it as a menace to the Establishment, some of the bishops condemned the society in pastoral letters, and several other writers attacked it in a series of books and pamphlets. Some objected to circulating the complete Bible among the poor, saying that the text with its contradictions and difficulties of interpretation would serve only to confuse them. Others objected because the society did not supply the Prayer Book with the Bible. Still others, like the Reverend Herbert Marsh, contended that the Evangelical organization threatened to undermine the authority of the church. For years this controversy continued, kept alive by dozens of brochures written by both sides.[25]

Orthodox churchmen constantly declared that, in view of the

[23] Ibid., pp. 208 ff., 502 ff. [24] Canton, op. cit., I, 360 ff. [25] Ibid., pp. 303 ff.

work of the S.P.C.K., there was no need for the British and Foreign Bible Society. The Evangelicals, however, felt that the older organization was inadequate. Certainly it lacked the vigor of their own society. Although well endowed, the S.P.C.K. in recent decades had failed to play an aggressive part in the religious life of the country. Each year it published a number of Bibles, tracts, and religious books, but it had been fired neither by the revival nor by the alarm caused by the French Revolution. Many of its religious pamphlets dated from the Queen Anne period and lacked the freshness of the Evangelical tracts. Moreover, it had done little to meet the increased demand for religious and moral works. For 1807 its total issues amounted to 177,506 works, of which 20,953 were Bibles and Testaments, and 118,004 were tracts. This compared very unfavorably with the output of the new Evangelical societies.[26]

For a time the members of the S.P.C.K. contented themselves with attacking the Evangelical Bible society. But calumny and abuse availed nothing, for the Evangelicals grew continually stronger, and their societies overshadowed the much older S.P.C.K. Finally, as a last resort, certain churchmen decided to adopt some of the tactics of their rivals. One of the first things they did was to rejuvenate the S.P.C.K. Starting in 1810, this organization established diocesan and district committees under the supervision of parish clergymen. It was the function of these committees to distribute the literature published by the S.P.C.K., to secure subscriptions for the society, and to enroll new members. In other words, they were to serve in the same capacity as the branch associations of the Evangelical Bible society.[27]

The S.P.C.K. next decided to refurbish its list of tracts. To make them more appealing it introduced several new ones of the more informal type. Among these were the "Instructive Tales" of Mrs. Trimmer, which had first appeared in the *Family Magazine*. Following the example of the Evangelical tract so-

[26] Allen and McClure, *Two Hundred Years; The History of the Society for Promoting Religious Knowledge*, p. 198 and *passim*.
[27] *General Account of the S.P.C.K.*, London, 1813, pp. 23 ff.

ciety, the S.P.C.K. also introduced its tracts into schools and established lending libraries. Through such devices it became once more a vigorous organization. In 1817 it produced a total of 1,307,582 publications, of which 84,077 were Bibles and Testaments, and 1,077,493 were tracts. That meant that over a period of ten years it had increased its annual output sixfold. Continuing to grow, the S.P.C.K. before the middle of the nineteenth century was circulating about 4,000,000 works a year.[28]

The regeneration of the S.P.C.K. was typical of what was happening within the church. A counter-reformation had started, due in part to competition with Evangelicalism, in part to a revival of genuine zeal. In either case the result was the same. Except for a few points of dogma, the orthodox became very much like the Evangelicals, and when this happened, it insured the progress of the revival and the development of a stricter moral code.

CHARITABLE AND VISITING ASSOCIATIONS

In the absence of public relief agencies, there was a genuine need for charitable enterprises. The industrial revolution was complicating the old disease of poverty, and the government, suffering from the paralysis of laissez-faire philosophy, merely tinkered with the antiquated system of parochial relief and did little otherwise to assist the unfortunate members of society. Consequently it was left for philanthropy to provide for the poor, to care for the ill, and to comfort the distressed. A large number of societies were founded for these purposes, and undoubtedly they reduced somewhat the incidence of suffering. Yet they failed miserably as relief agencies, partly because the problems confronting them were exceedingly difficult, but chiefly because religiosity and cant interfered with honest philanthropy.

Charity eventually became a secondary aim with most of the societies. If religiosity did not dominate them in the beginning, it did so eventually, with the result that philanthropy became subordinate to narrow moral and religious interests. This is what

[28] Allen and McClure, *op. cit.*, p. 198.

happened to the Society for Bettering the Condition and Increasing the Comforts of the Poor. At its founding in 1794, the members determined to study the problems of poverty in a scientific manner. They recognized that the well-being of the poor was of vital concern to the nation, and, reversing the common view that poverty generally resulted from vice, the members declared, "The vices and faults of the poor must be deemed the vices and faults of an unfavorable situation, rather than of individual delinquency." [29] This attitude did not survive for long. When members of the Clapham Sect organized a branch of the society in 1799, their aims were neither scientific nor genuinely charitable. They stated their purpose as follows:

The discovery and relief of cases of real distress, the assistance and rewarding of honest industry, the detection of fraud and imposture, the discouragement of idleness and vice, and the employment of children at an early age, so as to improve the condition and morals of the poor.[30]

In addition to policing the poor, the Clapham society, with true Evangelical zeal, was determined to further the revival. To this end it introduced a system of visiting. The parish of Clapham was divided into eight districts and several visitors were appointed for each one. Upon receiving an appeal for relief, a visitor first called on the applicant and his family to discover their degree of industriousness and the frequency with which they attended church. Then, if the case was considered deserving, the society would provide relief in the form of blankets on loan, whitewash for cottages, or aid for lying-in patients. The bestowal of such benefits, however, was contingent upon the piety and moral disposition of the needy.[31]

Visiting societies of this kind became extremely common during the first part of the nineteenth century. In the beginning many of them had a genuinely charitable purpose, but, as the revival progressed, they almost invariably became proselyting

[29] *Reports of the Society for Bettering the Condition and Increasing the Comforts of the Poor,* London, 1798–1808, II, 14 and *passim.*
[30] *Ibid.,* II, 343.   [31] *Ibid.,* II, 347.

agencies. Such was the course followed by the Benevolent Society. In 1803 it was primarily a philanthropic organization,
whose visitors were making about 300 calls a week and distributing approximately £150 a month to the poor. The crusading
spirit had not yet come to dominate it, for a report of the society
states that "it is neither the design or desire to add to the number of any particular sect." [32] As time went on this policy changed,
and the report of the society for 1829 clearly shows that the religious zealots were in control. Declaring that it is more important to convert the ill than to give them temporal relief, the
instructions for visitors urge them to instill the fear of God in
those they visit and, if they find them too weak to discuss their
sinfulness, to read them the Bible.[33]

One finds the same emphasis upon conversion in the reports
of the Ladies' Royal Benevolent Society. This organization,
which was founded in 1812 by members of the Church of England, advised its visitors that a time of sorrow or affliction was
particularly apt for awakening religious fervor and that they
should take advantage of these occasions to reclaim the wicked.
To assist them in this work, visitors were provided with a supply of homilies and tracts.[34]

The climax of the visiting movement came in 1828 with the
establishment, under the auspices of the Church of England,
of a General Society for Promoting District Visiting. This organization, planning a nation-wide system, sent circular letters
to the bishops and to several hundred clergymen, urging them
to start a visiting society in each parish. By this time enthusiasm
was strong, and the plan was rapidly adopted. In London alone,
by 1831, there were 25 local chapters of this organization, and
their 573 visitors were making a total of 163,695 visits a year.
The society instructed its visitors to conduct themselves as
follows:

[32] *The Nature, Design, and Rules of the Benevolent or Stranger's Friend Society*, London, 1803.
[33] *Report of the Benevolent Society*, London, 1830.
[34] *The Ladies' Royal Benevolent Society*, London, 1818.

You will gently and prudently lead their attention to religious subjects. . . . You will urge upon them the duty and privilege of observing the Sabbath, of prayer, and of public worship. You will point out to them as occasion may require, their relative duties, and avail yourself of opportunities of reproving open vice. You will pay particular attention to the young, the sick, and the aged. You will encourage parents to send their children to day and Sunday schools, and recommend grown-up persons who cannot read to attend evening schools. You will inform those who are without a Bible how they may obtain one, and suggest a weekly subscription for this purpose.[35]

This society pursued a more aggressive policy than its predecessors, for its visitors called upon every poor family in their districts, not waiting for an invitation or for the pretext of comforting the ill. To be sure, the society provided the needy with clothes, food, and fuel, and sometimes sent the ill to hospitals. That temporal relief was a secondary interest, however, appears from the reports of the visitors. These are concerned chiefly with the number of tracts distributed, the effect of reading the Bible to the bedridden, and remarkable conversions. Reports such as the following were typical, "E.R. is gradually sinking into the grave, but is quite resigned, for she has been taught to see herself a sinner and now trusts to be saved by grace." [36]

Sometimes, indeed, so ardent was the desire to convert people that the visitors must have done more to menace than to improve the health of the stricken. Reading the Bible was a favorite practice, and visitors were wont to herd as many auditors as possible into the sick room. One visitor reported with considerable pride, "No less than ten persons had assembled in the room of a poor invalid and the Bible was read aloud, the persons present putting whatever questions arose in their minds." [37]

Though the visitors did convert some people, they undoubtedly overestimated their influence upon the poor. More important, perhaps, was the effect upon the visitors themselves,

[35] *The Fourth Annual Report of the General Society for Promoting District Visiting*, London, 1832, p. 44 and *passim*.
[36] *Ibid.*, p. 33.   [37] *Ibid.*, p. 21.

for thousands of men and women belonging to the upper classes engaged in the work. Some of them were attracted to it by genuinely humanitarian interests, of course, but many became visitors because the practice had become fashionable. With little real sympathy for the poor and no training to cope with the problems that confronted them, the visitors frequently botched the business of charitable relief. Yet it was rather pleasant playing Lord or Lady Bountiful. One could talk in commiserating tones about the horrible conditions one saw in the slums and one found it flattering to hear the expressions of gratitude that flowed from the humble. Humility was a great virtue, especially in one's inferiors.

Despite their enthusiasm, the visitors were generally not equipped to instruct others in religion. Although they probably helped to create the sentimental form of piety that flourished in the nineteenth century, they did little to further the true spirit of Christian charity. That spirit, indeed, seemed to be waning. In 1827 it was remarked that the old-fashioned type of Christmas was fast being forgotten. Instead of a time to express good will toward men, Christmas had become just another occasion for superintending the morals of the poor. Blaming the religious enthusiasts for this, a writer in the *Morning Chronicle* (December 22, 1827) observed:

Among the most liberal of this class, the inclement season of Christmas is distinguished, not by a distribution of *beef* and *blankets*— but a comfortable dispensation of Bibles bound in *calf* and religious tracts in *sheets,* procured at cóst from Rivington's or the Society. The creature-comforts would too much pamper the flesh, and excite perhaps a spirit of insubordination in the "lower orders" highly offensive to the taste, if not threatening to the privileges of the mighty. A grovelling prostitution of body and soul among their inferiors, effected by half-starvation and drivelling, enervating cant of censurers of other people's enjoyments is most acceptable in the sight of the upper orders. Whether this be sheer hypocrisy or sour puritanism we will not decide.

Hypocrisy or Puritanism? Apparently it was a mixture of both. Certainly the societies were poor substitutes for some systematic way to cope with the problem of poverty, though they served, perhaps, to salve the conscience of a nation which had neglected to make an honest effort to improve social conditions. No doubt many visitors were at least superficially convinced that by distributing Bibles and tracts they were performing their duty to the poor, for it is easy to believe what one wants to believe. If Dr. Johnson had been alive, he might have described them, not as hypocrites, but as victims of "cant." Discussing this term, he had once remarked, "There is a middle state of mind between conviction and hypocrisy, of which many are conscious. By trusting to impressions, a man may gradually yield to them, and at length be subject to them." [38]

Serving a twofold purpose, to keep the poor subservient and to further the narrow principles of the revival, the societies symbolized the spirit of the first part of the nineteenth century. They were to remain, however, as a heritage to later Victorians. And perhaps the truest final judgment upon them is that pronounced by a Victorian clergyman who said:

In the last half century our societies have multiplied to such a degree that they have become a public nuisance. They crush, instead of promoting, individual charity, and tame our sympathy between man and man. Our social evils have come to that pass that it may be truly said, "Nec vitia nostra, nec remedia, pati possumus." [39]

---

[38] Boswell, *Life of Johnson*, IV, 122.
[39] Mark Pattison. "Philanthropic Societies," *Essays*, Oxford, 1889, II, 322.

CHAPTER SIX

THE MODEL FEMALE

THE BEGINNING of the nineteenth century found middle-class readers interested in a relatively new type of literature. Women, especially, were absorbed in books which described the proper training of a young lady. These guides to etiquette, for that is what most of them were, contained rules for decorous conduct, advised parents upon the reading and amusements of their daughters, and warned young ladies against the pitfalls of the fashionable world. The taste for such works, remarked one reviewer, had grown to be an "epidemic fashion." "It is astonishing how many female writers have ventured upon this subject! . . . some really valuable writers, and some mere old women." [1]

It was not surprising that books of etiquette were popular at a time when many people found themselves in a class superior to that in which they had been born. To the new middle classes, who were not quite sure of the proprieties to be observed in the upper walks of society, any information upon manners was naturally welcome. Nor was it surprising that the authorities upon this subject were, for the most part, women. As the educators frequently observed, it is the province of the female sex to rule upon manners. There was, however, a more specific reason for the flood of books upon the proper training of a young lady. It was noticeable that the writers were uniformly conservative in their views, so conservative, in fact, that they seemed to be leagued against the one person who had proposed a radical plan for educating women. The rebel was Mary Wollstonecraft, au-

[1] The *Annual*, IV (1805), 708.

thor of *Rights of Women,* which had first appeared in 1792. To many readers this book, with its novel and revolutionary theories, seemed profoundly shocking. The reaction to it had been generally unfavorable, but it had provoked discussion, and the other educators were evidently determined to counteract any influence it may have had by publishing their own views upon the proper role of women in society.

Mary Wollstonecraft was a pioneer in the struggle to win social emancipation for women, and her book was the first genuinely important work devoted to that cause. In *Rights of Women* she urged her sex to assert themselves, to throw off the gyves of convention, and to demand equality with men. For centuries, she said, women had been the willing bond servants of men, depending upon their sexual attraction to gain whatever favors they sought from their masters. To escape from bondage, she insisted, women must cultivate their intellect, find new occupations, and refuse to accept a subordinate role in life. *Rights of Women* was a straightforward appeal, free from sentimentality, and fired with the author's desire to better the condition of her sex. With its emphasis upon equal opportunities for women, it opened the door upon a new world—a world in which women would enjoy liberty, equality, and a kind of fraternal partnership with men. But one glimpse of this startling world was enough for the "old women" who set themselves up as authorities upon education. They began to scribble, the public read their books, and another century was to pass before women were to enjoy. the rights demanded by Mary Wollstonecraft.

If *Rights of Women* had appeared earlier in the eighteenth century, it might have provoked laughter, but certainly not alarm. Published at the time of the French Revolution, however, it was bound to have an unfavorable reaction, for it fell upon a frightened world. Everything was against it. *Rights of Women* shocked people not merely because it proposed radical changes, but because its author was considered a scandalous person. Everyone knew that she was an ardent republican, for in a book called *A Vindication of the Rights of Man* she had taken issue with that great conservative manifesto of the time, Burke's *Reflections*. The story of her affair with Imlay was whispered about, and her indiscretions were probably held against her as a writer. Finally, and nothing could have damaged her reputation more, she was a friend of Tom Paine, the scarifier of Toryism. Even Horace Walpole, that debonair sophisticate who was generally contemptuous of popular sentiment, held the same opinion as the middle classes where Mary Wollstonecraft was concerned. Writing to Hannah More in 1795, he had closed his letter to this pietistic lady with, "Adieu, thou excellent woman! Thou reverse of that hyena in petticoats, Mrs. Wollstonecraft." [2]

As for Mrs. More, the very title *Rights of Women* was enough to make her ruffle her feathers in indignation. Without having read the book, she told Horace Walpole her opinion of it in no uncertain terms:

I have been pestered to read *Rights of Women,* but I am invincibly resolved not to do it. Of all jargon, I hate metaphysical jargon; besides there is something fantastic and absurd in the very title. How many ways there are of being ridiculous! . . . So many women are fond of government, I suppose, because they are not fit for it. To be unstable and capricious, I really think, is but too characteristic of our sex; and there is perhaps no animal so much indebted to subordination for its good behaviour as woman.[3]

Had she taken the trouble to read *Rights of Women,* Hannah More would have discovered that Mary Wollstonecraft agreed with her that women were unstable and capricious. But she would have found no sympathy with her idea of keeping them subordinate. It was their subordination to the other sex, said Mary Wollstonecraft, which made them superficial creatures. But they need not remain so. Give them the same opportunities, she urged, and they would show the same degree of maturity as men. What Mary Wollstonecraft wanted most was the chance for women to cultivate their intellects. Although she believed that their health would improve if they exercised more,

2 *Letters of Horace Walpole,* ed. by Mrs. Paget Toynbee, XV, 337.
3 Wm. Roberts, *Memoirs of the Life and Correspondence of Hannah More,* I, 487.

she made it clear that she wished to have them develop the mental rather than the physical robustness of men. In *Rights of Women* she said:

From every quarter I have heard exclamations against masculine women; but where are they to be found? If by this appellation men mean to inveigh against their ardour in hunting, shooting, and gaming, I shall most cordially join in the cry, but if it be against the imitation of manly virtues, or, more properly speaking, the attainment of those talents and virtues, the exercise of which enobles the human character, and which raises females in the scale of animal being, when they are comprehensively termed mankind;—all those who view them with a philosophical eye must, I should think, wish with me that they may every day grow more and more masculine.[4]

Despite this temperate attitude, the opponents of Mary Wollstonecraft insisted that her plan of educating women would produce a breed of amazons. The *Lady's Monthly Museum*, for instance, published a case history which demonstrated the deplorable effect that reading *Rights of Women* had upon one family. Incredible though it seems, this account was written with utter gravity, and no doubt serious readers found it edifying rather than amusing. The writer said that she was the mother of four daughters. Her family had been a happy one, and the young ladies had always conducted themselves in the most exemplary fashion until they read *Rights of Women*. Thereupon the formerly proper young ladies had become lamentably and indecorously masculine. The eldest daughter now joined in the hunt with men, groomed her own horse, and wagered that she could outride any man in the neighborhood. The second daughter, taking a bookish turn, seldom spoke without quoting from some classic and regularly held debates in her study. The third young lady developed such a passion for anatomy and vivisection that it was impossible to keep a dog or cat in the house. The youngest daughter, who became a devotee of military exercises, went about boasting that she was strong enough to knock down an ox.[5]

[4] *Rights of Women*, Boston, 1797, pp. 19–20.
[5] *Lady's Monthly Museum*, III (Dec., 1799), 433–36.

Determined to save English womanhood from the fate of these young ladies, the educators who followed Mary Wollstonecraft invariably stressed the importance of extreme femininity. Instead of encouraging common interests with men, they urged women to be a species apart. It was not sufficient that women were distinguished from men in various respects that followed from physical and glandular differences. They were to become still more feminine by suppressing certain natural dispositions and by cultivating peculiar modes of conduct. A set of manners and attitudes distinctive to women was to surround them with an aura of protection and mystery. To move out of this orbit, the educators warned their readers, would be a serious breach of propriety. Speaking of the proper education of a young lady, Maria Edgeworth cited this prescription:

Her mind must be enlarged, yet the delicacy of her manners must be preserved; her knowledge must be various, and her powers of reasoning unawed by authority; yet she must habitually feel that nice sense of propriety, which is at once the guard and charm of feminine virtue.[6]

Invariably the educators tabooed the freedom for which Mary Wollstonecraft had pleaded. Instead of lowering the barrier between the sexes, they insisted upon raising it still higher. Banished was the idea of equality with men. Women were to accept their subordinate position and to stake all upon the bargaining power of their sexual attraction. It was to be their one forte, guarded by rules of decorum and made mysterious by the disguise of frailty. Gushing upon the importance of modesty, Hannah More said:

Oh! if women in general knew what was their real interest, if they could guess with what charm even the appearance of modesty invests its possessor, they would dress decorously from mere self-love, if not from principle. The designing would assume modesty as an artifice; the coquet would adopt it as an allurement; the pure as her appropriate attraction; and the voluptuous as the most infallible art of seduction.[7]

---

[6] *Practical Education*, London, 1798, II, 550.

[7] *Coelebs in Search of a Wife*, Philadelphia, 1884, p. 108.

Upon which Sydney Smith remarked, "If there is any truth in this passage, nudity becomes a virtue; and no decent woman, for the future, can be seen in garments." [8]

This comment must have struck the female educators as extremely indelicate. They were not accustomed to such frankness, and, for that matter, most of them probably did not think of modesty of attire in terms of coquetry. According to Evangelical teaching, a love of finery showed a worldly disposition, and there were many Evangelicals among the educators. When they described a model young woman, she usually expressed a proper disdain for fine clothes. Mrs. Sherwood's pattern female of the lower classes refuses to dress in silk or wear ribbons, saying, "It becomes everyone of us to dress decently, but surely, whatever the rich may think it right to do, it becomes not a poor servant girl to spend her little pittance on needless finery." [9] Her reservations about the rich only showed the proper deference the model female in humble life should exercise toward her superiors. In the books of the educators a model female of superior rank was generally almost as circumspect in her attire. Describing her middle-class heroine, Hannah More said she appeared "as neat as the strictest delicacy demands, and as fashionable as the strictest delicacy permits." [10]

The influence of the Evangelical moral code upon the educators was particularly observable in their attitude toward amusements. Most of them countenanced relatively few pleasures for a respectable young lady. In *Duties of the Female Sex,* a book which discussed proper pastimes for maid, wife, mother, and dowager, the Evangelical Thomas Gisborne forbade masquerades and Sunday concerts altogether. The theater, he conceded, was not completely corrupt, but, believing that it generally had a pernicious effect upon young ladies, he advised them to refrain from seeing plays. Nor would he allow them to indulge in card-playing. That pastime, he said, should be shunned by everyone except very old people. Gisborne did not exactly forbid

[8] *Essays,* p. 153 (*Edinburgh Review,* April, 1809).
[9] Mary M. Sherwood, *Works,* New York, 1858, III, 153.   [10] *Coelebs,* p. 108.

dancing, but he warned his readers that the ballroom was beset with many dangers. When young ladies attended a dance, therefore, they must carefully guard against making a vain display of their persons and refuse to accept strange and unprincipled men as partners.[11] The other educators were equally insistent that those who chose to dance must obey the proprieties or pay the piper. Never, said Sarah Trimmer, should a young lady indulge in "an improper display of personal beauty and indecorous agility." [12]

Fiction was a particular obsession of the educators. According to Mrs. West, novels, like strong wine, made young ladies giddy. But the effect was more lasting. "Had so many fascinating descriptions never been given of the pleasures, enjoyments, and advantages of rank and fortune," observed Mrs. West, "the elegantes of humble life would have been far less numerous, and we should have retained some valuable stuff, capable of being converted into the wives of traders and yeoman." [13] Joshua Collins believed that it would be wise for parents to establish an "immutable law" forbidding their charges to borrow books from the circulating libraries. "It is much to be questioned," said Collins, "whether any sort of fictitious representation of life and manners ought to be put into the hands of youth." [14] Erasmus Darwin was somewhat more liberal. Many novels contained objectionable passages, he remarked, but to expurgate such works would only excite curiosity. He believed that a better policy was to allow the passages to remain, and to have a governess or older person mark them with disapproval when reading with young ladies. Some books, however, like *Gil Blas* and *Tom Jones*, he considered too improper for any young lady to open.[15]

One of the less prudish educators was John Aikin, a doctor

11 *Duties of the Female Sex*, London, 1801, pp. 168 ff., 190 ff.
12 *Guardian of Education*, II (April, 1803), 104.
13 Jane West, *Letters to a Young Lady*, London, 1806, II, 439.
14 *An Address to Parents and Instructors*, London [1800], pp. 32 ff.
15 *A Plan for the Conduct of Female Education in Boarding Schools*, Derby, 1797, pp. 33–34.

and a Unitarian. Although he too excluded some reading as unfit for young ladies, he objected to the absurdly severe restrictions which other writers imposed. People who considered Pope's "Eloisa to Abelard" seductive could find a great deal of literature equally objectionable, he remarked, but to conceal "not only this poem but most of the real history of human life" showed "a distrust of good sense and principle." [16] This opinion shocked Mrs. Trimmer, who attacked Aikin for expressing it. After much ado about "poisoning" the mind of youth by "promiscuous reading," she concluded that "nothing can make us think otherwise of 'Eloisa's Epistle to Abelard' than as very unfit for a young person to read." [17]

The higher the rank of the model female, of course, the greater the degree of liberty permitted. Because Hannah More's *Hints for Forming the Character of a Princess* was intended for the instruction of Charlotte, heir presumptive to the throne, it placed fewer restrictions upon reading than books written for the guidance of ordinary young ladies. Nevertheless, it reflected the narrow views of its author. Shakespeare received only qualified approval. His tragedies could be read in their entirety, but some of his plays were to be read only in part, and others not at all. Novels, according to Mrs. More, were not generally suitable even for children of royalty, but she made a few exceptions, among which, rather curiously, was *Don Quixote*.[18] Much less liberal was the reading list prepared by Priscilla Wakefield for model females of the lower middle classes. Excluding novels and plays completely, she recommended only such works as the Bible, Mrs. Trimmer's *Family Magazine*, the *Cheap Repository*, Hanway's *Virtue in Humble Life*, Watts's *Poems*, and Barbauld's *Hymns*.[19]

Despite their contempt for fiction, the educators were fre-

[16] *Letters to a Young Lady on a Course of English Poetry*, London, 1804, pp. 81–82.
[17] *Guardian of Education*, III (July, 1804), 292–93.
[18] *Works*, VII, 72, 199–213.
[19] *Reflections on the Present Condition of the Female Sex*, London, 1798, pp. 142–43.

quently the authors of novels and short stories. In justice to them, however, it should be said that they seldom wrote merely to entertain readers. Their fictional works, they explained, were intended to serve as an antidote to some of the more vicious books of the time and to attract patrons of the circulating libraries to serious lessons in conduct and morality. Several of these educators, therefore, wrote stories in which a model female was the heroine. In their narratives she embodied all the virtues recommended in the etiquette books. Her sense of decorum was faultless, her delicacy beyond reproach. No matter what the cost, and sometimes it was life itself, she always obeyed the proprieties.

One of the best examples of prudence in humble life is found in *Susan Gray*. Mrs. Sherwood, who first published this story in 1802, allows her heroine few happy moments. Orphaned at an early age, Susan finds a temporary protector in Mrs. Neale, a wealthy old woman who teaches her to be tidy and sends her to school. While living with Mrs. Neale, Susan is converted, and from this time she becomes exceedingly pious. Unfortunately her benefactress dies, and Susan is forced to become the assistant of a laundress named Mrs. Bennett. The heroine, still in her teens, now has no other occupation except washing and ironing. But she never complains about her work. What does pain her is to find that Mrs. Bennett and her young friend, Charlotte Owen, are wicked creatures who are always thinking about fine clothes. Susan herself is never beguiled by such idle thoughts, and when Mrs. Bennett offers to buy her a new hat or a ribbon, she flatly refuses to indulge in such fripperies.

One day, at Mrs. Bennett's bidding, Susan delivers some shirts to an army captain. This gentleman, admiring her good looks, attempts to become better acquainted with her. Although he treats her with respect, she rebuffs him. A few days later he meets her in a lane and again tries to converse with her. But Susan, unlike Pamela, believes that it is improper for a poor girl to encourage the attention of any man above her station. The captain, after several fruitless attempts to be friendly, eventually enlists the aid of Mrs. Bennett, who brings him to her house. Terrified at his presence, Susan eludes her pursuer by jumping from a window and escaping to a near-by town. Here she finds employment working in the fields, but within a few weeks she falls ill, weakened, not from hard work, but from the shock to her sensibilities. While she is languishing upon her deathbed, a clergyman visits her, and to him she confides her story. Then, utterly resigned and giving vent to many pious platitudes, Susan dies in true Evangelical style.

But the story does not end with the death of Susan, for Mrs. Sherwood generously includes the sermon preached at her funeral. And to make the moral unmistakable, she tells the reader that the army captain, who was really a cad, eloped with the vain Charlotte Owen, only to desert her a few weeks later. Charlotte thereupon pursues a sinful course for a few years and then dies under horrible circumstances. In conclusion Mrs. Sherwood addresses the reader as follows: "Remember Susan Gray and let her example be ever in your mind; and let it not be your wish to be rich and great, to seek for distinction and pleasure in this world, but to do your duty in that humble station in life in which it has pleased God to call you." [20]

Despite its lugubrious moral, *Susan Gray* was extremely popular. As a short story, it was a good miniature of the model female, but for a full-length portrait one must turn to *Coelebs in Search of a Wife*. In this novel, published in 1809, Hannah More produced the best example of a pattern young lady of superior rank. Since she had frequently condemned the practice of reading novels, however, Mrs. More felt she must apologize for writing one herself. Her explanation was:

I wrote it to amuse the languor of disease. I thought there were already good books enough in the world for good people, but that there was a large class of readers whose wants had not been attended to—the subscribers to the circulating libraries.[21]

This was no compliment to the readers who bought up eight editions of *Coelebs* in two months, but they could have excused

---

[20] Sherwood, *Works*, III, 203-4.   [21] Roberts, *op. cit.*, III, 103.

their indulgence, for even strict Evangelicals praised the book, putting it in a class by itself. In a panegyric on *Coelebs,* the *Christian Observer* remarked, "It may be very true that novels are mischievous, but we cannot allow this work to be called a novel." [22] Strictly speaking, perhaps it is not a novel. The plot is meager, the characters are unreal, and the dialogue often sounds like a sermon. Nevertheless, no single work better reveals the temper of the early Victorians.

Coelebs in Search of a Wife portrays both a model male and a model female. The hero is a young man who has been brought up according to a strict plan of education. When his parents die and he is left alone in the world, he decides to search for a wife. His quest brings him to London, where he is introduced to several middle-class families in which there are daughters of marriageable age. Coelebs, after carefully observing the young ladies, invariably finds them deficient in some respect. The daughters of his first host are pretty, but he refuses to consider them further when he discovers that they have no interest in domestic duties and fritter away their time reading *The Sorrows of Werther, Perfidy Punished,* and similar works of fiction. When he meets the Ranbys, he concedes that the daughters are good-natured girls, but he decides that none of them would make a suitable wife, for all lack an adequate knowledge of religion and dress in "transparent and scanty clothes." The hero therefore moves on to the next mart, continuing his quest, but finding no one to suit his exacting demands.

Finally Coelebs arrives at the home of his father's old friend, Mr. Stanley of Hampshire. In this serious household he finds nothing at fault, and here at last he meets his model of female perfection. Lucilla, the eighteen-year-old daughter of the family, is pretty, modest to an extreme, and, according to the author, possesses a sprightly but not a saucy wit. The reader has few opportunities to judge her wit, however, for Lucilla generally remains silent except when she is asked to express her views upon manners, morals, or religion. Upon these occasions she speaks

[22] *Christian Observer,* VIII (Feb., 1809), 109.

sententiously, but often cuts herself short for fear of saying more
than modesty warrants. Coelebs, impressed by her air of propriety, follows her about with appraising eyes and is delighted
to learn that she is a prudent home economist and spends much
of her time instructing her younger brothers and sisters. What
most impresses him, however, is to find that visiting the poor is
one of her regular occupations. One day he follows her to a
humble cottage in the neighborhood, and entering on tiptoe,
he discovers Lucilla at the bedside of a dying woman reading
the penitential psalms from a large Bible.

When Coelebs is thoroughly convinced that Lucilla possesses
all the virtues necessary in a wife, he asks her to marry him.
Lucilla, ever mindful of the proprieties, meekly refers him to her
father, who gladly accepts Coelebs into the family. In fact, it
turns out that years before the fathers of these two noble speci-
mens had, in the best comic-opera tradition, agreed to train them
according to a strict formula, hoping that some day they would
meet and marry.

It was apparent that the author of *Coelebs* held no brief for the
independent or assertive woman. This was somewhat remarkable, for Hannah More herself was an aggressive person. She
was now an elderly woman, but years before, when a young
girl, she had come up to London seeking a career. There she had
managed to meet the important figures in the literary world, and
before long she could boast of being a friend of the great Dr.
Johnson and of the famous actor, David Garrick. With their
encouragement, she published some essays and poetry which
established her reputation as an accomplished writer. Eventually,
having also written a couple of successful plays, she became a
prominent member of that exclusive group of literary ladies
known as the Bluestockings.

Later, when many of her earlier friends were dead, Hannah
More had attached herself to the rising Evangelical party and
turned to writing tracts. These works proved even more popular than her secular writings, and Hannah More gained the reputation of being a great moralist. From the sale of her various

works she had amassed a substantial fortune and, despite all the prejudices against her sex, she had contrived to have two distinct and notable careers. Her life, indeed, was an epitome of what an independent woman might achieve. Not so her writings. Her bloodless heroines never dreamed of having a career, and Lucilla Stanley, who made it a rule never to read controversial works, would have been a dullard in any literary salon.

The only lively girl in *Coelebs* is Amelia Rattle, and this character the author apparently introduced for the purpose of satirizing Mary Wollstonecraft's idea of an independent woman. When Miss Rattle, accompanied by her mother, visited the Stanleys, she entered the drawing-room and "threw herself back on the sofa at nearly full length." Having assumed this indecorous position, she proceeds to monopolize the conversation, while Lucilla sits by silent and proper. Miss Rattle, who is very much the scholar, rattles on about her various studies. They include geography, history, music, botany, and astronomy. She has also studied several languages and attended lectures on chemistry and experimental philosophy. Despite these numerous intellectual interests, Miss Rattle finds time to attend dances and parties and she attempts to entertain the Stanleys by describing the gay social life of London. The serious Stanleys listen politely, but they are not amused by this account of Miss Rattle's worldly pursuits. Nor is the frigid and proper Coelebs, who shows his disapproval of the frivolous young woman in his account of her departure from the Stanleys. Although Hannah More intended it to illustrate the masculine independence of Miss Rattle, this incident serves as an amusing side light upon the priggish disposition of the hero. Coelebs describes the occurrence as follows:

Mr. Stanley conducted Lady Rattle, and I her daughter; but as I offered to hand her into the carriage, she started back with a sprightly motion and screamed out, "O, no, not in the inside, pray help me up to the dickey. I always protest I will never ride with anybody but the coachman, if we go ever so far." So saying, with a spring which showed how much she despised my assistance, the little hoyden was seated in a moment, nodding familiarly to me, as if I had been an old friend.

Then, with a voice emulating that which, when passing by Charing Cross, I have heard issue from an overstuffed stage vehicle, when a robust sailor has thrust his body out the window, the fair creature vociferated, "Drive on, coachman!" He obeyed, and turning round her whole person, she continued nodding at me till they were out of sight.[23]

When Coelebs has sufficiently recovered, he and Mr. Stanley discuss Miss Rattle in pitying terms. "Here is a mass of accomplishments," said Coelebs, "without one particle of mind, one ray of common sense, or one shade of delicacy." [24]

The didactic purpose of the novel is obvious. Throughout the volume Coelebs critically examines and evaluates the young women he meets, and he, supposedly, represents the view of what every man wants in a wife. Mrs. More was not a very good judge of masculine tastes, however, and there were protests from the sex which she had maligned. Charles Lamb, having borrowed *Coelebs* from "a very careful, neat lady," returned it with the following quatrain:

> If ever I marry a wife
> I'll marry a landlord's daughter;
> For then I may sit at the bar,
> And drink cold brandy and water.[25]

The Reverend Sydney Smith, in a splendid review of the book, called *Coelebs* a typical piece of Evangelical propaganda. Never exercising any discrimination, the exemplary characters avoided all amusements, as if their virtue were made of such frail stuff that it could stand no trial. "The excellent Mr. Stanley is uniformly paltry and narrow," wrote Smith, "always trembling at the idea of being entertained, and thinking no Christian safe who is not dull." One would never suspect that in her salad days Mrs. More had been a dramatist of note, for, as Smith observed, "Coelebs and Lucilla, her *optimus* and *optima*, never dance and never go to a play. They not only stay away from the comedies of Congreve and Farquhar, for which they may easily be for-

---

[23] *Coelebs,* chap. xxiii.   [24] *Ibid.*
[25] *The Letters of Charles Lamb,* Troy, New York, 1902, II (June 7, 1809).

given; but they never go to see Mrs. Siddons in *The Gamester* or *Jane Shore*." [26]

The puritanical character of the novel, although repugnant to Sydney Smith, recommended it to serious readers, and the minute analysis of conduct helped to make *Coelebs* a favorite of young ladies. It was easily the most popular of all the books written to teach propriety. But the others were not neglected, and, so far as instruction was concerned, it made little difference whether one read Mrs. More, Thomas Gisborne, or Mrs. Sherwood, for the pattern of female perfection was always very much the same. Indeed, the model female figured so frequently in literature that she became a stereotype. Even Byron was familiar with this famous character as she appeared in the works of the educators. Hence his description of Donna Inez in *Don Juan:*

> In short she was a walking calculation,
> Miss Edgeworth's novels stepping from their covers,
> Or Mrs. Trimmer's books on education,
> Or "Coelebs wife" set out in quest of lovers,
> Morality's prim personification
> In which not Envy's self a flaw discovers;
> To others' share let "female errors fall,"
> For she had not even one—the worst of all.
>
> Canto I, stanza 16

The model female was much more than a stock character in literature. Many young ladies took her for their prototype, as one may gather from the resemblance of the Victorian woman to the model female. But the influence of the educators was apparent long before the accession of Victoria. In addition to teaching conduct, they usually suggested certain occupations for young ladies, and their recommendations had a direct bearing upon the new role adopted by women in the first decades of the nineteenth century.

Because they were principally interested in prescribing for young ladies of the middle and upper ranks, relatively few of the educators had much to say about the problem of earning a

[26] *Essays*, p. 153 (*Edinburgh Review*, April, 1809).

living. Those who did deign to treat this subject usually recommended such conventional occupations as teaching, working in millinery establishments, or shopkeeping. Occasionally, to be sure, they suggested a new type of employment, but they stressed the idea that women were not to compete with men unless it was to fill some position in which they could serve to protect feminine sensibilities. This was the motive Priscilla Wakefield had in mind when, with a curiously morbid form of prudery, she remarked:

Every undertaker should employ women for the express purpose of supplying the female dead with those things which are requisite. How shocking is the idea of our persons being exposed, even after death, to the observation of a parcel of undertaker's men.[27]

It is uncertain whether anyone acted upon this particular suggestion, but shortly after it was made. The Ladies' Committee of the Society for Bettering the Condition and Increasing the Comforts of the Poor decided to investigate certain occupations to determine whether they were not better suited to women than to men. The report made by these ladies shows that they were just as prudish as the educators. It was recommended, for instance, that daughters of clergymen and army officers should be trained to teach in academies for girls, since the practice of employing men "might be injurious to the character of the female sex." Particularly obnoxious were the French drawing and dancing masters, "tinctured as most of them must be with foreign habits and vices." [28] Certain other employments were recommended, not because the ladies of this society wished to promote the independence of their sex, but merely to protect feminine delicacy. Although written as early as 1804, the following report is Victorian even in its diction:

The personal attendance of male hair dressers, shoemakers, and staymakers in the dressing rooms and private apartments of our fair country women has been frequently noticed, not only as indecorous

---

27 *Reflections on the Present Condition of the Female Sex*, p. 165.
28 *Extract from an Account of the Ladies' Society for the Education and Employment of the Female Poor*, London, 1804, pp. 6 ff.

but derogatory to the character and intrinsic purity of the sex. It should seem natural for female delicacy to accept as an attendant at the toilet the assistance of a virtuous and well-educated Englishwoman in preference to men unknown, unaccredited, and not otherwise recommended than by having been imported from the shores of France or Italy. It should also seem natural for ladies who feel what is due either to their character or to the unprotected of their sex to desire to frequent those shops only from whence the employment and assistance of women are not entirely excluded; and to avoid those where files of athletic men, ranged in order behind the counter, are employed like Hercules in the service of Omphale in the most minute, trivial, and effeminate occupations of the female sex.[29]

The educators, in addressing young ladies of the superior classes, urged them never to engage in masculine pursuits or to do anything to jeopardize the dignity of their rank or the delicacy of their sex. These restrictions greatly limited the activities in which women could properly engage. In fact, for a lady of some social standing, virtually the only sanctioned occupations outside the home were teaching Sunday school, distributing Bibles and tracts, and visiting the poor. And these were the employments which the educators invariably encouraged. According to Hannah More, who was easily the most popular authority upon this question, every young lady should become an amateur social worker. In her *Strictures on the Modern System of Female Education*, this distinguished patron of Sunday schools had argued that, by instructing the poor and visiting them in their homes, women of the upper ranks would avoid habits of indolence themselves and "give the best practical answer to the popular declamations on the inequality of human conditions."[30] Later, when she wrote *Coelebs*, Hannah More gave still greater encouragement to the practice of visiting, for she made it Lucilla Stanley's most praiseworthy occupation. This book, more than any other work, appears to have set the fashion.

Consider, for instance, the effect which *Coelebs* had upon Marianne Francis. From her letters this young lady, who was a

[29] *Ibid.*, p. 8.   [30] *Works*, VI, 63.

niece of Fanny Burney, appears to have been a rather intelligent person. She was also a distant relative of Arthur Young, at whose home in Bradfield she spent much time. It was probably through her association with him that she became an Evangelical, but the interests which she developed soon after her conversion appear to have been chiefly stimulated by reading her favorite author, Hannah More. In February, 1809, Marianne Francis wrote to Mrs. Piozzi, "I have read *Coelebs* with great delight—delight that was increased, I am ashamed to say, by finding the sentiments on religion and education a counterpart to my own." [31] It was about this time that Marianne Francis began visiting the poor in charity schools, at the workhouse, and especially in their homes. She had her own school at Bradfield, where she instructed the children of the neighborhood twice a week. When she heard a sermon, she took notes in order to retail its substance to others. A student of theology, she sometimes sent religious books to her friends, hoping to convert them. Her chief missionary work, however, was among the poor. Describing the daily routine of this disciple of Hannah More, a daughter of Arthur Young wrote:

When at Bradfield she sleeps over the servants' hall, with a pack-thread tied round her wrist and placed through the keyhole, which he [Arthur Young] pulls at four or five times, till he awakens her, when she gets up and accompanies him in a two hours' walk on the turnpike road to some cottage or other, and they take milk at some farmhouse; and she distributes tracts (religious ones), and questions people about their principles, and reads to them and catechises them.[32]

The various societies which came into existence during the first few decades of the nineteenth century greatly encouraged the practice of visiting, and most of the domestic missionaries were associated with one or another of these organizations. By 1821 the British and Foreign Bible Society alone had no fewer

[31] Letters from Marianne Francis to H. L. Piozzi, John Rylands Library, MS 583, p. 33.
[32] *Autobiography of Arthur Young*, ed. by M. Betham-Edwards, London, 1898, p. 472.

than 10,000 lady visitors.[33] A still larger number were probably engaged in distributing tracts or calling from house to house on behalf of one of the numerous charity associations. To be sure, the question of propriety arose. Was it consistent with female delicacy for ladies to visit the unstately homes of England? This was a nice problem, but C. S. Dudley, of the British and Foreign Bible Society, helped to settle it by deciding that circumstances justified the practice. If women had an important part in the proceedings of the Bible Society, he argued, one might consider it indecorous. But men conducted the public meetings and took care of all important business; the ladies merely visited the poor. Inasmuch as their motives were purely benevolent, they transgressed no rules of decorum.[34]

Having settled the question of propriety, Dudley observed that the habit of visiting the poor and doing other works of charity had produced a remarkable change in the character of the female sex. As a result, he said, writing in 1821, "Woman has assumed a higher title to our admiration and respect." This improvement he attributed to "the admirable writings of many enlightened females, and especially to those of one venerable character who may justly be called the moralist of her sex."[35] Needless to say, the moralist of her sex could be no one but Hannah More.

Even non-Evangelicals admitted that Hannah More's influence upon manners was very great. Lucy Aikin, writing to her American friend, the Reverend William Ellery Channing, remarked:

It has always been the practice of the better kind of country ladies to distribute benefactions among the cottagers, and often to carry, as well as to send them, aids in sickness. In towns of moderate size the same things were done; but Hannah More in her *Coelebs*, by representing her *pattern* young lady as regularly devoting two evenings in a week to making her rounds among the village poor, unfortunately made it a fashion and a rage.[36]

---

[33] C. S. Dudley, *An Analysis of the System of the Bible Society*, p. 501.
[34] *Ibid.*, pp. 345 ff.   [35] *Ibid.*, p. 343.
[36] *Correspondence of W. E. Channing and Lucy Aikin*, p. 396.

It is interesting to note that visiting was not an important feature of the larger societies until shortly after the publication of *Coelebs*. That book first appeared in 1809, and the first ladies' auxiliary of The British and Foreign Bible Society in England was formed in 1811. Undoubtedly Lucy Aikin was right in attributing the popularity of visiting in the first instance to Hannah More's novel. *Coelebs* started the fad among ladies of the Evangelical party, she said, and eventually, because that party gave "the tone to society," visiting became a fashion with women generally. Continuing her discussion, Lucy Aikin wrote:

The practice of thus supervising the poor has become so general that I know no one circumstance by which the manners, studies, and occupations of English women have been so extensively modified, or so strikingly contradistinguished from those of a former generation. By these female missionaries numberless experiments have been made and projects started. Some have addressed themselves to the bodies of the poor, others to their souls, and there has been much quackery in both departments. Some have distributed Calvinistic tracts, others bread and soup tickets. Some have applied themselves to clothing children, others to teaching them, others to reading to the sick and infirm.[37]

Lucy Aikin merely confirms what is evident in the reports of the societies.[38] In the absence of a better system, the charitable assistance given by the visitors accomplished some good, she readily admitted. But when visiting became a fad, "a positive demand for misery was created by the incessant eagerness to relieve it." As a result, improvidence was encouraged. Some of the poor, knowing that the good ladies would take care of their families, squandered "their wages on drink and dissipation." Wives, formerly industrious, stopped sewing for their children, who were now clothed in the cast-offs of their betters. Hypocrisy increased, for the indigent often "put on a little saintliness" in order to make them appear more deserving, or, hoping to flatter the ladies, assumed "a fawning, dependent servile spirit, unworthy of free men." [39]

Describing the effect which visiting had upon members of her

[37] *Ibid.*, pp. 397–98.   [38] See above, chap. v.   [39] *Correspondence*, p. 90.

own rank and sex, Lucy Aikin observed, "I think it has given rise among the ladies to much spiritual pride and self-inflation, much of an imperious, pragmatical, meddling habit." Some of them became so enthusiastic about superintending the poor that they neglected literature and the arts and made home life intolerable for their fathers and husbands. To Lucy Aikin, who had a genuine reverence for the teachings of Christianity, the religiosity of the visitors was particularly objectionable. Most of them, though too ignorant to be able to instruct others, insisted upon catechizing the poor. In one infant school the lady-managers thought it would be a good plan for the babies to memorize "the interpretations of prophecies concerning the twelve tribes of Israel." They desisted only when a curate interfered.[40]

But all this business of supervising the poor, giving them tracts, and selling them the Bible was not entirely a matter of exaggerated fervor or mistaken benevolence. In part, at least, it was motivated by expedient political interests, by the prevailing belief that it was necessary to keep the poor docile. Commenting on the bibliolatry of the visitors, Lucy Aikin wrote to the Reverend W. E. Channing, "You know well, too, how the precepts of Christianity have been pressed into the service of a base submission to all established power." [41] Although it was not necessarily her intention, by soothing the distresses of the humble the model female probably helped to keep the poor from grumbling about the system of government. Thus she had a share in maintaining the conservative political order.

The model female, however, was as much the victim of reactionary conservatism as the poor. She found her place in society, but her position remained inferior to that of men. She had new occupations and interests, and she could command certain privileges due her sex, but she was a slave to convention and propriety. Hannah More and the other educators had scotched the ideas of Mary Wollstonecraft and scotched them so successfully that it was to take even longer to secure the rights of women than to establish the rights of free men.

[40] *Ibid.*, pp. 129, 398.   [41] *Ibid.*, p. 129.

CHAPTER SEVEN

THE IMPROVEMENT
OF THE MASSES

BY 1830 there was a noticeable difference in the standards of all classes of society, but perhaps the most remarkable change had occurred in the habits of the common people. They were no longer the ignorant and brutish populace of the eighteenth century. Although not much better off economically, most of them had come to observe certain amenities and to be fairly law-abiding. Their amusements were less gross, and to a marked degree they were more sober and cleanly. Exceptions could be found, of course, but as a class they had definitely improved their standards.

What accounts for this change? Although there were many contributing factors, the most important reason for the improvement of the masses was the development of popular education. Speaking of the effect which the growth of literacy had upon manners, Leslie Stephen remarked, "Two centuries ago the reading part of the nation was mainly confined to London and to certain classes of society. The most important changes which have taken place have been closely associated with the changes which have entirely altered the limits of the reading public." [1] Stephen was speaking of two whole centuries, but within this period the most significant expansion in the size of the reading public occurred between 1780 and 1830. By the end of this time about half the population was literate. That meant there were now seven or eight million readers as compared with an esti-

[1] *English Literature and Society in the Eighteenth Century*, p. 25.

mated million and a half before the introduction of Sunday schools.[2]

The existence of this vast reading public distinguished the new generation from all previous ones and was responsible for many other distinctive characteristics of the time. It was not merely the growth of literacy, however, which altered the standards of the common people. So far as book learning was concerned, their education was generally meager. Many never got past the primer stage and never learned so much as to write their names. But even a slight degree of education was often sufficient to alter their way of living, inasmuch as many of them, for the first time, learned certain elementary principles of conduct. Furthermore, the educators of this period were quite as much interested in disciplining the lower classes as they were in teaching them their letters. Much was dependent, therefore, upon the character of the educational systems.

The introduction of these systems was achieved in the face of great obstacles, for the shadow of the French Revolution hung over the nation for decades, intimidating people and creating opposition to any thoroughgoing plan to educate the masses. As a result the schools had to depend upon private contributions for their support. Not until 1833 did Parliament appropriate any money for popular education, and not until 1870 was there anything remotely resembling a public school system.[3] Further handicaps limited both the amount and the quality of instruction given in free schools. Nevertheless, by comparison with any previous period, great advances were made. Circumstances had brought the nation to a stage where education was to be general, and thousands of new schools were founded upon one plan or another.

[2] These figures are necessarily partly conjectural, for the first census was not taken until 1801. The population of England and Wales in 1831 was 13,896,797. In 1780 it was probably about half of that. From various statistics of the number of children in school, some of which are given later in this chapter, it would appear that about half the population could read in 1831, while probably not more than 25 percent were literate before the Sunday school movement.

[3] John W. Adamson, *English Education, 1789-1902*, Cambridge, 1930, pp. 34 ff.

SCHOOL SYSTEMS

Although Sunday schools were eventually to become much
more numerous than they had been during the eighteenth century, at the end of that period they nearly came to grief. It was
rumored that the Sunday schools were being used by conspirators against religion and the state to promote atheism and
Jacobinism. Nothing could have been more absurd, but after
the frightening decade of the French Revolution many people
were inclined to credit this report. Among those who helped to
spread it was Bishop Horsley of Rochester. Apparently Horsley
had been reading Robison and Barruel, for in a charge to the
clergy of his diocese, published in 1800, he explained that a
conspiracy had caused the downfall of established institutions in
France. Alleging that the conspirators had now shifted their
operations to England, Horsley said that it was part of their
plan to employ Sunday schools, especially those of the Methodists, to promote atheism and rebellion.[4]

So fantastic were these rumors that even the schools of Hannah More, that pillar of the established order, fell under suspicion. The trouble started at Blagden, where the local curate
objected to the Methodist principles of one of her teachers.
Hannah More dismissed the master, but the quarrel continued
and she finally had to close the school. Meanwhile reports of
this affair got into the newspapers and periodicals, and what had
started as a local dispute became a national controversy. People
took sides for or against Hannah More—her enemies insisting
that she had used her schools to promote Methodism, atheism,
and sedition—her friends defending her with great indignation.[5]

The charges of atheism and sedition were, of course, un-
grounded, and Hannah More was not a Methodist. What she
wanted was a revival within the Establishment. She had devoted her proselyting activities to that end, but, as one of
the more prominent Evangelicals, she was disliked by orth-

[4] *Gentleman's Magazine*, LXX (Nov., 1800), 1076 ff.
[5] *DNB;* Wm. Roberts, *Memoirs of the Life and Correspondence of Hannah
More,* III, 114 ff.

odox churchmen, who were now genuinely disturbed by the progress of the revival. Indeed they were probably much more alarmed by the growing power of the Evangelicals than they were by the rumor of a conspiracy. No doubt people like Bishop Horsley really believed that the enlightenment of the masses might lead to skepticism and political rebellion, but they apparently exaggerated their fears upon this score, knowing the propagandist value attached to such damning labels as "atheism" and "Jacobinism." What alarmed them most was the prospect that Methodist and dissenting Sunday schools, by instructing children in the principles of Nonconformity, would wean large groups of people from the Establishment. There was also a feeling that Evangelicals like Hannah More might eventually turn Methodist and take their Sunday scholars with them. Hence orthodox churchmen endeavored to suppress the schools which were not under their immediate supervision.

As a result of unfavorable propaganda the Sunday schools came into disrepute in some quarters, and for a few years the tendency was to close schools rather than to found new ones. But the alarmists could not completely dampen enthusiasm for these institutions. Too many people believed that the Sunday schools served a great need. Even those who might be opposed to teaching the poor to read could not escape the fact that popular education achieved other results. It was frequently said that the establishment of a Sunday school in a community improved its whole character, and no one could validly object to training the masses to be more industrious and law-abiding. Besides the Methodists and dissenters refused to abandon the task of educating the poor, and orthodox churchmen had no alternative but to develop more schools of their own.

Eventually opposition to the Sunday schools completely subsided, and when, in 1816, a committee of Parliament made an investigation of these institutions, it reported that they were performing a great social service for the nation. Several Sunday school directors appeared before the committee, and uniformly they attested that children who attended their classes were more cleanly, better-behaved, and more law-abiding than others. Some of the supervisors said that none of their pupils had ever been charged with delinquency. The investigation also revealed that Sunday school children often reformed their parents by dissuading them from using profanity and shaming them into being more cleanly in their habits. Frequently the parents turned over a new leaf after hearing their children read the books and tracts which they brought home from school. One supervisor told the tale of a little girl who had borrowed Legh Richmond's *Dairyman's Daughter*. While she was reading it to her mother, her father overheard the story and was so impressed by it that he abandoned his former practice of spending Sunday at the local public house and became a regular churchgoer. After listening to testimony of this kind, the committee of Parliament concluded that every encouragement should be given to the establishment of additional Sunday schools.[6]

All over England Sunday school directors were teaching children, not only their letters, but also to be neat, well-mannered, and pious. When Sunday schools were first introduced it was customary to pay some "deserving woman" a small stipend to conduct the classes. The Methodists had early adopted the plan of employing volunteer teachers, however, and by 1800 other denominations were following this practice. The results were said to be much better, since men and women who offered their services were generally more conscientious than paid instructors. It was the duty of the teachers to hear the lessons of the pupils, to shepherd them at church services, and to supervise the lending library of the school, from which children were allowed to borrow religious books and tracts. The teachers also paid frequent visits to the homes of their pupils, where they consulted parents upon the conduct of their charges and advised them in domestic matters. Thus the Sunday school supervisors, most of whom were drawn from the middle ranks of society, exerted considerable influence upon their communities.

By 1824 there were no fewer than 62,000 Sunday school teach-

6 *Parliamentary Reports*, IV (1816), 155 ff.

ers in England and Scotland.[7] They had their own society, which had been founded in 1803 to promote their common interests. Called the Sunday School Union, this organization printed catechisms, prayer books, spellers, tracts, and sermons. It also published a periodical for children and another for the teachers. The Sunday School Union was chiefly important, however, for the influence which this large and unified group could exert upon public opinion. When, in 1837, a bill came before Parliament which would permit Sunday racing at Notting Hill, the union helped to defeat it by submitting a petition signed by 6,600 of its teachers. In the same year the society protested against having men work at the post offices on Sunday, and as a result this practice was at least partly discontinued. Later in the Victorian period members of the union heard that Parliament was to consider a proposal to open the British Museum and the National Gallery to the public on Sunday. They immediately circulated petitions in all parts of the country and, when Parliament met to discuss the measure, the society presented it with 4,880 separate petitions. These were signed by 603,000 teachers and parents, who indicated that, in their opinion, gaping at the Elgin Marbles or viewing the paintings of Holbein and Reynolds were unsuitable Sabbath occupations. Faced by this overwhelming evidence of sentiment, the House of Commons defeated the measure by a vote of 378 to 50.[8]

The lobbying activities of the union help to show the broad social implications of the Sunday school movement. Far more important, however, was the fact that millions of people were receiving some education. By 1828 there were more than 900,000 Sunday school pupils. Still further additions would bring this number to about 3,000,000 in the middle of Victoria's reign.[9] If it had not been for Sunday schools, many children would have grown to maturity without any formal supervision. But having attended Sunday classes for a few years, they had learned to scrub

[7] *Annual Report of the Sunday School Union*, London, 1824, p. 8.
[8] W. H. Watson, *The Sunday School Union*, London, 1869, pp. 123 ff.
[9] John Wade, *History of the Middle and Working Classes*, London, 1833, p. 112. W. H. Watson, *The First Fifty Years of the Sunday School*, p. 160.

their faces, to dress more neatly, and to read simple English. Furthermore, as a group they were noticeably more religious, industrious, and law-abiding than their ancestors had been. One may say with assurance, therefore, that of all the educational systems of the early nineteenth century, the Sunday schools did most to change the standards of the masses. The specific results of popular education, however, must await discussion until other educational movements have been considered.

The first decades of the nineteenth century produced an interesting experiment in adult education. Earlier, especially in Wales, mature men and women had sometimes learned to read by attending Sunday schools. In England the Quakers had established a few schools exclusively for adults, but there was not much interest in such institutions until 1812, when an auxiliary of the British and Foreign Bible Society established one at Bristol. It was definitely an experiment, for while the founders were eager to give more people access to the Bible, there was some uncertainty as to whether it was possible to teach mature individuals. When it proved perfectly feasible, additional schools were provided at Bristol, and within two years more than 1,500 scholars were enrolled. A similar plan was adopted soon afterwards at London, Plymouth, Sheffield, Salisbury, Norwich, and in several other cities.[10]

Most adult schools did not teach writing, for the objection was raised that if the poor learned to write there would be an epidemic of forgeries. The curriculum was confined to instruction in reading and religion, and to the inculcation of moral principles. According to reports this training produced eminently satisfactory results. The scholars developed proficiency in reading the Bible, became more cleanly in their personal habits, and showed great improvement in their conduct. No matter how aged the pupil or how hardened the sinner, the schools apparently worked wonders. That, at least, appears from the amusing testimony given by a visitor to the schools at Bristol, who reported:

[10] Thomas Pole, *A History of the Origin and Progress of Adult Schools,* Bristol, 1814.

In one of these schools was a man of eighty-eight years of age advanced in his alphabet to spelling words of two syllables, and anxious for improvement; who, we were informed by the conductor, was much improved in his moral character since attending as a learner. Another man in the same room was privately pointed out to us as having lived unlawfully with a woman for the space of twenty years; but, since his attendance in the school, he has been so convinced of the sinfulness of his conduct as to induce him to marry her.[11]

Perhaps the informant exaggerated the accomplishments of the octogenarian, and possibly the marriage of the tardy but repentant swain was due in part to the persistence of his bride. Nevertheless, it would appear that the adult schools, besides teaching many to read, exerted much the same sort of disciplinary influence as the Sunday schools. By doing so, they shared in changing the standards of the masses.

Next to the Sunday schools, the most important contribution to popular education in the first decades of the nineteenth century was the monitorial system. Although this plan had been employed before this time, it was not widely adopted until about 1800, when Joseph Lancaster, a young Quaker schoolmaster, introduced it in his school. The details of the program were simple enough. Lancaster acted as supervisor and taught the older boys. They in turn heard the lessons of the younger children.

The chief advantage of the monitorial system was that one schoolmaster could serve for as many as three or four hundred pupils. If the masses were to be educated, it was necessary to have some cheap mode of instruction, since schools had to depend upon private contributions for their support. Schoolmasters come cheap, however, and when only one was needed to teach several hundred children, the cost of instruction was reduced to a minimum. The introduction of the monitorial system, therefore, held the promise that eventually it would be possible to provide schools for all. Much impressed by the plan, George III contributed £100 a year to establish additional schools and at an interview with Lancaster said, "I heartily approve of your sys-

11 *Ibid.,* pp. 65–66.

tem, and it is my wish that every poor child in my kingdom be taught to read the Bible." [12]

Others, not so pious as the king, were eager to promote the monitorial system in order to make popular education general. Liberals like James Mill, Francis Place, and Henry Brougham believed that Lancaster's plan was superior to any which had so far been introduced to educate the common people. Without doubt it was. Although the monitorial system had serious deficiencies, it had distinct advantages over the Sunday school system. It provided a full-time course of instruction and gave children the opportunity to learn writing and arithmetic as well as reading. Moreover, Lancaster and his supporters, unlike many founders of Sunday schools, were genuinely interested in promoting the welfare of the masses. They wanted to give them the best instruction possible and, because they considered popular education a right, and not a privilege, they kept their schools from being mere charitable institutions.

The monitorial system, although introduced in several places, soon encountered opposition. Lancaster had founded his schools upon nonsectarian principles. That is, he confined religious instruction to Bible-reading and to teaching the general principles of Christianity. Inasmuch as children of various denominations attended his schools, this practice would seem to have been the logical one to follow. But certain orthodox members of the church thought otherwise. To them it was just another malicious plot to weaken traditional institutions.

The first person openly to attack Lancaster was Mrs. Sarah Trimmer. Her criticism appeared in 1805 under the title *A Comparative View of the New Plan of Education*. Reviewing this treatise, Sydney Smith referred to the author as "a lady of respectable opinions and very ordinary talents; defending what is right without judgment, and believing what is holy without charity." [13] It was an apt characterization, for nothing could have

---

[12] David Salmon, *The Practical Parts of Lancaster's Improvements and Bell's Experiments*, Cambridge, 1932, p. ix.
[13] *Essays*, p. 84 (*Edinburgh Review*, Oct., 1806).

been more absurd than some of the objections she raised to Lancaster's system, but many people considered Mrs. Trimmer an authority upon education, and the church and state party endorsed her views.

Mrs. Trimmer was opposed to Lancaster's schools chiefly because they failed to teach the specific doctrines of the Established Church. She had always held that it was dangerous to teach the poor anything more than to read, however, and she now advanced this old argument once more, affirming that further education would make the lower classes discontented with their lot. When she attacked other features of the new system, Mrs. Trimmer proved more original in her remarks. Lancaster had given silver medals as a reward to boys who acted upon what he termed "noble principles." To Mrs. Trimmer this practice seemed almost seditious, for boys taught to consider themselves noble, she said, might aspire to become "nobles of the land and to take the place of the hereditary nobility." She also objected to the method of punishing boys who came to school with dirty faces. In order to shame them into washing, Lancaster stood them up before the class and had one of the girls scrub their faces. Mrs. Trimmer's prudish comment upon this practice was, "It is inconsistent with the modesty of the female sex, at that age or any age, to perform such an office before a gazing multitude of the other sex; nor is this the way to guard a girl against future seduction." [14]

Mrs. Trimmer may have been partly motivated by jealousy, for George III, who had once visited her Sunday schools, had become the patron of Lancaster. As a churchwoman, however, she was genuinely opposed to nonsectarian education, and there were others equally disturbed by this innovation. John Bowles, the professional propagandist, wrote a pamphlet in which he declared that Lancaster's system of instruction "was incompatible with the safety of the Established Church and in its tendency subversive of Christianity itself." Bowles, resorting to what was

[14] *A Comparative View of the New Plan of Education,* London, 1805, pp. 39, 46, and *passim.*

now a favorite argument to defeat any progressive measure, suggested that the new schools would promote deism.[15] Another of Lancaster's opponents was the Reverend Herbert Marsh, who affirmed that nonsectarian education would weaken both religious and political institutions. "By detaching men from the Church," he said, "we create divisions in the state which may end with the dissolution of both." [16]

It was apparent that England was still suffering from the conservative reaction to the French Revolution when members of the church and state party resorted to such arguments to check the progress of popular education. They were afraid that, if educated, the masses would demand a larger share in government and they were equally afraid that nonsectarian institutions would wean members from the Establishment. It was the same fear, in fact, that had created opposition to Methodist and dissenting Sunday schools. Yet, ironically, the attempt to destroy the Lancastrian system eventually resulted in the erection of a still larger number of schools. This happened because orthodox churchmen, failing in their efforts to suppress the nonsectarian institutions, were driven to the expedient of establishing their own system of monitorial schools.

Mrs. Trimmer was partly responsible for the idea. In criticizing the schools of Lancaster, she had declared that the Reverend Andrew Bell, and not Lancaster, was the originator of the monitorial system. An orthodox clergyman, Bell had formerly been a superintendent of schools in India, where, indeed, he had employed monitors some years before Lancaster had started his experiment. Bell was now living in England, and Mrs. Trimmer brought him out of retirement to champion her cause. With her encouragement he published an account of his own system, in which he endorsed her opinion that it was best to limit instruction for the poor to reading. He then introduced his plan into a few schools. Finally, in 1812, a group of orthodox churchmen, alarmed at the progress of nonsectarian education, decided to

15 *A Letter to Samuel Whitbread*, London, 1807.
16 "The National Religion the Foundation of National Education," a sermon by Rev. Herbert Marsh; quoted by James Mill, *Schools for All*, London, 1812, p. 72.

establish a system of schools under the auspices of the church. For this purpose they formed the National Society for the Edution of the Poor and employed Bell to act as supervisor. Once embarked upon this program, the church greatly added to the number of monitorial schools.[17]

Meanwhile supporters of the Lancastrian plan, in order to encourage the founding of more schools, had established a society called at first the Royal Lancastrian Association and later the British and Foreign School Society. For a time Lancaster supervised the schools of this organization, but he eventually proved incompetent. The patronage he had received had apparently made him conceited, and, after quarreling with his associates and squandering money intended for the schools on personal luxuries, he finally resigned. Under the capable direction of other members, however, the British and Foreign School Society continued to flourish.[18]

Thus, with two monitorial systems in competition with each other, an increasingly large number of children were provided with instruction in day schools. By 1820 more than 145,000 pupils were attending monitorial institutions, and by 1828 the total number in unendowed day schools amounted to approximately 1,000,000.[19] With almost as many children enrolled in Sunday schools, England was rapidly becoming a literate nation. But the process had been going on ever since Raikes had started his experiment at Gloucester. Many adults had already profited by the greater educational opportunities of their generation, and there were various signs that the common people were improving their standards.

SIGNS OF THE TIME

Historians have been prone to underestimate the effect of educational developments in the period 1780–1830. To be sure, neither the Sunday nor the day schools provided a very satisfactory educational system. Too often those who supervised the

17 Salmon, *op. cit.*   18 *Ibid.*
19 *Parliamentary Papers*, VII, 341–44; Wade, *op. cit.*, p. 112.

schools considered them mere reformatories, the chief purpose of which was to furnish moral instruction for the poor. The Lancastrian schools, however, gave a fair elementary training, and the other schools at least taught children to read and introduced them to better habits. This meant much by contrast with the former absence of any education, and the masses responded in a remarkable fashion to the meager opportunities offered them.

The best authority upon the improvement of the working classes in this period is Francis Place. He had himself been born of humble parents and knew from experience the conditions which prevailed among the poor of London at the end of the eighteenth century. But when he contrasted manners in the period 1820–1830 with those existing thirty or forty years before, he was not merely reminiscing. For Place kept voluminous records of the social changes of his time, filling hundreds of scrapbooks with pamphlets, newspaper clippings, letters, and his own comments. These documents are the more valuable because Place was a scrupulous observer of conditions. His biographer, Graham Wallas, said of him: "My own opinion, formed after consulting independent evidence in newspapers and elsewhere for a large number of Place's statements, is, that his accuracy on all questions of fact was most remarkable." [20]

With this comment anyone who has worked with the Place Collection will probably agree. But it is difficult for even the most scrupulous critic to escape some sort of bias, and Place, although accurate in recording facts, sometimes erred in his interpretation of them. When he discussed the social improvements that had occurred in the lower ranks, he was inclined, probably because he was a skeptic and a Benthamite radical, to underestimate the influence of religious and conservative forces in effecting the changes he observed. The improvement of the working classes he attributed almost entirely to popular education. True, the schools had probably done more for the poor than tons of tracts and regiments of district visitors. Never-

[20] *The Life of Francis Place, 1771–1854,* London, 1918, p. vii.

theless, the education of the masses, especially that share which fell to Sunday schools, was so closely associated with the religious revival that it is impossible, for a clear understanding of conditions, to separate them. Place gives almost no credit to the Sunday schools, and as one of the founders of the Lancastrian Association, he was inclined to overemphasize the importance of the schools established by that society and to underestimate the influence of Bell's monitorial system. Otherwise his observations upon the improved standards of the working classes seem entirely trustworthy and they are probably the most knowing comments that have been made upon this subject.

Writing in 1829, Place said:

I am certain I risk nothing when I assert that more good has been done to the people in the last thirty years than in the three preceding centuries; that during this period they have become wiser, better, more frugal, more honest, more respectable, more virtuous than they ever were before.[21]

Although less emphatic than Place, James Mill made very much the same sort of observation when he wrote of the lower classes:

In manners, in all the little moralities of daily intercourse, there is, even within the memory of men still living, a prodigious amelioration. There is a gentleness and civility in their deportment towards one another, not to speak of their superiors, rarely met with a century ago. Riot and drunkenness are greatly diminished.[22]

Numerous exceptions could, of course, be found. There were remote hamlets where life crept in its petty pace, just as it had for centuries. Rural workers in these communities had perhaps never heard of the new gospel of Evangelicalism, may never have attended a Sunday school, and were often innocent of all book learning. There were also the new industrial towns in which conditions of life were possibly even worse than they had been for the London poor of the eighteenth century. Nor could one expect decent standards to prevail in the mining districts, where

21 B.M., Add. MSS 27,828, p. 61.
22 *Westminster Review*, VI (Oct., 1826), 264.

the workers, many of them women and children, were doomed to spend most of their waking hours underground.

A prominent labor leader, Francis Place was vividly aware of the distressful circumstances under which thousands of people were forced to live. But while admitting that exceptions existed, he was convinced that as a class the poor had considerably bettered their social standards. On the other hand, and this made the change the more remarkable, their economic status had not improved. According to modern authorities, the real income of the British worker was approximately the same in 1825 as it had been at the time of the French Revolution.[23] Making virtually the same comment in 1826, Place wrote, "Real wages have not increased, but frugality, sobriety, and better management and self-respect have increased." [24]

In London, said Place, a separation had occurred between "those who are informed and those who remain in ignorance; they no longer associate in common as they formerly did." Yet even the most wretched members of society were not quite so wretched as they had been a few decades earlier, for "the meanest, the most ignorant and most depraved, with some exceptions, are bettered by the example of the informed workmen." [25] They were not so squalid, their children were not so bandy-legged, and their manners had improved. This was particularly noticeable to one visiting the slums. Accompanied by his wife, Place walked through the district of Petticoat Lane and Spital Fields one day in 1826, and coming home wrote the following account:

We walked leisurely, and people who were standing on the pavement moved out of the way to let us pass; not an offense was given; not an improper or even impertinent word was spoken in our hearing. Ten or twelve years ago only, and still more so twenty years ago, we should not have ventured in the same manner to have gone from one end to the other of this long Rosemary Lane. We should have been assailed with the most opprobrious language, should have

---

[23] J. H. Clapham, *An Economic History of Modern Britain,* Cambridge, 1930, I, 131, 602, and *passim.*
[24] B.M., Add. MSS 27,828, pp. 129–30.
[25] *Improvement of the Working People,* London, 1834, pp. 9–10.

been blackguarded from one end of lane to the other, as I and my two eldest daughters were one Sunday afternoon about fifteen years ago in Spital Fields and along the road to Bethnal Green. Nothing can more strongly mark the great change of manners among even the most unfortunate of the people than the conduct I have noticed.[26]

A still greater change had taken place in the class of skilled workmen. "Formerly, and even within my own recollection," wrote Place, "the education and manners of all sorts of workmen in London were so nearly alike, that they may be said to have differed in no material particular." Skilled and unskilled laborers were equally untutored. "Few could write, none read books of any use to them, and very few even looked at a book of any sort." Having no interest in bettering their condition, most of them spent their leisure time in the pursuit of the grosser pleasures. "The whole body was much more dissolute and profligate than they are now, and drunkenness was the conspicuous and prevailing vice." If anything, the better paid workmen were more corrupt than the others, for they had more money to spend on debauchery. "Now," said Francis Place, writing in 1829, "the difference between skilled workmen and common labourers is so strongly marked as was the difference between the workman and his employer." As educational opportunities increased, standards had rapidly improved among skilled laborers, who were now "more sober, more moral, and better informed than were the generality of their employers at the time alluded to." Many of them had, despite low wages, managed to acquire a little property or to insure in a benefit club, and now that drunkenness was "no longer the prevailing and conspicuous vice among workmen," they visited the public house less frequently and spent more time in their homes.[27]

The greater cleanliness of the common people was of itself sufficient evidence of their improved standards. Place explained that instead of spending their money on gambling and drink, as they formerly did, many of them used their earnings to buy

---

26 B.M., Add. MSS 27,828, pp. 129–30.
27 *Improvement of the Working People*, pp. 5–6.

household equipment and decent apparel. Perhaps, too, the influx of Sunday school teachers, tract distributors, and district visitors into the cottages and tenements of the poor encouraged neater habits. Certainly those who had attended school had been taught the virtues of soap and water. Another thing, quite apart from education, which had contributed to the better appearance of lower-class women was the development of the cotton textile industry. Formerly the "wives and daughters of journeymen, trademen, and shopkeepers had worn leather stays, quilted petticoats, and woolen gowns." These garments were almost never washed. Cotton had become so cheap, however, that women had turned to making their gowns and petticoats from this material, and, because it was easy to wash, "cleanliness followed almost as a matter of course." [28]

The change was observable also in the greater respect for law and order. To be sure, the total number of convictions increased during the third decade of the nineteenth century, but the records of arrests are misleading. In the old days, when the police had been notoriously inefficient, many criminals escaped detection. Now relatively few went unpunished, for the laws were much more stringently enforced. Yet the number of crimes committed had probably decreased, for the rank and file had become much more law-abiding. "Those who commit crimes are in a class by themselves," said Francis Place, "and consequently the comparative number of crimes is lessened." [29]

Especially noteworthy was the great reduction in crimes of violence. In the old days, when highwaymen roved the countryside, a traveler considered himself fortunate to reach his journey's end without being robbed. It was equally hazardous to venture by night into certain parts of London, for thieves and murderers padded the dark streets of the metropolis. Now one could feel fairly secure of life and limb. According to James Mill, there was "not only a diminution, but almost a cessation of the more atrocious crimes." [30]

[28] B.M., Add. MSS 27,827, pp. 53-54.
[29] B.M., Add. MSS 27,826, II, no. 5.
[30] *Westminster Review*, VI (Oct., 1826), 264.

Even the law itself was becoming less barbarous. In 1823 Peel succeeded in getting Parliament to remove about a hundred felonies from the list of those punishable by the death penalty, though horse-stealing, sheep-stealing, and housebreaking remained capital offenses until 1832.[31] Paradoxically, as penalties became less severe, crime decreased. The explanation was that the masses, even before the reform of the penal code, were becoming more respectful of law and order. This tendency, which increased as the nineteenth century progressed, could be attributed to the extension of popular education, said Francis Place. Statistics show that he was probably right. When a survey was made, it revealed that criminal convictions were most numerous among completely illiterate groups and in geographical areas which had relatively few schools. Conversely, it was shown that the incidence of crime greatly diminished among the literate and in sections where better provisions for education had been made.[32]

To an older person who could recall conditions existing among the common people at the close of the eighteenth century, these various changes were truly astonishing. Still greater improvements were to come, but Hogarth's London had already vanished. Looking back in 1824 to the time of his youth, Francis Place observed:

We never see now, as we used to see thirty years ago, groups of drunkards lying on the stairs on a Sunday morning in the summer time as was then common; we now no longer hear the voice of the rude drunkard at midday in the public houses and respectable streets, bawling out obscene songs. We no longer see women dressed in linsey woolsey, or quilted petticoats which were never washed, and in leather stays saturated with perspiration. We no longer see groups of servant girls standing in the streets to hear songs [for singing] which the prostitutes themselves would now pelt those who attempted to sing them. A mighty change has taken place, and the consequences are seen in the health and longevity of the offspring of the mass of the people.[33]

---

[31] E. L. Woodward, *The Age of Reform*, Oxford, 1938, p. 451.

[32] Joseph Bentley, *The State of Education Contrasted with the State of Crime*, Manchester [1838?].

[33] B.M., Add. MSS 27,827, pp. 50–51.

Thus it happened that the low-lived brutish masses of the eighteenth century were being transformed into the more decent, law-abiding common people of the Victorian era. They had their foibles and follies, as every reader of Dickens knows, and they sometimes engaged in Grundyism quite as much as their superiors. But they formed, nonetheless, a solid citizenry. As compared with the populace of the eighteenth century they were more humane, better informed, and more genuinely civilized. And so they have remained, for the better standards attained by the common people survived the passing of the Victorian period and today the ordinary Englishman is heir to them.

CHAPTER EIGHT

CHANGING TASTE AND
TEMPERAMENT

FROM THE TIME of Defoe there had been a tendency to level distinctions among readers. Books read in the servants' hall were often identical with those read by the master or mistress. The novel, portraying characters from all ranks and gauged to the comprehension of the uneducated reader, was particularly a democratic form of literature. It appealed to the large number of women readers who had been superficially educated in boarding schools and it appealed equally to readers and auditors among the lower ranks of society. There was, therefore, a great demand for fiction toward the end of the eighteenth century. According to James Lackington, the bookseller, even the poor farmers and peasants, who formerly spent their evenings telling ghost stories, now listened to "their sons and daughters read tales, romances, etc." They also delighted in some of the better novels. "You may see *Tom Jones, Roderick Random,* and other entertaining books stuck on their bacon racks," he said, "and if John goes to town with a load of hay he is charged to be sure not to forget to bring home *Peregrine Pickle's Adventures,* and when Dolly is sent to market to sell eggs she is commissioned to purchase *The History of Pamela Andrews.*" [1]

Writing in 1791, Lackington estimated that the sale of books was more than four times greater than it had been twenty years earlier. For this he himself was partly responsible. Having de-

[1] *Memoirs,* pp. 254–56.

veloped a large trade in secondhand books, Lackington had demonstrated to other booksellers the advantage of marketing cheap books. The demand for them, he predicted, would become even greater in a short time, since Sunday schools were rapidlv teaching the lower orders to read.[2]

This prediction, of course, proved true. During the early decades of the nineteenth century interest in reading developed even further than Lackington could have anticipated. Both the Sunday and monitorial schools added millions of new readers, and, because there was a growing tendency to frown upon cards, dancing, and the theater, people of all ranks read more than formerly. And the more they read, the more important it became to have some knowledge of books. Literature had become a favorite topic of conversation, and it was necessary for social reasons to develop a bookish taste. Commenting upon this change, a magazine published in 1826 said, "Some degree of reading and information . . . has become indispensable to respectability in every circle."[3]

Yet, despite this great avidity for books, taste had altered remarkably since Lackington had made his observation upon the popularity of novels. It had altered because, during the first decades of the new century, the temperament of readers had changed. There was now a much more censorious attitude toward literature. Speaking of the Methodists, Robert Southey remarked: "An Index Expurgatorius cannot be published in England, but as their people read nothing but what is recommended to them, an Index Commendatorius answers the same purpose."[4] This could have been said just as well of Evangelicals belonging to other denominations, for many of them read only the books prescribed by their leaders. Unlike eighteenth-century readers, they neglected *Tom Jones* and *Roderick Random*. Byron and Scott were of course exceedingly popular writers during the first part of the nineteenth century, but good Evangelicals did not read Byron, and those who abjured all novels

[2] *Ibid.*   [3] *Panoramic Magazine,* I (Jan. 31, 1826), 1–5.
[4] *Quarterly Review,* IV (Nov., 1810), 506

could not consistently except *Waverley* or *Ivanhoe*. Hannah More was scandalized when a clergyman told her he had bought an edition of Byron's minor poems, though he "boasted that he had burned *Don Juan*." Distinguishing between Byron and Scott, Mrs. More called the first an "anti-moralist," the second a "non-moralist." No one, she believed, should read "Byron and his compeers in sin and infamy." With Scott it was a somewhat different matter. One could not read him "for profit," to be sure, since it "would be difficult to find another specimen of such admirable works with so few maxims for the improvement of life and manners." Nevertheless, she would not prohibit him "to the mass of readers." [5]

But a censorious attitude was not confined to the Evangelicals. The public had become timorous of literature during the period of the French Revolution and continued to be so for some time afterwards. Fearing propaganda of a skeptical or Jacobinal nature, reviewers carefully examined books for any expression of infidelity or political radicalism, and some of the secular magazines were almost as wary as the Evangelical periodicals. None of them, however, displayed such an absurd fear of books as the *Guardian of Education*. To Mrs. Trimmer, the editor of this magazine, the word "philosopher" conjured up a vision of subversive and atheistical Frenchmen plotting to undermine happy English homes. In discussing a reading program for children, therefore, she cautioned parents against "books of Chemistry or Electricity, and all that might lead them prematurely to making philosophical experiments." [6]

On the other hand, if an author paid sufficient deference to the religious and moral cant of the times, and provided he said nothing at variance with the particular religious beliefs of any large sect, his works were sure to receive favorable notice in certain magazines. Under these circumstances writers frequently purported to have some serious ethical or utilitarian interests, in

[5] Wm. Roberts, *Memoirs of the Life and Correspondence of Hannah More*, IV, 181–82, 203–7.
[6] *Guardian of Education*, II (July, 1803), 403.

order to sell their works. Some of them even went so far as
frankly to disavow any claim to literary merit, demanding that
their works be judged solely upon the soundness of their moral
views. Mrs. West, for instance, while virtually admitting that
The Infidel Father was a poor novel, contended that it had a
noble purpose. In her preface she wrote:

> The rage for novels does not decrease; and though I by no means
> think them the best vehicle for "the words of sound doctrine" yet,
> while the enemies of our church and state continue to pour their
> poison into unwary ears through this channel, it behoves the friends
> of our establishments to convey an antidote by the same course; es-
> pecially since those who are most likely to be infected by false prin-
> ciples will not search for a refutation of them in profound and scien-
> tific compositions.
>   The particular design of this present work is to show the superior-
> ity which religious principle possesses, when compared with a sense
> of honour, moral fitness, or a love of general applause. The story is
> confessedly subordinate to this aim; and those who dislike it will
> observe that the *argumentative* part is not affected by the faults of
> the *narrative*.[7]

In making this statement Mrs. West undoubtedly knew that
many readers would applaud it. It would particularly commend
her book to that large section of the reading public which had
few cultural traditions, those thousands and perhaps millions
who now formed the largest literate group in the nation. Not
that the number of educated and discriminating readers had
decreased. If anything, they were more numerous than ever. On
their shelves could be found splendid editions of the Greek and
Roman writers, the works of Shakespeare, Milton, and Dryden,
the novels of Fielding, Smollett, and Fanny Burney, Boswell's
Life of Johnson, bound volumes of *The Tatler* and *The Rambler*, and the poetry of Pope, Burns, and Cowper. Even Coleridge
and Wordsworth, while not so generally accepted, had their
admirers. But there was a far larger group of readers who knew
little and cared little about such writers. They ranged from the
Sunday school graduate, who could not afford anything more

---

7 Jane West, *The Infidel Father*, London, 1802, Vol. I, "Introduction."

expensive than a tract, to affluent though recent members of the middle class, who could afford the finest calf editions, but who had never developed a taste for their contents.

The chief requirement of this large group of new readers was that literature should have a serious aim. When they read fiction, they liked to think that it conveyed some useful lesson. Those whose taste had been strongly influenced by the revival, however, preferred definitely moral and religious works. Some of them read the older Protestant divines like Jeremy Taylor, Richard Baxter, and William Law. Extracts from these older writers were frequently published in the Evangelical magazines, which also helped to form the taste of readers by printing strongly partisan criticisms of current literature. Several of the religious periodicals enjoyed a large circulation, but still more widely read, still more democratic in that they appealed to all classes of readers, were the tracts. These pamphlets were so cheap, so easy to obtain, and so expressly designed to promote religion and morality that they were eagerly read by young and old, by rich and poor. Only one other source of instruction was more frequently consulted by all ranks and degrees of people; that was the Bible.

At no time, either before or since, has the Bible been so familiar to English-speaking people as it was during the nineteenth century. Hardly a dwelling in England or the United States was without a copy. Read and reread, it influenced the speech of two nations and the style of scores of writers. No matter what their estate, people could quote long passages from Scripture and identify references by chapter and verse. In a crisis they opened the Bible at random and frequently made decisions according to the text revealed. It served at all important events—at birth to supply a name, at marriage to inspire holiness, at death to console the bereaved. One consulted this commonplace book throughout life's journey, and sometimes, clasping it in a death grip, carried it to the grave.

To be sure, the Bible had always been important to Christian culture. Never before, however, had all ranks and degrees of people read it so frequently and so thoroughly. Never before had almost every household possessed a copy. But now the Bible societies were publishing millions of copies, and their agents, by house-to-house canvassing, were endeavoring to provide one for every home. In former times, when illiteracy was common, a Bible would have been of little use to most people. Now millions could read, and the Bible was often the first book children encountered. In some schools it served as a common reader, and in all schools it was an important part of the curriculum. This was fortunate in many respects, for the Bible was sometimes the only excellent literature that children read. One book at least they knew, a book unequaled for the sustained quality of its simple, rhythmical English, containing the noble principles of Christianity.

Familiarity with the Bible could not but have its good effects. To it may be owing a considerable share of the integrity and idealism found in English character. To it also one might attribute the emphasis which many Victorian writers placed upon justice tempered by mercy, fortitude in the face of adversity, hope that yields not to despair. Nevertheless, under Evangelical influence, devotion to the Bible often resulted in bibliolatry. Later on, of course, a literal and completely authoritarian interpretation of Scripture was to be largely responsible for the Victorian conflict between science and religion. In the early decades of the nineteenth century, while this conflict had not yet developed, bibliolatry frequently narrowed the judgment. Considering the Bible the source of all dogma, the Evangelicals referred to it not only to determine matters of faith, but to test the righteousness of particular practices. Even when Scripture made no predication upon a subject, they attached a good deal of significance to a casual mention of it or, for that matter, to the absence of any reference to it. Consequently people both affirmed and denied the lawfulness of the stage, upon the basis of a few chance references to the theater in the Bible. When certain zealots attacked fiction, others defended it by citing the use of

parables in Scripture.[8] And the most bibliolatrous group, because they discovered that Christ and his apostles never used it,
strongly objected to satire.[9]

It is possible also that the emphasis put upon Bible-reading in
school developed a more credulous attitude among ordinary
readers. Children taught to believe every word of the first book
they read were inclined perhaps to accept everything that appeared in print as gospel truth. Many Evangelicals did this, but
since they read almost nothing but prescribed religious and moral
works, their reading only enforced their religious beliefs.

Next to the Bible in authority were the religious periodicals.
Widely read, these magazines not only guided readers to other
literature, but helped to determine their conduct. There were
a number of them, for, as interest in reading grew, the various
denominations had been quick to realize the growing importance of periodical literature. Although some of the religious
magazines survived for only a few years, there were four which
lasted for several decades and proved to be extremely popular.
They were the *Methodist Magazine,* the *Evangelical Magazine,*
the *Christian Observer,* and the *Eclectic Review.* Today these
Evangelical periodicals are among the most important records of
the revival, for they reveal its character and intensity and contribute to an understanding of the serious attitude that developed early in the nineteenth century.

The *Methodist Magazine* was really a continuation of Wesley's
Arminian Magazine. Akin to it in many respects, though Calvinistic rather than Arminian in its views, was the *Evangelical
Magazine,* which a group of Baptists, Congregationalists, and
churchmen had introduced in 1793. Both were intended for the
poorer and lower middle classes and, catering to this public, they
seldom if ever rose above the cultural or intellectual capacity of
their readers. By 1807 each of these periodicals was said to have
a monthly circulation of 18,000 to 20,000 copies.[10]

8 *General Chronicle and Literary Magazine* (July, 1812), pp. 340–42.
9 *Christian Observer,* II (Nov., 1803), 655–57.
10 *Edinburgh Review,* XI (Jan., 1808), 341.

After examining several issues of the *Methodist* and the *Evangelical*, Sydney Smith exclaimed, "In reading these very curious productions, we seem to be in a new world, and to have got among a set of beings, of whose existence we had hardly before entertained the slightest conception." [11] Here was a brand of piety unknown to this rational-minded clergyman. Here was a display of fanaticism the equal of which he had never before seen. Even the advertisements reflected a somber, austere type of enthusiasm. A single issue of the *Evangelical* contained the following:

Wanted, by Mr. Turner, a shoemaker, a steady apprentice; he will have the privilege of attending the ministry of the gospel—premium expected.

Wanted, a man of serious character who can shave.

A young person in the millinery line wishes to be in a serious family.

A single gentleman can be accommodated with lodging in a small serious family.

To let, a genteel first floor in an airy situation near the tabernacle.

Wanted, a governess of Evangelical principles and corresponding character.[12]

Whatever the Evangelicals might profess, said Sydney Smith, it was clear from their periodicals that they stressed certain aspects of religion more than other Christians. They constantly endeavored to make men more religious than it was consistent for human nature to be. Their hatred of pleasure caused them to be fearful of enjoying harmless pastimes and unappreciative of the gifts of God. By emphasizing the more mysterious parts of Christianity, they neglected to teach practical righteousness. They acted as if every internal feeling was a monition of God and must therefore govern their decisions. Finally, they interpreted every stroke of good or bad fortune as an instance of divine interference and referred it specifically to the actions of those concerned.[13]

[11] *Ibid.*, p. 342.
[12] Quoted by Smith, *Edinburgh Review*, XI (Jan., 1808), 352.
[13] *Edinburgh Review*, XI, 355 ff.

This last feature of Evangelicalism was particularly noticeable in the *Methodist Magazine* and in the *Evangelical Magazine*. Both contained a large number of anecdotes showing the remarkable intervention of the deity in causing a sudden cure, a death stroke, or a miraculous conversion. Some were cited to prove that virtue frequently receives an immediate reward. Others showed the punishments meted out to those who profaned the Sabbath, swore, played cards, or indulged in other forbidden practices. One issue of the *Methodist Magazine*,[14] for instance, contained the following illustrations of immediate reprobation for violating the Sabbath. In Burton on Trent, a minister had warned the inhabitants against profanation of the Lord's Day, but a tailor disregarded the warning and walked the length of the town to buy meat. On his way home he fell dead. At Alcester, in Warwickshire, a bold young lady vowed to dance as long as she could stand. Going to the village green on Sunday, she started to dance but fell ill of a violent disease to which she succumbed.

Anecdotes showing providential interference were apparently sent in by subscribers, who frequently named the place and the individuals concerned. This was true of some of the following accounts plucked from the *Evangelical Magazine*. The Reverend James Moody of Paisley was very fond of music, dancing, and the theater. Sometimes he even indulged these tastes on Sunday. Although two of his godly servants remonstrated with him, he persisted in these pleasures until his sight began to fail. Then, fearing that he would become blind, he turned his mind to serious thoughts. He attended an Evangelical chapel, where he heard a stirring sermon. Convinced by it that he was a sinful creature, he abandoned his vain and worldly pursuits.[15] Another anecdote told what happened to David Wright. This man suffered from scrofulous legs and was, in addition, an atheist. With some difficulty he was persuaded to attend church, where a sermon preached by a Mr. Coles immediately converted him.

14 *Methodist Magazine*, XIII (Aug., 1790), 432.
15 *Evangelical Magazine*, XV (May, 1807), 194.

After that he was troubled no more by either scrofula or infidelity.[16] There was also an account of a young man who, when stung by a bee, gave vent to various dreadful oaths and imprecations. As he was blaspheming, a second bee stung him on the tongue.[17] Another contributor cited the case of a clergyman who, instead of fulfilling his ministerial duties, was playing cards. When it came his turn to deal, he fell dead. He was the third person of his neighborhood within a few years to be "summoned from the card table to the bar of God." [18]

As Sydney Smith said, the frequent appearance of these anecdotes in their magazines showed the importance Evangelicals attached to a belief in providential interference. This did not mean that other Christians put no faith in an active deity. But most religious groups had wisely refrained from interpreting the significance of every event that did not come within the normal course of affairs. By stressing the idea of divine intervention, the Evangelicals did much harm, said Smith. It was a dangerous practice to test the merit of an individual by counting his strokes of good fortune or to judge his demerit by the number of his misfortunes. It was dangerous, because it implied that the wealthy were virtuous, the poor, wicked. It fostered supersition, gave the clergy too much power, and controverted the Christian precept that man receives his retribution, not on earth, but in the life hereafter.[19]

Even some of the Evangelicals objected to the type of enthusiasm displayed in the *Methodist Magazine* and the *Evangelical Magazine*. Taking note of Smith's observations, the editors of the *Christian Observer* admitted that the tone of these periodicals was regrettable. What they objected to chiefly, however, was the use of "low absurd expressions." "The truth is," they remarked, "that while the age in general has advanced in refinement, many of these good people have been contented to stand still." [20]

16 *Ibid.*, XV (Oct., 1807), 444.   17 *Ibid.*, XV (Aug., 1807), 363.
18 *Ibid.*, XV (June, 1807), 262.   19 *Edinburgh Review*, XI, 356.
20 *Christian Observer*, VII (June, 1808), 384.

The editor of the *Christian Observer* was Zachary Macaulay, father of the celebrated historian. Macaulay was a prominent member of the Clapham Sect, and the *Christian Observer* was the mouthpiece of that group. Because it was designed for readers of the upper ranks of society, who might be offended by the vulgar fanaticism of the other Evangelical organs, the *Christian Observer* pretended to be more tolerant in its views. It even went so far as to declare that George Burder, a Congregational minister, had placed too many restrictions upon a good Christian when he declared that the only lawful amusements were "walking, riding, books on history, biography, and natural philosophy, and music in moderation." [21]

The *Christian Observer* meddled in politics more than the other Evangelical magazines. At its inception in 1802 the editors declared that their purpose was to act as the friend of revealed religion and civil government, and to oppose impiety, skepticism, and sedition.[22] But, like many other conservative writers of the period, they constantly used the familiar device of associating liberal opinions with skepticism. So frequent was this practice that the *Edinburgh Review* declared that the *Christian Observer* "appears to have no other method of discussing a question fairly open to discussion than that of accusing their antagonists of infidelity." [23]

The main interest of the *Christian Observer* was to further the revival and moral reform. To this end, it tried to reconcile the Arminians and the Calvinists with each other and declared that, with regard to the issues upon which these two groups differed, its own policy was one of neutrality. It was difficult to be neutral upon the questions involved, however, and despite its profession the *Christian Observer* favored slightly a moderate type of Calvinism. In accord with Evangelical moral principles, it condemned the theater, dancing, and novel-reading, but having a socially superior class of readers it more frequently discussed fine points of conduct than the other Evangelical maga-

21 *Ibid.*, IV (April, 1805), 234 ff.   22 *Ibid.*, I, iii–iv.
23 *Edinburgh Review*, XII (April, 1808), 181.

zines. Was it proper to read newspapers on Sunday? Did a Christian who failed to hold daily prayers for the servants of his household neglect his duty? How much evil was attached to the practice of having servants say "not at home" when one was indisposed to receive callers? Needless to say, the answers to these questions favored the enforcement of stricter manners.

In its reviews the *Christian Observer* uniformly lauded Evangelical writers such as Cowper, Wilberforce, and Hannah More. Sometimes it condemned secular works on principle, but it was never as bitterly denunciatory as the *Eclectic Review*, which a group of Nonconformists introduced in 1805. The editors of this magazine explained that it was intended "for those numerous and respectable classes of society, not of the learned professions, but possessed of general intelligence." It would be their policy, they declared, "to blend with impartial criticism an invariable regard to moral and religious principles." Yet in practice few critical journals at any time have displayed more bigotry. The *Eclectic Review* condemned on principle whole classes of literature. At its introduction, it promised to exclude from its pages "the refuse of the circulating library and the theater," [24] and in issue after issue the editors expressed their scorn for satire and romances.

One might expect that the *Eclectic Review* would have little use for Byron. It called "Beppo" "licentious in its morals, occasionally vulgar and profane in its expression, and rather tedious in its narrative." A year later, when it reviewed "Mazeppa," it described Byron as a particularly dangerous writer, who beguiled the reader by the charm of his poetry and at the same time outraged all better principles. His was poetry "such as no brother could read aloud to his sister, no husband to his wife— poetry in which the deliberate purpose of the author is to corrupt by inflaming the mind." The *Eclectic Review*, having thus warned its readers against the wicked lord, promised that in the future it would pass over his productions in silence.[25]

[24] *Eclectic Review,* Vol. I, "Prospectus."
[25] *Ibid.,* IX (June, 1818), 55; XII (Aug., 1819), 149.

More surprising was this periodical's estimate of Samuel Richardson, who had formerly been praised for his decorous views and his model characters. Dr. Johnson had considered him the most moral and instructive of all novelists, but Richardson could not pass the rigorous scrutiny of the Evangelical editors of the *Eclectic Review*, who spoke of him as follows:

We recognize with pleasure his genius, his morals, and his regard to religion such as he apprehended it to be; but we cannot dissemble that his views of Christianity are general and obscure. Not only in his novels, but in his letters, as well as those of his correspondents, the sacred terms of Lord and God are lightly and therefore profanely used as unmeaning expletives. Sir Charles Grandison, a gentleman who talks of the goodness of his heart, renounces no vanity of this world. His family prayer, which every christian should in his conduct at least openly avow, he conceals; and with all his declamation against duelling Sir Charles . . . is himself a duellist. To reconcile the modern fine gentleman with the disciple of Christ is impossible. Richardson was hardy enough to attempt it; but his failure was inevitable.[26]

Because they held strict religious views, the Evangelical magazines were somewhat more partisan than other periodicals. But the first quarter of the nineteenth century was a time of unyielding political partisanship, and most periodicals were on the side of the conservative powers. The *British Critic* and the *Anti-Jacobin* strongly opposed any critical opinion directed at church or state. The *Edinburgh* and the *Quarterly Review,* though conducted respectively by Whigs and Tories, had much in common. Both were almost as reactionary in their political opinions as they were in their literary judgments. Neither wished to see any drastic change in the established order.[27] Politically, the nation was dominated by conservatism, and both directly and indirectly a conservative political atmosphere aided the moral reformers.

The popularity of tracts, for instance, was due in part to repressive political measures which made other forms of cheap literature scarce. Distributed free or sold for a penny, the tracts were almost the only form of cheap literature. Normally people

26 *Ibid.*, I (Feb., 1805), 126.
27 Walter Graham, *English Literary Periodicals*, New York, 1930, p. 244 and *passim*.

would have read newspapers, but a series of taxes imposed on the press had made them prohibitive to a large section of the population. In 1789 the tax upon a single newspaper had been a penny and a half. This was inordinately large, but during the troublesome period that followed the tax kept increasing, until 1815, when it amounted to fourpence.[28] This levy was not reduced until 1836 nor finally abolished until 1855. Ostensibly imposed to raise revenue, the tax operated and was intended to operate as a check upon the free expression and dissemination of opinion. To a large degree the conservative group succeeded in their aim, for in 1821 only about 500,000 copies of newspapers circulated each week among a population of more than 12,000,000. A further restriction was placed upon the press in 1819, when Parliament passed a bill imposing the newspaper duties on pamphlets and magazines which sold for sixpence and contained news of a political nature. It exempted monthly periodicals, however, as well as religious and moral publications.[29]

These provisions definitely limited millions of readers in their choice of literature. But they did not kill the zest for reading. Deprived of newspapers and other cheap literature, people read what was available—that is, the religious and moral tracts. As a result, these publications circulated by the millions, and without serious competition they enjoyed almost ideal conditions in which to shape the opinion of readers.

Yet one must not forget that many would have read the tracts in any event. The upper classes, who could afford more expensive literature, read them and read them with enjoyment. Some ardent Evangelicals even preferred them to other works. This was true of James Lackington, who, after his second conversion, gave up other forms of reading and confined himself to tracts. Tracing the steps in this process, he wrote:

The reading of these tracts increased the serious impressions which had been made before on my mind; and as I thought that most of

---

[28] W. H. Wickwar, *The Struggle for the Freedom of the Press, 1819–1832*, London, 1928, p. 29. The duty of fourpence was subject to a discount of 20 percent, provided publishers complied with certain special regulations.
[29] *Ibid.*, pp. 30, 138 ff.

them were, upon the whole, well calculated to awaken my poor neighbours in the village around to a sense of their wicked way of life, I sent for about 3,000 of them, and many of them I have already given away to farmers, labourers, soldiers, etc. The more I employed my time and money in attempts to be serviceable to the souls and bodies of my fellow-creatures, the more was I disposed toward religious duties and enabled to enter into the spirit of religion, and I wished for the mind that was in Christ with some degree of ardour. Mrs. Lackington also partook much of the same disposition; so that no books now pleased us so well as those that treated of divine subjects. We had sometime before given up novels, romances, and books of a trifling nature. Now we even neglected history, voyages, travel, etc., not that we thought it wrong to read them, but because we found more pleasure and satisfaction while engaged with those that treated of divine truths and religious duties.[30]

Arthur Young experienced a similar change in his reading habits. Prior to his conversion he had delighted in all types of literature; after it he found pleasure only in religious works. To these he became extremely devoted. He read the sermons of Isaac Watts and Samuel Ogden, of Sherlock and Secker. He read the works of Richard Baxter and John Owen and published extracts from their writings. He read Bryant's *Authenticity of Scriptures,* Scott's *Christian Life,* Butler's *Analogy,* and Wilberforce's *Practical View.* Above all he read and reread the Bible.[31] Only once, apparently, after his conversion, did he read a novel. A lady had pressed *Marie Menzikoff* upon him, recommending it as a "true history." It fascinated him, he admitted, but reading it gave him a sense of guilt, and to his diary he confessed:

It has unhinged my mind and broken my attention to better things, which shows how strongly pernicious this reading is, and what a powerful temptation to vice such productions are sure to prove. Oh! the number of miserables that novels have sent to perdition.[32]

Young could not have objected to all narratives, however, for he, with his friend Marianne Francis, was fond of distributing tracts to the poor, and the most popular tracts were those which told a story. Frequently, as in the three famous tracts

[30] *Confessions,* pp. 165–66.
[31] *Autobiography of Arthur Young,* ed. by M. Betham-Edwards, pp. 282 ff.
[32] *Ibid.,* p. 421.

written by Legh Richmond, the story was an account of a sinner's conversion. If Young preferred a "true history," he must have liked Richmond's *Dairyman's Daughter,* for this urgently worded tale was based upon the life of Elizabeth Wallbridge, a resident of the Isle of Wight. This tract was probably more widely read during the nineteenth century than any other work except the Bible, and to it were attributed many conversions.

There is practically nothing in *The Dairyman's Daughter* that can be called a plot. Richmond meets the heroine when he officiates at the funeral of her sister. They become better acquainted, and she tells him her story. For several years she had worked away from home as a servant. During most of this time she had been vain, possessed of little true religious feeling, addicted to fine clothes. Then one Sunday she went to church, chiefly to display her finery, but after listening to a sermon on the text "Be Ye Clothed with Humility," she became convinced of her sinful nature. Her conversion followed, accompanied by strong feelings of piety. Shortly afterwards she came home to live with her aging parents on their dairy farm, where she found her sister dying of tuberculosis. Elizabeth converts her, and the sister dies happily. Then Elizabeth is stricken with the same malady. It is at this time that Richmond begins his visits and correspondence with her. To him the dairyman's daughter pours forth her pious thoughts, but she never presumes upon her acquaintance with the clergyman, for she is extremely conscious of her humble station. The nearer she approaches death, the greater her spiritual ardor. At length, after a lingering illness, she dies with complete resignation, uttering many pious sentiments.[33]

So much for the events, but no summary can reproduce the characteristic tone of a tract. Written in extremely sentimental language, the tracts abounded in biblical quotations and pious platitudes. Morbid, they frequently prolonged a death scene for several pages, for the Evangelicals believed that the serene death of a pious person proved that what they taught was true. Thus

[33] Legh Richmond, *Annals of the Poor,* Philadelphia, 1814.

the circumstances of a person's death became extremely important. Even Mrs. Trimmer, a non-Evangelical, held these views. When she banned David Hume, she explained that she objected to him because of his writings and because the "urbanity of his manners and the calmness of his death have rendered him the pride and boast of his disciples." [34] In the tracts a pious person died lingeringly, with calm resignation. Frequently he rallied just before his demise to convert some member of his family. A large audience crowded around his bedside to hear his last words and, almost invariably, no matter how weak he had been, he found sufficient strength just before the end to utter many pious sentiments.

In addition to the religious tracts, there were many based upon moral themes. Some of these were straightforward diatribes against swearing, Sabbath-breaking, and indulging in finery. More popular, however, were the tracts which introduced moral precepts under the guise of fiction. These moral stories, like those of Hannah More, frequently appeared both in penny pamphlets and in more expensive editions, for they appealed equally to the lower and the upper ranks of society. Some writers, indeed, while employing the customary formula for a moral story, published their works only in book form. But there was little to distinguish them from the works intended to circulate as tracts.

The moral stories, like the religious periodicals, contained innumerable instances of divine intervention. In a sense, of course, it is the business of any moral story to show that virtue is rewarded and vice punished, and moral stories have always been popular. The eighteenth century was fond of them, but in that period writers were content to let the moral adorn the tale. Now, the moral did not adorn the tale so much as the tale the moral. Virtue and vice were equated in terms of profit and loss, and earthly rewards and punishments were measured out by rule of thumb. Strongly propagandist in their aims, writers apparently felt that it was easier to persuade readers to virtue by promising

---

[34] *Guardian of Education,* II (Jan., 1803), 1–3.

them immediate dividends than by assuring them of a reward in heaven or suggesting that virtue is its own reward. So frequently was this their practice that some people felt that the emphasis upon providential interference might do more harm than good to decent moral principles. As Sydney Smith had warned against it in the periodicals, Samuel Bailey tried to discourage it in fiction by writing:

It is injurious to the cause of good morals to invest virtue with false powers, because every day's experience may detect the fallacy. . . . Many of our writers of fiction, with the best intentions, injure the cause which they support, by rewarding virtuous conduct with accidental good fortune.[35]

Such warnings had little effect. Even stories for children often stressed the idea of providential interference. These, to be sure, differed little from the stories read by adults, and sometimes young and old read the same improving literature. Several women writers, however, specialized in tales for children, notably Elizabeth Hamilton, Mrs. Hurry, Mary Leadbeater, and Mrs. Sherwood. These ladies produced a type of fiction in which one dominating purpose was manifest—the desire to inculcate a prudential morality by adducing an earthly system of rewards and punishments. The battleground upon which virtue and vice contested sometimes varied—Mary Leadbeater placed her stories in Ireland, Elizabeth Hamilton set hers in Scotland, and, for several of hers, Mrs. Sherwood used the background of India —but inevitably the stories illustrated some moral which it took no searching of the text to find.

The moral stories written for children proved so popular that they frequently supplanted the traditional storybooks. Writing to a friend, Charles Lamb said:

"Goody Two Shoes" is almost out of print. Mrs. Barbauld's stuff has banished all the old classics of the nursery, and the shopman at Newberry's hardly deigned to reach them off an old exploded corner of a shelf when Mary asked for them. Mrs. Barbauld's and Mrs. Trimmer's nonsense lay about in piles.[36]

---

[35] *Essays on the Formation of Public Opinion*, London, 1837, 3d ed., p. 206.
[36] *The Letters of Charles Lamb*, Troy, New York, 1902, II, 75.

CHANGING TASTE 197

Wordsworth, writing presumably in 1804, also commented with regret upon the waning popularity of the traditional stories. In "The Prelude" (Book V, lines 341 ff.) he wrote:

> Oh give us once again the wishing-cap
> Of Fortunatus and the invisible coat
> Of Jack the Giant-Killer, Robin Hood,
> And Sabra in the forest with St. George!
> The child, whose love is there, at least doth reap
> One precious gain, that he forgets himself.

Yet a few years later Wordsworth, who was rapidly becoming a good Victorian, praised the religious and moral tracts which were supplanting the fairy tales. In a letter to Francis Wrangham (June 5, 1808), he remarked, "I am entirely of accord with you in chiefly recommending religious books for the poor." He had discovered in his walks that ballads and penny tracts circulated among the agricultural laborers of the Lake District "in great abundance." Although some of these works seemed objectionable, "either for the superstition in them, or more frequently for indelicacy," Wordsworth believed that most of them had an excellent influence. "I have many times wished that I had talents to produce songs, poems, and little histories, that might circulate among other good things in this way," wrote Wordsworth. "Indeed, some of the poems which I have published were composed not without hope that they would answer this purpose." [37]

The desire for improvement had become so great that even among the upper classes parents sometimes substituted moral tales in the nursery for the books they had read themselves when children. This practice was strongly recommended by Mrs. Trimmer, who felt that fairy tales were not only inferior but actually vicious. She explained that when she was a child, reading "Blue Beard" had given her the "horrors." Believing that it must often produce this effect, she declared, "This is certainly a very improper tale for children." "Little Red Riding Hood" and "Cinderella," she granted, were "perhaps merely absurd."

[37] *The Letters of William and Dorothy Wordsworth*, ed. by Ernest De Selincourt, Oxford, 1937, I, 221 ff.

Nevertheless, she warned parents against "the harm, as well as the impropriety, of putting such books as these into the hands of little children." [38]

No doubt many parents heeded this oracle, but today the moral stories seem much more likely to produce the "horrors" than fairy tales. Consider, for instance, *The History of the Fairchild Family,* published by Mrs. Sherwood in 1818. According to the *Dictionary of National Biography,* "most children of the English middle classes, born in the first quarter of the nineteenth century, were brought up on the *Fairchild Family.*" It is a book of novel length, centering around incidents that occur in a family consisting of parents and three children.

Mrs. Sherwood followed a principle formulated by Hannah More, namely, that the chief purpose of juvenile literature is to teach children that they are naturally depraved creatures. The parents of the Fairchild family constantly reiterate this doctrine to their children, who, being naturally sinful, are constantly involved in difficulties. Since each peccadillo of the children gives the parents an opportunity to discuss the evil inherent in human nature, there is no end of sermonizing. If the children filch preserves or get mud on their clothes, the Fairchilds act as if they had committed enormities. It is not surprising that young Henry, aged seven, is afraid to admit that he has taken an apple from a young tree, the fruit of which Mr. Fairchild has forbidden the children to touch. Mr. Fairchild discovers that the apple is missing, however, and eventually detects the criminal. Thoroughly shocked that Henry has lied about his misdeed, he thrusts him into a dark closet to meditate upon his wicked nature. Only after Henry has owned his sinful heart and begged for pity does Mr. Fairchild restore him to the Eden of the family circle.

Like many later Victorians, Mrs. Sherwood delights in morbidity. Three deaths occur in the story. The first of these illustrates what happens to sinners. Miss Augusta Noble is introduced as the child of the wealthiest family in the neighborhood.

She is much more wicked than the Fairchild children, for she regularly disobeys her governess, lies, steals, and even mocks the piety of the young Fairchilds. Although her elders have forbidden her to play with fire, Miss Noble persists in doing so. The disobedient young pyromaniac is finally punished, however, for one day her dress catches fire and she is burned to a crisp. The second person to die is Charles Trueman, a very different sort of child from Miss Noble. Though humbly born, he has developed great piety and seriousness, and in his discussions with young Henry Fairchild he talks with all the sobriety of a mature Evangelical. Charles Trueman realizes that he has but a short time to live, but the thought does not disturb him, since he is willing to quit a sinful world. Although everyone knows he is ill, no attempt is made to discover the nature of his malady or to cure it. As a result he eventually dies, but like a true Evangelical he expresses many pious sentiments just before the end, much to the edification of the Fairchilds, all of whom are at his bedside. The third death, that of an old gardener, is apparently introduced for the sake of morbidity alone. Hearing that the old man is dead, the Fairchild children ask their father if they may accompany him when he goes to view the corpse. He consents, saying that it is good for children to become acquainted with death. Before they leave, he discourses at large upon man's mortality and quizzes the children upon references to death in the Bible. The Fairchilds then depart to view the corpse, which is described with morbid realism. As they stand before it, Mr. Fairchild, always alert to such opportunities, talks further upon death, describing the corruption of the body and the sinful nature of man.

Today *The History of the Fairchild Family* seems to epitomize the worst sort of child psychology. Yet it was substituted for healthy tales of the imagination like "Cinderella" and "Jack the Giant Killer." At first it seems incredible that children could have enjoyed the moral stories, but apparently they did, especially if they had no opportunity to read Mother Goose tales. Illustrations helped to make the stories interesting, and the writers who knew their craft often used melodrama and suspense to good effect. A good many children, therefore, may have enjoyed the moral stories almost as much as the young Fairchilds did. At one point in Mrs. Sherwood's story the family servant brings home a book for each of the children. This event occasions the following dialogue:

"Indeed, John, you are very good," said the children. "What beautiful books."

"How many beautiful pictures in mine," said Henry, "it is about a covetous woman— 'The History of the Covetous Woman.' I never read that story before."

"My book," said Emily, "is 'The History of the Orphan Boy' and there are a great many pictures in it; the first is a picture of a funeral —that must be the funeral of the little boy's papa or mama, I suppose."

"Let me see, let me see," said Henry, "Oh how pretty. And what is your book, Lucy?"

"There are not many pictures in my book," said Lucy, "but there is one at the beginning; it is the picture of a little boy reading to somebody lying in bed, and there is a lady sitting by. The name of the book is 'The History of the Good Child,' who was made the instrument of turning his father and mother to the ways of holiness." [39]

This dialogue may not sound very realistic today, but it had a genuine ring to the Victorians. Millions of children were reading stories like *The History of the Covetous Woman* and *The History of the Orphan Boy*. And millions of adults were reading books which had the same Evangelical emphasis. Stories of conversion they could understand, for conversion was a common experience. Moral tales had a strong appeal, for the Victorians made a shibboleth of morality. Works of this kind were equally popular in the United States, where writers like E. P. Roe, continuing the tradition, had a large following until recent decades.

The taste for moral and religious literature in the first quarter of the nineteenth century was at once a cause and a product of the growing seriousness of the times. Today, when one thinks of the writers of that period, the romantic poets come first to

[39] Mary M. Sherwood, *Works*, New York, 1858, II, 138.

mind, but there were thousands then who read Legh Richmond in preference to Sir Walter Scott. While the works of Shelley and Keats gathered dust, booksellers sold millions of tracts. In homes where Coleridge and Wordsworth were unknown, Hannah More and Mrs. Trimmer were read and reread. People were now getting their opinions from books as never before, and the religious and moral works strongly impressed readers. If there was a good deal of cant in what they read, they hardly recognized it as such, for canting had become a habit of the times. If their favorite authors frequently expressed fanatical views, a generation which produced Joanna Southcott, John Wroe, and so many other mad fanatics could easily digest the milder fanaticism of the Evangelicals. Many readers testified that a single book or tract had changed the whole course of their lives. Children who were being brought up on works like *The Fairchild Family*, however, would not have to change their beliefs. They were conditioned to make good Victorians.

CHAPTER NINE

CENSORS AND REFORMERS

THE MORAL REFORMERS of the early nineteenth century frequently censured the life and writings of the famous Lord Byron. He, in turn, though generally more occupied with satirizing his fellow poets, occasionally aimed his ridicule at the reformers. In "English Bards and Scotch Reviewers" he wrote:

> Whet not your scythe, suppressors of our vice!
> Reforming saints! too delicately nice!
> By whose decrees, our sinful souls to save,
> No Sunday tankards foam, no barbers shave;
> And beer undrawn, and beards unmown, display
> Your holy reverence for the Sabbath-day.

These lines could refer to the activities of only one group, the Society for the Suppression of Vice. Like the earlier reform societies, this organization was composed of private citizens who were determined to enforce the vice laws. It was, in fact, a direct successor to the eighteenth-century associations, but, instituted in 1802, in the midst of a zealous reform movement of which it was a part, it was destined to have a longer career than its predecessors. The founders fervently denied any intention to compete with the still existent Proclamation Society. Their plan, they said, was to coöperate with the older organization in making a vigorous onslaught upon vice. Eventually the Society for the Suppression of Vice absorbed the Proclamation Society, and Wilberforce and his friends transferred their interest from the original association to the more recent one. But Wilberforce's name did not appear upon the list of members published in

1803, and the society was not, in the beginning, dominated by the Evangelicals.

Several familiar names appeared upon the society's first list of subscribers: John Bowdler, author of *Reform or Ruin;* Charles Rivington, the publisher; Patrick Colquhoun, a famous London magistrate; and that eminent friend of virtue, Sarah Trimmer. The society also enrolled a few titled aristocrats, several clergymen, the Lord Mayor of London, and other officials. Prominent among those who served upon the committee was John Bowles, the professional propagandist of the church and state party; and it is possible that Bowles, who had not yet fallen into disgrace for stealing government money, was the father of the Society for the Suppression of Vice. At any rate a writer in the *Annual Review* ascribed to Bowles the *Address to the Public* with which the organization introduced itself, and both the contents and the bombastic style of this manifesto indicate that he may very well have been the author of it.[1]

The *Address to the Public* declared that a society to suppress vice was urgently needed, in order to avert the moral collapse of the nation. Referring to the alleged conspiracy against religions and governments, the author of this brochure explained that "Infidelity, Blasphemy, Treason, and Licentiousness have been let loose among us upon design." Various associations had been formed to promote Jacobinism and infidelity, with the result that vice had been increasing "with almost unexampled rapidity." The only way to avert this pernicious tendency, urged the writer, was to establish a reform society such as had existed in the time of Queen Anne. With an organization of this sort, it might be possible to stem the "encroachments vice is daily making." Otherwise there was a grave possibility that "religious principles would be swept away."[2]

Continuing in this vein for a hundred pages, the *Address to the Public* made every possible effort to trade upon the fears

[1] *Annual Review for 1804*, III, 225 ff.
[2] *Part the First of An Address to the Public from the Society for the Suppression of Vice*, London, 1803, p. 37 and *passim*.

that had arisen in the closing years of the eighteenth century, and it is a good illustration of the fact that the development of social conservatism owed almost as much to reactionary political sentiment as it did to the religious revival. As propaganda, it may have been effective, since the nation was still suffering from the delusion that there was a conspiracy against governments and religions. More critical observers, however, saw that the *Address to the Public* was as nonsensical as it was perfidious. To say that treason and irreligion were rife was ridiculous, for political reformers were asking merely for moderate changes in government, and the people were showing more interest in religion than they had for a century. To revive the bogey of conspiracy was absurd, for Jacobinism had gone out of fashion, Napoleon was now in the saddle, and the real menace to England was the possibility that his army might invade the country. Furthermore, to pretend that a society which devoted most of its energies to the detection of petty Sabbath-breakers would serve as a bulwark against the conspirators, granted that any existed, seemed foolish. Satirizing the society upon this point, one of its critics remarked:

It does not appear that the publicans who suffered tippling during divine service acted upon order from the Jacobin Club; nor that shopkeepers who have been convicted of pursuing their ordinary callings on the Sabbath day have any connection with the French Encyclopedists, or the illuminated in Germany.[3]

A hundred years earlier, when Defoe had scored the Societies for the Reformation of Manners, he had objected to their prosecuting only the poor, and now Sydney Smith, whose clear voice came like an echo of the eighteenth century, denounced their successor for a like reason. Since it did not bother the wealthy, said he, it should be called "a society for suppressing the vices of persons whose income does not exceed £500 per annum." Smith also condemned the society for using informers, for limiting membership to worshipers in the Established Church, and,

3 *Annual Review for 1804*, III, 129.

most of all, because he believed that it was impossible for a group of this kind to keep from becoming pharisaical:

It is hardly possible that a Society for the Suppression of Vice can ever be kept within the bounds of good sense and moderation. . . . The loudest and noisiest suppressors will always carry it against the more prudent part of the community; the most violent will be considered the most moral; and those who see the absurdity will, from fear of being thought to encourage vice, be reluctant to oppose it.[4]

The public, though not unsympathetic with the aims of the society, often sided with its victims, for the members generally singled out petty offenders and were merciless in their prosecutions. Furthermore, Englishmen had always objected to prying personal investigations, and the practice of using spies to secure its evidence made the society unpopular. When it endeavored to organize branch associations, therefore, it did not succeed as well as the Bible and tract societies. A few branches were established, to be sure—one at Bath, one at Hull, and another at York—but for the most part it was left to the original group at London to rescue the nation from vice.[5]

In the range of its activities the Society for the Suppression of Vice outdid the earlier reform associations. Like them it declared war upon profane swearers, Sabbath-breakers, and keepers of gambling resorts and brothels. But it went further than the former agencies when it proposed to suppress lotteries and to prosecute people for cruelty to animals and the use of false weights and measures. Indeed almost any practice considered vicious might fall under its censure. When a citizen of Margate

[4] *Edinburgh Review*, XXVI (Jan., 1809), 336.

[5] *Occasional Report of the Society*, London, 1812. In this report the committee of the society expresses satisfaction that a branch organization had also been formed at Oxford, under the patronage of the Vice-chancellor. A copy of the "Proceedings" at Oxford is included, in which it is solemnly stated that vice had increased of late at the university, since easy access to London permitted the undergraduates too much intercourse with the world. It goes on to affirm the intention of the members to suppress various rampant vices. But the Oxford report was apparently a hoax. According to a note (signed P.B.) on the copy in the Bodleian Library, no society was formed at Oxford, though some wag, pretending that there was, sent the London society a spurious account of its proceedings. The members apparently thought it was genuine and printed it in their report.

complained to the society about the frequency of masquerades in his town (his chief objection was that his servants neglected their duties to attend them), the association warned the innkeepers of Margate that their licenses might be suspended if they rented their premises for masquerades. When residents of Brighton notified the society that gentlemen's servants frequently went swimming in the nude at the public beaches, it posted a warning that anyone who bathed in this "most indecent manner" would be prosecuted. Upon another occasion this organization did prosecute an old man for telling fortunes, with the result that he was convicted and sentenced to serve six months in prison.[6]

The chief concern of the society, however, was to enforce the Sabbath laws and to suppress the sale of objectionable books and prints. These activities are so closely associated with the development of Sabbatarianism and the growth of moral censorship that it will be better to consider them in connection with these larger issues.

SABBATARIANISM

Contrary to popular belief, the Victorians were not chiefly responsible for making the English Sunday a gloomy day. Although they had a number of Sabbath laws which they strictly enforced, they had inherited most of them from former times. More important, they had inherited an attitude of mind which closely associated piety with joylessness. As early as the first decade of the nineteenth century Robert Southey described the English Sunday as follows:

All public amusements are prohibited by the daemon of Calvinism; and for private ones, half of the people seriously believe that were they to touch a card on Sunday, they should immediately find the devil under the table, who is said to have actually appeared upon such an occasion to an old lady at Bath. The Savoyard who goes about with his barrel-organ dares not grind even a psalm tune upon the Sabbath. The old woman who sells apples at the corner of the street has been sent to prison for profanation of the Lord's Day by

---

[6] *Statement of the Proceedings of the Society,* London, 1804; *The Trial of Joseph Powell, the Fortune-Teller,* London, 1808.

the Society for the Suppression of Vice: the pasty-cook, indeed, is permitted to keep his shop-window half open because some of the society themselves are fond of ice-creams. Yonder goes a crowd to the tabernacle as dismally as if they were going to a funeral; the greater number are women;—inquire for their husbands at the ale-house, and you will find them besotting themselves there because all amusements are prohibited as well as labour, and they cannot lie down like dogs and sleep. Ascend a step higher in society,—the children are yawning, and the parents agree that the clock must be slow, that they may accelerate supper and bedtime. In the highest ranks, indeed, there is little or no distinction of days, except that there is neither theater nor opera for them, and some among them scruple at cards.[7]

Most of the prohibitions to which Southey refers dated from the sixteenth and seventeenth centuries. After the Reformation the civil authorities, having taken over various functions hitherto performed by the church, had attempted to regulate public conduct on Sunday by introducing rules which forbade people to engage in weekday occupations and amusements. There was even a law, dating from the reign of Elizabeth, which imposed a fine of a shilling upon anyone who absented himself from public worship on the Sabbath. Although this law remained upon the statute books until the middle of the nineteenth century, the magistrates, after the time of Cromwell, appear never to have invoked it. But other Sabbath regulations, forbidding anyone to make a journey on Sunday, to keep a butchershop open, or to sell liquor during service time, had frequently been enforced, especially by the Societies for the Reformation of Manners. Even after these organizations were defunct, the authorities occasionally punished Sabbath-breakers, and at no time in the Georgian period was the English Sunday very cheerful.

But it was the temper of the English, much more than their laws, that made Sunday a cheerless day. For the English did not cease to be Puritans when they stopped believing in Puritanism. Although churches were poorly attended and English reformers, with a good deal of truth, constantly asserted that irreligion was

[7] *Letters from England*, London, 1808, III, 186 ff.

the prevailing spirit of the eighteenth century, foreigners who visited England in this period were amazed at the austerity of the English Sabbath. What astonished them most was that certain harmless practices were forbidden while others, more gross, were permitted. One of these visitors, Carl Philipp Moritz, while staying at a London lodging house, was reprimanded by his landlady's son for whistling on Sunday. On the other hand, Moritz discovered that in more exalted company virtually no respect was paid to the Sabbath. At Oxford he spent a Sunday night at the Mitre in the company of several clergymen, who sat well into the morning, getting drunk, swearing, and jesting about passages in Scripture.[8]

Another German visitor observed that both the clergy and the laity performed their religious duties in a phlegmatic manner. In the cathedrals, he said, "one is struck by the irreligious and careless air with which they acquit themselves." Nevertheless, the outward observance of the Sabbath was extremely strict. Because the law forbade working on Sunday, most people were idle. But they could not enjoy their leisure. Dancing and singing in public were strictly forbidden, and one could not even go for a sail on the Thames, since bargemen were generally not allowed to ply their trade on Sunday. Consequently, wealthier people fled to the country to escape spending a gloomy day in London, and the poor, seeking cheer in a cup, crowded the taverns.[9]

Agreeing that the English Sunday was a cheerless day. F. A. Wendeborn remarked:

The Sabbath-day is kept in England with more outward decency than I have seen in many countries; and in churches and meeting-houses outward decorum and seeming devotion are very observable, particularly in the country, at some distance from the metropolis. About London, the public houses are on Sunday very full indeed; but the ear of the passenger is not struck with music and dancing, as is too much the case abroad, nor is there card-playing, except that of late some houses of people of quality at the west end of the town,

---

[8] *Travels of Carl Philipp Moritz in England in 1782*, London, 1924, pp. 24, 146 ff.
[9] M. De Archenholtz, *A Picture of England*, London, 1797, pp. 166 ff.

have, on Sunday resounded with musical concerts, and card-tables have been in use. Upon the whole Voltaire's description of the manner in which the Sunday passes in London contains much truth when he says, "Point d'opéra, point de comédie, point de concert, à Londres, le dimanche; les cartes mêmes y sont si expréssement defendues, qu'il n'y a que les personnes de qualité, et ce qu'on appelle les honnêtes-gens, qui jouent ce jour-là; le reste de la nation va au sermon, au cabaret, et chez des filles de joie." [10]

From such comments it appears that even before the French Revolution the English Sunday was rather dour. The reaction to that event, however, served to increase the emphasis upon a strict observance of the Sabbath. As has been shown, the upper classes became more frequent attendants at public worship and gave up certain forms of entertainment.[11] Various schemes were also introduced during the revolutionary decade to encourage the poor to go to church on Sunday. At Winton, Durham, for instance, some of the more affluent residents instituted benefit societies for the lower classes. Anyone enrolled in these organizations was entitled to three or four times the sum he paid in, provided that during the course of a year he had regularly attended church services.[12]

Another plan to attract the poor to church was introduced at Brentford by Sarah Trimmer, who, wishing to have it more generally adopted, imparted the details of it to the Association for Preserving Liberty and Property. Her letter to this organization reads almost like "A Modest Proposal," but Mrs. Trimmer was not capable of writing satire, and the irony is entirely unconscious. Dated December, 1792, the letter observes that a mob had recently made "a seditious attempt to plant the tree of liberty at Kennington Common upon the Sabbath day." From this action Mrs. Trimmer concludes that the enemies of the nation planned to use Sunday as a particular time to incite "an idle licentious mob." She suggests therefore that a scheme used at Brentford be encouraged:

10 *A View of England towards the Close of the Eighteenth Century*, London, 1791, II, 269.
11 See above, chap. iii.   12 S. Trimmer, *The Oeconomy of Charity*, II, 208 ff.

The necessities of the lowest order of people, notwithstanding the great sums which are annually expended on the parish poor, is indisputably very great in the depth of winter. The dearness of provisions is already felt by them. In a short time we may expect to see their necessities increased by hard weather, and there is great reason to apprehend that advantage will be taken of this distress to instigate them to insurrection, if not timely prevented by the interposition of benevolence. I therefore beg leave to recommend the raising subscriptions in order to furnish *Sunday gifts* for such of the poor as shall attend public worship and absent themselves from alehouses, etc. . . . A large fund will not be requisite for these purposes, for so fond are the poor of receiving gifts that I will venture to say, a single loaf of bread kindly bestowed upon them will give higher satisfaction than a much more considerable acquisition. . . . I am fully persuaded that a Sunday gift accompanied by a judicious printed admonition may put a whole neighborhood of people into good humour with their superiors, and set their minds in a proper train for a whole week.[13]

There is no evidence that the Association for Preserving Liberty and Property encouraged this plan, nor does it appear to have been adopted except in Brentford. Nevertheless Mrs. Trimmer's modest proposal shows the willingness of the conservatives of this time to make religion serve political ends, and it is impossible to doubt that the general tendency of the conservative reaction to the French Revolution was to increase Sabbatarianism.

More important in this respect, however, was the traditional Protestant emphasis upon the Old Testament. From the time of the Reformation, and more especially at periods when a religious revival was in progress, the English had endeavored to apply the severe restrictions imposed upon the Jewish Sabbath to the Christian Sunday. Many of their Sabbath laws, indeed, appear to have been adopted directly from commandments in the Old Testament. In Exodus they read, "Remember the Sabbath day, to keep it holy. Six days shalt thou labour, and do all thy work; but the seventh day is the Sabbath of the Lord thy God; in it thou shalt not do any work, thou, nor thy son, nor thy

---

[13] B.M., Add. MSS 16,921 f.131.

daughter, thy manservant nor thy maidservant, nor thy cattle, nor the stranger that is within thy gates." Elsewhere in the Old Testament one found interdictions which forbade gathering sticks, kindling a fire, cooking or baking, traveling, or conducting business on the Sabbath.

The custom of observing a strict Sabbath had been so well established by the eighteenth century that, despite the irreligious character of the age, in many circles formal restrictions continued to be respected. With the coming of the religious revival, Sabbatarianism became still more common. Almost every organized activity of the Evangelicals, in fact, was designed in some way to further a strict Sabbath. In their periodicals and tracts they featured anecdotes of persons who had suffered severe punishment for indulging in Sunday amusements. Through their district visitors they brought pressure upon the poor to attend services and to abstain from levity on the day of rest. Still more influential, perhaps, were their Sunday schools, which, by keeping children in class most of the day, accustomed them to spending the Sabbath in church and prevented them from playing games. A few of the more naughty boys, to be sure, might at recess steal out to the graveyard to pitch farthings on tombstones, but woe to those whom the master caught at this sinful occupation.

Anyone among the upper ranks who professed to be a good Evangelical was bound to obey the Sabbath ritual. Ordinarily one attended church services at least twice a day. At sermon time, especially if one attended the church of a strict clergyman, a worshiper might hear a sermon such as the one the Reverend George Burder preached on "Lawful Amusements." On week days, he said, a Christian might walk for exercise, read history, biography, and natural philosophy, and occasionally enjoy the company of "intelligent and pious persons." But on Sunday a good Christian must refrain from all amusements, including "journeys merely for the purpose of pleasure" and "paying and receiving visits." [14] After morning service a good Evangelical

14 "Lawful Amusements," London, 1805.

would go home, where, if the household obeyed the Old Testament injunction against cooking, he would have to nourish himself on cold meats. The rest of the day until afternoon or evening service might be passed in reading the Bible or some other religious work.

Inasmuch as the Evangelicals frequently imposed their views upon others, many who were not strict believers in all matters came to accept their views upon keeping the Sabbath. One occasionally sees a reflection of this tendency in the non-Evangelical literature of the time. Jane Austen, for instance, was undoubtedly expressing her own beliefs in *Persuasion* when she has her heroine decide that Mr. Eliot would not be a suitable match. The young lady admitted that "he was a sensible man, an agreeable man, that he talked well, professed good opinions, seemed to judge properly as a man of principle." On the other hand, and this was very much against him, he never expressed any "burst of feeling, any warmth of indignation or delight, at the evil or good of others." Worst of all, "she saw that there had been bad habits; that Sunday travelling had been a common thing; that there had been a period of his life (and probably not a short one) when he had been, at least, careless on all serious matters." [15]

Evangelical influence was already strong by the first decade of the nineteenth century, and Sabbatarianism appears to have characterized that period as much as it did any Victorian decade. In 1804 a writer in the *Annual Review* remarked:

Like a truly industrious nation, we endeavour to make the rest from labour more irksome than toil itself; and by the gloomy denunciations of a mystical superstition, to convert leisure into misery. The progresss of ascetic fanaticism is deplorable; reason and cheerfulness sicken at its presence; the tongue whines an unintelligible jargon; the imagination is haunted by starting fiends and fires of hell; and these puritanic sectuaries, as a remedy for the pains of mind, which their indiscreet teachers wander to inflict, are seen to seek in dram drinking a refuge from the devil. Not only their private, their public morality is debauched. Whole bodies of volun-

---

[15] *Persuasion,* chap. xvii.

teers have been persuaded to withdraw from Sunday drills, as if a special interposition of Providence would resist Sabbath invasion.[16]

Since this comment appeared just about the time that the Society for the Suppression of Vice was organized, one might well ask why it was necessary to have a private association to enforce the Sabbath laws. Actually, of course, there was no need for such a society, inasmuch as public opinion was proving to be a strict enforcing agency. Nevertheless, some recalcitrant proprietors, refusing to obey the law, still kept their butcher shops open on Sunday or continued to sell liquor during service time. As soon as it was organized, the vice society began to prosecute these offenders, and by 1804, 623 shopkeepers and publicans had been convicted of breaking Sabbath laws. But a mere recording of the number of convictions gives no adequate idea of the extensive activities of the association, for its policy was to warn offenders first, and to bring them before a magistrate only after they had refused to heed the warnings. According to the reports of the society, a written admonition was generally sufficient. Pleasure-seekers were also threatened with prosecutions, apparently, for the society briefly notes that it had successfully employed this method to stop "the shameful practice of rowing machines and boat races on Sunday." [17]

Although, as Sydney Smith had observed, the society did not prosecute wealthy offenders, upon one occasion it sent an admonition to the royal household at Windsor. This happened when members of the association heard that a number of workmen were employed in and about the palace on Sundays. Believing that the king would not knowingly tolerate such an abuse, the committee of the society brought it to the attention of their president, the Earl of Dartmouth, who promptly dispatched a letter on the subject to the surveyor of works at Windsor.[18]

No one could complain that the Society for the Suppression of Vice neglected an opportunity to further Sabbatarianism, but

[16] *Annual Review for 1804*, III, 323.
[17] *Statement of Proceedings of the Society*, London, 1804.   [18] *Ibid.*

the eagerness to form societies knew no bounds, and in 1809 another association, called the Society for Promoting the Observance of the Sabbath, was inaugurated. Unlike its predecessor, this organization had no function other than to enforce the Sabbath laws. The members were apparently very diligent, for in 1812 the new society reported that it had prosecuted 446 offenders in the previous twelve months.[19]

Despite their numerous prosecutions, however, neither of these societies had more than a small share in the development of nineteenth-century Sabbatarianism. In the final analysis public opinion was the real enforcing agency. And so strongly in favor of a strict Sabbath was public opinion that even royalty was forced to accede to it. A demonstration of this fact occurred in 1809, when old Bishop Porteus, the friend of the Evangelicals, heard that a club, of which the Prince of Wales was a member, customarily held its meetings on Sunday. Having secured an audience with the prince, the Bishop remonstrated with him, and before he left he secured a promise that thereafter the club would meet on Saturdays.[20] Now it would be ridiculous to pretend that the future George IV had been converted, especially since he continued to sow successive crops of wild oats. Like most members of the aristocracy and royalty, the Prince of Wales was not very much affected in his private life by the reformers of the time. But when he submitted to the Sabbatarian views of the Evangelicals upon this occasion, he showed that even royalty did not dare affront this large and censorious section of the people. This victory was a milestone on their triumphant march to glory. In the seventeenth century, when Puritan severity would have denied all amusements on Sunday, James I had issued his *Book of Sports,* in which he insisted upon the right of the people to enjoy harmless pastimes on Sunday. In the early years of the nineteenth century the sportive future king, far

19 *Christian Observer,* XI, 851 (Appendix).
20 Robert Hodgson, "Life of Porteus," in *Works of Bishop Porteus,* London, 1811, I, 249.

from taking any such action against the Sabbatarians of his day, bowed to their will.

CENSORSHIP

At first the Society for the Suppression of Vice left the prosecutions of blasphemous publications to the Proclamation Society. Only after it had absorbed the latter organization did it take a prominent part in the attempt to suppress skeptical writings, and most of its prosecutions of this offense come within the period 1819–1823. It was at this time that the society endeavored to ban the publications of Richard Carlile, a bookseller who specialized in the works of Paine. Carlile fought the society as none of its other victims dared do. When he was sent to prison in 1819 for selling *The Age of Reason*, he arranged to have his wife and sister keep his shop open for the sale of deistical works, When they, too, were tried and convicted, other associates of Carlile took over the business. Meanwhile the irrepressible Carlile further embarrassed the government by issuing, while still in prison, a weekly periodical called the *Republican*. Through the pages of this magazine he continually attacked the vice association and gave it unfavorable publicity by printing the reports of its prosecutions. The *Republican* also demanded that the nation adopt more democratic principles, particularly freedom of speech and freedom of the press. The vice society eventually prosecuted this periodical, too, but it failed to stop the circulation of deistical works or to crush the spirit of Richard Carlile, who, believing that every trial for blasphemy served only to advertise his publications, gloated over each prosecution. Carlile undoubtedly enjoyed the role of martyr, which he played in the grand manner. Nevertheless, he was sincerely devoted to democratic principles, and he did creditable service toward the eventual establishment of a free press.[21]

The period starting with the French Revolution had been characterized by repression and suppression, and now, while

[21] W. H. Wickwar, *The Struggle for the Freedom of the Press, 1819–1832*.

Carlile was warring with the Society for the Suppression of Vice, occurred the final struggle to subdue republican opinion. A new society, called the Constitutional Association, was formed in 1820. This organization, like the old Association for Preserving Liberty and Property, was particularly designed to prosecute so-called seditious works. A strong antiliberal group, it included the Duke of Wellington, six bishops, twenty peers, and about forty members of the House of Commons.[22] With two societies vigorously prosecuting publishers, it seemed for a few years as though they might succeed in shackling the press completely. Various booksellers were tried and convicted for vending Palmer's *Principles of Nature* and the political and skeptical writings of Paine. Under threat of prosecution, the publisher of Shelley's "Oedipus Tyrannus; or, Swellfoot the Tyrant" withdrew the work from circulation. Another publisher, William Clark, who had issued a pirated edition of Shelley's "Queen Mab" was convicted and sentenced to four months in prison.[23]

But the war on booksellers continued for only a few years. Despite the fact that their members contributed hundreds of pounds, the societies found the prosecutions extremely expensive. The liberals kept fighting them, and public indignation was aroused by the merciless treatment of the poor booksellers, who were prosecuted in preference to the owners of large establishments. Furthermore, it was becoming increasingly apparent that nothing could impede the growth of democratic sentiment. In 1823, therefore, the Constitutional Association called off its trials for sedition and, as the members fell away, the organization was soon extinct.[24]

At the same time the Society for the Suppression of Vice ceased its prosecutions of blasphemy, although it was to remain in existence until much later in the nineteenth century. It had been definitely worsted in its contest with Carlile, for it had not prevented the sale of skeptical works. Indeed, by giving

[22] *Ibid.*, pp. 180 ff.
[23] Walter E. Peck, *Shelley*, New York, 1927, II, 175; Wickwar, *op. cit.*, p. 262.
[24] *Ibid.*, pp. 180 ff.

them considerable publicity, it had probably done more than Carlile to familiarize the public with them. When, in 1823, Parliament discussed the activities of the society, Joseph Hume asserted that it had given so much notoriety to otherwise little-known works that the members should really be called "pro-moters and not suppressers of vice." [25] Nor was this remark in-tended to be taken entirely in jest. According to the *Westminster Review* the circulation of deistical works had greatly increased as a result of the prosecutions for blasphemy. Before the trials of Carlile and his associates only about a hundred copies of *The Age of Reason* were sold each month; after these prosecutions the monthly sale of this book soared to approximately nine hundred copies.[26]

Many sincerely religious persons had been opposed to the trials for blasphemy, knowing that they failed to suppress skep-tical works and knowing that the purpose of the prosecutions was not to protect orthodox faith so much as to maintain estab-lished political institutions. The old order was changing, how-ever, and the time was not far distant when England would be forced to make concessions to the principles of democracy. The failure to suppress so-called blasphemous works, indeed, might be interpreted as a harbinger of defeat for the political reac-tionaries. It was in no sense an indication that the masses favored skeptical views. Without the publicity given to deistical writ-ings, venders could have sold few copies of *The Age of Reason* and similar works, for the general reading public much pre-ferred the Evangelical or near-Evangelical books and tracts of their time. In fact, though political conservatism was weakening, social conservatism was growing stronger each year. This trend was particularly noticeable in the development of popular senti-ment upon the question of obscenity.

The Proclamation Society appears to have been little con-cerned with moral censorship, though its reports are so scanty that one cannot affirm this with certainty. It may have threat-

25 *The Parliamentary Debates*, VIII, 709 ff.
26 *Westminster Review*, II (July, 1824), 12 ff.

ened publishers of bawdy works, but it probably did not prosecute any. Nevertheless, there had been a few trials for obscenity
during the eighteenth century, and these, because they established legal precedents, had an important bearing upon sub-
sequent cases. The first conviction for this offense occurred in
1727, when Edmund Curll, the enemy of Pope, was found guilty
of having published a scurrilous book called *Venus in a Cloy-
ster*. At the trial Lord Hardwicke, the attorney-general, declared
that any work which tended to corrupt the morals of the king's
subjects might be considered an obscene libel. The publication
of such a work, moreover, was a punishable offense, for any act
prejudicial to morals could be construed as a breach of the
peace. This interpretation established a precedent which, in the
absence of any statutory provision for prosecuting obscenity,
made it possible to convict offenders. Later in the century, when
John Wilkes and a few other publishers of bawdy literature were
put on trial, the decision rendered in the case of Curll was re-
affirmed, and by the end of the century it had become part of
the common law.[27]

Prosecutions for obscenity had been very infrequent, however, until the institution of the Society for the Suppression of
Vice. Then they became rather numerous. For the first several
years of its existence, indeed, the association was much more
concerned to suppress obscenity than blasphemy. The details
of its activities in this field are somewhat obscure, however,
since the society, not wishing to advertise objectionable works,
refrains from mentioning them by name in its reports. Very
often it prosecuted individuals, not for selling obscene books,

---

[27] *State Trials*, XVII, 153–60; XIX, 1075 ff. Later in the nineteenth century,
because it was a slow and costly business to secure convictions under the common
law, the Society for the Suppression of Vice helped to have specific laws enacted
to provide for prosecutions of obscenity. The first of these (1 and 2 Vict. c. 38)
made it possible for a magistrate to punish anyone who exposed an obscene print,
picture, or exhibition to public view. The second (20 and 21 Vict. c. 83), known
as Lord Campbell's Act, permitted a magistrate to issue a search warrant, which
allowed the police to enter the premises of anyone suspected of keeping, with
intent to publish or sell, indecent books, papers, and prints, and to seize and
destroy such works. See *Occasional Report of the Society*, London, 1868; also *The
Law Journal Reports* (new series), XXXVII, 89 ff.

but for vending ballads, prints, and devices of an allegedly las-
civious character. It also prosecuted itinerant salesmen who sold
snuffboxes with some sort of pornographic representation under
the lid.[28]

According to the reports of the society there was considerable
trafficking in these forms of pornography in the first decade of
the nineteenth century. The business was conducted by a group
of foreigners, who employed several hundred agents to sell their
wares. Under some pretext the salesmen frequently gained entrance to boarding schools, where they sold foreign prints, objectionable ballads, and indecent books to the students. To prevent this commerce, the society sent letters to heads of seminaries
and public schools, issued several warnings to the peddlers, and
prosecuted those against whom it had evidence. These methods,
it was affirmed, succeeded in destroying the sale of objectionable
works to schools.[29]

Although the members of the vice association probably exaggerated the number of people engaged in this business, there is
no reason to doubt that the practice existed or that the mer-
chandise was often genuinely pornographic. This appears from
the fact that in each of its thirty or forty prosecutions for obscenity in the period from 1802 to 1817 the society secured a
conviction. Later on, however, when it concentrated rather upon
prosecuting what the members considered obscene literature, it
was not always so successful. It failed, for instance, to obtain a
conviction in the case of William Benbow, who was tried in 1821
for having published "lewd stories, songs, and pictures" in his
Rambler's Magazine and for selling a certain French novel. The
latter, it was proved, had been translated into English thirty
years earlier and could be obtained at most large circulating
libraries.[30]

Still, the effectiveness of the society's campaign to suppress
certain types of literature cannot be judged entirely by the num-

[28] *Part the Second of an Address to the Public,* London, 1803.
[29] *Report of the Society,* London, 1825, pp. 29–31.
[30] Wickwar, *op. cit.,* p. 221.

ber of convictions secured. For the threat of being prosecuted
was often sufficient to cause venders to abandon the sale of objectionable works or, if they continued to sell them, to force
them to carry on the business very clandestinely. The *Christian
Observer* was probably right, therefore, when it stated that as a
result of the society's vigilance, "many of those polluting publications, which are now only sold by stealth and with peril to the
vender, might have been seen a few years ago exhibited in the
shops of respectable booksellers." [31] But—and this may help to
explain the reticence of early Victorian writers—the threat of
prosecution also made booksellers hesitant to print works which
were neither cheap nor pornographic. When Byron sent his
publisher the first two cantos of *Don Juan*, Murray was reluctant
to print them, fearing that a prosecution might follow.[32] When
Don Juan did appear, although the vice society took no action
against it, many reviewers denounced it as indecent and immoral.

This sort of reception, even more, perhaps, than the fear of
prosecution, kept authors from publishing anything that might
appear at all questionable. For, in the final analysis, the public established its own standards of decency. Its estimate of Byron
showed how censorious it had become in less than a generation.
Although his works were extremely popular, the Evangelicals
banned him, and many other people considered him a corrupting influence. Yet Byron, for all his piquancy, never spoke out
as freely as dozens of writers in the eighteenth century, and it
seems safe to say that had he written in that period no one would
have thought it daring to read his works.

Still better proof that public opinion had grown extremely
strict may be adduced from the views of enlightened people upon
the subject of moral censorship. Almost no one protested when
the Society for the Suppression of Vice prosecuted obscene works.
Now this was curious, for many people were opposed to the
principles upon which it acted. When it had tried to prevent
Carlile and others from selling so-called blasphemous publica-

[31] *Christian Observer*, X (March, 1811), 184.   [32] Wickwar, *op. cit.*, pp. 264 ff.

tions, the liberals had denounced the organization as one of the worst enemies of a free press. Yet, despite the fact that its trials for obscenity occurred at a time when liberals were fighting for the right to print what one wished, even the champions of freedom did not believe that the suppression of indecent literature abridged this right. Quite to the contrary, some of them definitely favored this kind of censorship. Even Richard Carlile, much as he hated the vice society, approved of its efforts to suppress indecency. Attacking it for other reasons, he remarked:

The first avowed object of your society was to seek out the persons who were instrumental in disseminating obscene books and prints. Had you confined yourself to this, no honest or moral man would have complained of or objected to your conduct as a society.[33]

Carlile was undoubtedly sincere in making this statement. He disliked anything that might be considered lewd, and when the vice society prosecuted William Benbow for selling the allegedly obscene *Rambler's Magazine,* Carlile denounced Benbow, who also trafficked in deistical writings, for selling what he considered a very objectionable publication.[34]

Joseph Hume, a member of the House of Commons, took a similar stand. While attacking the society in Parliament for prosecuting blasphemous works, he commended its efforts to suppress obscenity, saying that it had done creditable service in this field.[35] It is possible, of course, that Hume made this reservation because he knew where the public stood upon the question of obscenity. But, writing in his notebooks, where he was not compelled to defer to prejudice or propriety, Francis Place also applauded the association for having helped to destroy the sale of eighteenth-century ballads and other bawdy works. Yet Place, who was one of the foremost agitators for a free press, had nothing but contempt for the society's endeavors to suppress other types of literature.[36]

Thus the liberal reformers of government and the conserva-

---

[33] The *Republican,* II (Feb. 25, 1820), 182 ff.
[34] *Ibid.,* VI (July 19, 1822), 225 ff.   [35] *The Parliamentary Debates,* VIII, 733.
[36] B.M., Add. MSS 27,825, pp. 144–45.

tive reformers of manners, though bitterly opposed to each other upon most issues, agreed upon the question of moral censorship. This harmony of opinion characterized most Englishmen, and the writers of the time, knowing the disposition of their countrymen, generally took care not to offend their sensibilities. Meanwhile, as we shall see in the following chapter, several older authors were considered so indelicate that they could be tolerated only in expurgated editions.

CHAPTER TEN

CENSORS AND EXPURGATORS

IN HER *Strictures on Female Education* Hannah More had referred to the habit of reading novels as "one of the most universal as well as the most pernicious sources of corruption." She had devoted several pages to censuring this pastime, and, while she had not insisted that her readers abstain from all works of fiction, she had warned them that "novels, which chiefly used to be dangerous in one respect, are now become mischievous in a thousand." [1] Shortly after publishing this treatise, Hannah More received a note of congratulation from her friend and counselor, the Reverend John Newton. He had only one objection to her book. Said he, "I hoped your just censure of novels would have extended to the proscription of the whole race without mercy and without exception." [2]

The Evangelicals, as it appears, sometimes differed in estimating the degree of culpability attached to reading polite literature, but hardly any of them allowed a greater measure of freedom than Hannah More, and they seldom missed an opportunity to censure certain types of books. The leading Evangelical periodicals were particularly intolerant. Many of them asserted that for a Christian the drama was completely unlawful. Satire they condemned because it was malicious or because Christ and his apostles never used it. Fiction, except for the stories that appeared in their own tracts, they considered one of the chief snares

[1] *Works*, VI, 23, 93.
[2] Wm. Roberts, *Memoirs of the Life and Correspondence of Hannah More,* III, 77–78.

of the devil. "Novels, generally speaking, are instruments of abomination and ruin," said the *Evangelical Magazine*. "Even books of an opposite description—books which combine important instruction and untainted pleasure—will, if they preclude punctual attention to the duties of our representative stations, be read too much." [3]

The Evangelicals, by constantly printing statements of this kind, made it clear that they were generally opposed to books as a source of entertainment and suspicious of their intellectual content. Their strongest censure, however, was reserved for the theater. Typical of their sentiments upon this subject were the views expressed by the Reverend Rowland Hill in a tract called *A Warning to Professors*. Nothing could be "more corrupting and loose" than a comedy, wrote Hill, for in this species of drama "treachery and intrigue are brought forward as matters of merriment and fun; while the solemnities of the marriage contract are treated with ridicule and contempt." Yet tragedy, with its tendency to exalt pride, ambition, and revenge "by all the aids of oratory" had, perhaps, a worse effect upon the upper ranks "than comedy has in its filthy, frothy influence on all the thoughtless rabble." "As for those contemptible things called farces," added Hill, "they seem to be designed only to show how far the mind of man can put up with the most paltry ribaldry and nonsense." [4]

After browsing through some of the Evangelical magazines, where he had encountered numerous proscriptions of this sort, Robert Southey exclaimed, "What must be the effect of a confederated and indefatigable priesthood, who barely tolerate literature, and actually hate it, upon all those classes over whom literature has an influence!" [5] The chief effect of Evangelical censorship was to create the belief that literature was a constant threat to the moral integrity of readers, unless it conformed to certain very strict standards. Many adherents of the faith, follow-

[3] *Evangelical Magazine*, I (Aug., 1793), 78–79.
[4] *A Warning to Professors*, London, 1833.
[5] *Quarterly Review*, IV (Nov., 1810), 506–7.

ing what they were taught, refused to attend the theater or to read novels or plays. But censorship extended its influence beyond the circle of strict Evangelicals, for others, who remained unsympathetic with their religious teachings, were eventually impressed by their constantly reiterated proscriptions. As a result, public opinion veered toward the Evangelical position and, while it did not go so far as to condemn all novels and plays, it ruled that literature should be less outspoken than at any previous time.

One might observe that the theater and fiction had always had their enemies, that censorship was nothing new. Even during the middle years of the eighteenth century, to say nothing of the age that produced Jeremy Collier, occasional attacks upon the stage had appeared, emanating from the studies of die-hard English puritans, or coming, like a cold blast, from Calvinistic Scotland. Why, then, was it only in the nineteenth century that censorship had such a pervasive and lasting effect? In the first place, it had the advantage of operating in a sympathetic milieu. The earlier attacks upon literature had made little impression upon the typical reader, who was inclined to consider them the products of fanaticism. Now there were dozens of writers like Rowland Hill and thousands of serious-minded Evangelicals who obediently followed the proscriptions of their leaders. There was also a vast and impressionable group of new readers, products of the various educational systems, upon whom the censors could easily foist their opinions.

Furthermore—and this fact alone may have had an important bearing upon the excessive timidity of early nineteenth-century readers—the censors had become much more severe. When Jeremy Collier and his confreres had attacked the Restoration drama, they could point to examples of real grossness, but the theater had reformed since that time, and later writers, like John Home, Sheridan, and Mrs. Inchbald, had been careful not to offend their audiences. But even these authors were now furiously assailed. After reading Mrs. Inchbald's "The Wedding Day," Rowland Hill went into a tantrum because the play abounded in "oaths" like "egad," "dam'me," "heavens," and "faith." "Faith" was really an oath, he explained, for it meant "by faith of the Gospel." Mrs. Inchbald's works had been recommended to him as "the most pure and chaste of the age," but he had discovered that "The Wedding Day" dealt almost exclusively with "debauchery." Describing what he considered the most objectionable scene, Hill showed that he might have been an interesting subject for psychoanalysis when he wrote, "A young fellow clasps a young girl in his arms before all the spectators; what folly not to suppose that every impure passion is not immediately excited by such scenes as these." [6]

John Styles, a popular Methodist preacher, refused to admit that the theater had reformed. "The works of Congreve and Dryden," he wrote, "are absolutely pure when compared with the vile disgusting offspring of the profligate Kotzebue." But Styles, having a passionate hatred of all plays, was hardly capable of discriminating between the products of various periods of the drama. Of Shakespeare he said, "Barefaced obscenities, low vulgarity, and nauseous vice so frequently figure and pollute his pages that we cannot but lament the luckless hour in which he became a writer for the stage." The sentimental dramatists were equally offensive, for in their works, so long as the hero had "a good heart," he was excused for being "a libertine, a despiser of God, and a trampler on his laws." According to Styles the theater created false notions, encouraged profligacy, and increased the number of suicides. Its effect upon women was particularly degrading, so degrading, in fact, that Styles recommended "that in the choice of a wife, a gentleman should preemptorily reject every female who had been four times to the theater in the course of the last two years." [7]

Whole classes of literature were now condemned on principle. In the eighteenth century, moralists like Johnson and Defoe had employed satire to ridicule vice. But the Evangelical critics, believing that ridicule seldom acted as a corrective, argued that

[6] *An Expostulary Letter*, London, 1795, 32 ff.
[7] *Essay on the Stage*, London, 1806.

satire generally had a pernicious effect. According to the *Eclectic Review*, some of the most famous satirists of the past had written merely to amuse their readers and were quite insincere in their attacks upon evil. "Were Horace and Juvenal supposed to be more chaste and temperate because they satirized debauchery and drunkenness?" asked the reviewer. Too frequently, he said, the satirist aimed his blows, not at general faults which the reader could remedy in himself, but at known persons whose shortcomings, when exposed, provoked only malicious laughter. Thus the satirist, instead of serving as a moralist or even as the purveyor of innocent amusement, frequently corrupted the reader.[8]

The *Eclectic Review* was equally harsh in its treatment of sentimental writers, though, as has been shown,[9] the eighteenth-century sentimentalists, who were themselves often revolting from the coarser literature of their time, had been unstinting in their praise of virtue and morality. But their platitudes were too general, too completely unrelated to the specific doctrines of the revival to suit the Evangelicals. Thus, when the *Eclectic Review* discussed the sentimental style of writing, the comment was: "It is doubtful whether it has been productive of any good; and that it is the prolific parent of evil cannot be denied." [10]

When they named particular authors, the censors did not hesitate to denounce some of the greatest writers of the previous century. One might expect that the diction of Swift would occasionally offend squeamish readers and that some of the more obscure poems of Pope would be kept from children. But one is surprised to read "that the most ingenious compositions of these eminent wits are also the most pernicious and inexcusable." [11] Even Addison, whom a recent critic has called the first Victorian, was criticized because he used ridicule in portraying the character of Sir Roger, thereby failing to make him serve as an exemplary person.[12] Nor was Addison the only eighteenth-

[8] *Eclectic Review*, II (May, 1806), 372 ff. [9] See above, chap. ii.
[10] *Eclectic Review*, II (Feb., 1806), 140–41.
[11] Edward Mangin, *An Essay on Light Reading*, London, 1808, p. 153.
[12] H. Murray, *The Morality of Fiction*, Edinburgh, 1805, p. 90.

century moralist to lose prestige. Samuel Richardson, who had been so eager to correct the thinking of his time, the author who, according to Samuel Johnson, had "taught the passions to move at the command of virtue," even Richardson was now censured, because he had introduced various indelicate scenes which he described in minute detail, because he failed to stress religious principles, and because the tendency of *Pamela* was to encourage servant girls to rise above their allotted station in life.[13]

It was this unmitigated type of censorship, then, combined with the generally conservative temper of the time, that helped to create an extremely timid view of literature. In deference to it contemporary writers toned down their works and frequently supplied them with introductions in which they professed to have some lofty aim. But the works of older authors still remained, filled with errors, sprinkled with offending phrases, with corruption lurking for the reader on almost every page. The only way to make these productions conform to the stricter standards of the age was to purge them of their faults by publishing them in expurgated editions. This procedure was frequently adopted.

One should remember, however, that in expurgating great works of the past, nineteenth-century editors violated no tradition. It had been a common practice in the previous century to bring older writers up to date by revising the original text, and no one had objected when John Wesley and other reformers expurgated passages offensive to their religious and moral beliefs. There was still less reverence for original texts in the theater, for producers felt free to emend the plots of old plays, to exclude certain characters or to introduce new ones, and to delete lines that seemed superfluous or offensive. Thus the practice had precedent on its side, as one of the expurgators observed:

The custom of altering the works of authors appeared to me to be so well established in the vocal and dramatic world that it was sufficiently understood and acknowledged; and as my alterations had in view the cause of religion and morality, I trusted that this superior

---

[13] *Ibid.*, p. 99.

object would secure to the *Collection* an indulgence beyond that due to mere compilation.[14]

Even without an eighteenth-century tradition in their favor, the expurgators might easily have vindicated their efforts by referring to more recent practices. The fears caused by the French Revolution had been strongly prejudicial to literature, and there had been no hesitation in suppressing ideas and opinions which were deemed objectional for political, moral, or religious reasons. When contemporary writers were denied freedom of expression, why should the licentious passages of older authors be permitted to appear in print? Indeed, as compared with the strict Evangelicals who indiscriminately banned all novels and plays, the expurgators might consider themselves liberals, taking a middle course at a time when the most severe censors could not tolerate polite literature in any form.

THE ALTERATIONS OF JAMES PLUMPTRE

The most assiduous emendator of literature in the nineteenth century was James Plumptre. Born in 1770, he had attended Cambridge, where, after graduation, he became a fellow of Clare Hall. Later, having taken holy orders, he secured the living of Great Gransden, Huntingdonshire. Plumptre was not an Evangelical. Unlike many who were, he professed to have a great admiration for literature. He was himself the author of a few plays, and he constantly opposed those who asserted that the theater was unlawful. This degree of liberality did not count for much, however, for Plumptre was strongly influenced by the moral reformers of his time. An admirer of Hannah More and Sarah Trimmer, he endorsed their strict views upon the subject of censorship, and, when he published his first volume of expurgations, a collection of songs, he explained that he had undertaken the revisions after finding in the works of these two ladies the suggestion that many old English ballads should be altered in the interest of decency. Any profit that might accrue

[14] James Plumptre, *Letters to John Aikin,* Cambridge, 1811, p. xxix.

from this volume he promised to turn over to the Society for the Suppression of Vice. It seemed fitting to do so, he remarked, since his expurgated songs were intended to supersede those which the society was trying to prohibit.[15]

In revising the text of older writers Plumptre was guided by three principles. He wished (1) to make literature serve a definitely moral purpose, (2) to remove objectionable ideas and situations, and (3) to delete expressions which he considered gross or impious. To Plumptre the worth of a literary production depended chiefly upon the number of moral sentiments it contained. Even ballads and songs, he believed, should have some wholesome and pointed lesson. In revising the works of older writers, therefore, he found it necessary, not only to delete expressions, but, in many instances, to introduce additional lines and stanzas. He differed in this respect from his contemporary, Thomas Bowdler. Although the latter made frequent deletions when he edited Shakespeare, he seldom, in any single instance, added more than a short phrase to the text. Plumptre, on the other hand, frequently assumed the role of a collaborator and appended his own infelicitous lines to some of the great poetry of the past. He seems never to have realized the inferiority of his compositions, or, if he did, he felt that his substitutions and additions were justified by his aim. "With me," he declared, "the cause of morality and religion is paramount." [16]

The revisions were intended in the second place to remove ideas and situations which Plumptre considered too offensive to appear in print. He particularly objected to any form of impiety, but his notion of what constituted irreverence was, especially for a clergyman, very confused. According to Plumptre, to swear by the pagan gods of Greek mythology was just about as culpable as to swear by the Christian Deity. Consequently, when he expurgated a text, he generally removed all "heathen" references. No one should use the "language of Scripture" without proper reverence, he said, though he included within this category such

15 *A Collection of Songs*, London, 1806–8, "Preface," I, xiv ff.
16 *Ibid.*, I, xxvii.

words as "worship," "adore," and "create." Believing that it was equally wrong for men to form conjectures about the nature of "the invisible world," he would have forbidden all representations of heaven or hell on the stage. Nor would he have allowed witches or conjurers to appear in a play, holding that the introduction of such characters encouraged the belief that they really existed.[17]

To these proscriptions Plumptre added the following. Scenes of romantic love should be barred, inasmuch as they often encouraged young people to enter upon unhappy unions. It was wrong to introduce profligate characters, especially if they appeared in an amiable light. Murder and suicide should never be enacted on the stage, and when characters died in view of the audience, their last moments should be marked by a spirit of resignation and penitence. Such were some of the beliefs that guided Plumptre in making his expurgations. Yet he constantly affirmed the lawfulness of the stage. In fact, the proscriptions given above were all contained in his *Discourses on the Stage,* a work which he had produced to defend the theater against the attacks of those who believed it to be a completely unchristian institution.[18]

Plumptre's third purpose in altering the works of his betters was to delete offensive words and phrases. As has been shown,[19] there were signs at the end of the eighteenth century that people were becoming slightly prudish in their choice of language. This tendency increased as other forms of social conservatism flourished. There was probably no single reason for the development of various verbal taboos, though the middle-class emphasis upon rather artificial rules of propriety had more to do with it, perhaps, than the religious revival or the reaction to the French Revolution. At any rate when Plumptre deleted words that had been acceptable in other times, he was merely trying to make the older writers comply with the greater delicacy of his own age.

[17] *Four Discourses on Subjects Relating to the Amusement of the Stage,* Cambridge, 1809, pp. 25 ff.
[18] *Ibid.*   [19] See above, chap. ii.

If he was not so prudish as the later Victorians who substituted "limb" for "leg," he was, nevertheless, unprecedentedly squeamish. He expunged the word "whore" and he would not allow "damn" to appear even as "d---." But the substitutions he made often violated meaning much more than the original expression outraged delicacy. In one instance he changed the wording of a lusty sailor song from "I don't care a damn" to "I don't mind your bam." In another song he altered "damn ye" to "thank ye." Even the devil must be given his due, Plumptre insisted, for to call him "the old one" or "old Geman" was to use improper levity toward a subject which should excite only horror.[20]

Plumptre published his first expurgated edition in 1805. This work, which was a collection of songs, he expanded to three volumes within the next few years.[21] In addition to various songs by Plumptre, the anthology contained numerous selections from Shakespeare, Pope, Goldsmith, Cowper, Burns, and other distinguished poets. The stanzas of these writers frequently appeared in grotesquely altered versions. Perhaps the worst example of Plumptre's patchwork is a poem called "The Parish Priest," which is a composite picture of the poor priest in *The Canterbury Tales* and the country parson in "The Deserted Village." But the poem as Plumptre published it is really the work of four different writers, for he used Dryden's adaptation of Chaucer, and to the lines taken from Goldsmith he added some of his own.

The poet most frequently represented in the anthology was none other than James Plumptre. His verses, whatever else they lacked, always contained some pointed lesson. A typical composition was "The Onion," which went as follows:

> A plant there's in my garden grows,
> In all my taste a sharer.
> Its scent to me outvies the rose,
> The lily is not fairer.

---

[20] *A Collection of Songs,* I, lxiii ff.

[21] There is no copy of the 1805 edition in the British Museum, though the preface to it is included in later editions.

My food, my physic, my delight—
No longer for to fun ye on,
My rhyme and reason shall unite
In praising of the onion.

I envy not the great man's meal,
French cookery and kickshaws,
Disguising mutton, beef and veal,
His dishes I'd not like those.
The onion is the poor man's sauce,
With that he n'er can do ill,
A relish 'tis to bread and cheese
And e'en to water-gruel.

"The Onion" was apparently intended to persuade the lower classes to be content in their humble station and not to hunger for the savories enjoyed by their betters. What the poor may have thought of this anti-Jacobin song does not appear, but Plumptre said that it had "given offence to the delicate taste" of some of his friends. Apparently even the mention of such a vegetable was noisome in polite circles. Plumptre insisted upon printing the song, however, explaining that he had written it specifically for those who were destined to be hewers of wood and onion eaters.[22]

Plumptre's verse appeared the more execrable when he used it to patch out the poetry of some of the best English authors. Typical of the sort of revisions that occur throughout the anthology were those made in several lyrics of Shakespeare. The following song from *Cymbeline* is first given in its original version:

Hark! Hark! the lark at heaven's gate sings,
  And Phoebus 'gins arise,
His steeds to water at those springs
  On chalic'd flowers that lies:
And winking Mary-buds begin
  To ope their golden eyes:
With everything that pretty is,
  My lady sweet, arise:
  Arise, arise!

---

[22] *A Collection of Songs*, I, lxxvii.

Calling his moralized adaptation of the poem "The Sluggard,"
Plumptre published it in this form:

> Hark! Hark! the lark at heaven's gate sings,
>   The sun begins to rise;
> While murmurs break from bubbling springs
>   Mid flow'rs of thousand dies;
> And winking Mary-buds begin
>   To ope their golden eyes,
> With everything that pretty is,
>   For shame, thou sluggard, rise.

The reference to Phoebus was changed, of course, because of its
heathenism, and the steeds had to be omitted because they suggested a pagan myth. The same ludicrous fear of heathenism led
Plumptre to delete references to Juno and Ceres from the song in
The Tempest beginning:

> Honour, riches, marriage-blessing,
> Long continuance and increasing.

Plumptre also included, in an emended form, the cuckoo song
from *Love's Labour's Lost*. Shakespeare's refrain is:

> The cuckoo then on every tree,
> Mocks married men; for thus sings he,
>   Cuckoo;
> Cuckoo, cuckoo: O, word of fear,
> Unpleasing to a married ear!

In Plumptre's version, though there is more repetition, the references to cuckoldry are omitted:

> The cuckoo then on every tree,
> Begins his song, for thus sings he:
> Cuckow—cuckow—he then doth sing,
> Announcing the return of spring.

Elsewhere in this song the editor made further revisions. It
was doubtless prudery which caused him to substitute "carda-
mine" as the name of the flower to which Shakespeare gave the
more colloquial term, "lady-smocks." More to be expected was
the alteration of "turtles tread" to "turtles coo." Plumptre not

only changed this lyric, but added another stanza, in which the cuckoo, like the author, "gets hoarse in song" while announcing the return of summer.

One of the most amusing alterations was that made in a song from *As You Like It*. In the *Collection* the familiar

> Under the greenwood tree
> Who loves to lie with me

was changed to:

> Under the greenwood tree
> Who loves to work with me.

There appear to have been two reasons for altering the verb in this instance: the lying posture probably seemed indelicate if not suggestive to the editor, and, as a moralist, he was eager to encourage industry. The last verse of this song Plumptre omitted entirely, doubtless because he found it too cynical for inclusion in his anthology.

From such efforts it would appear that Plumptre was a rather simple-minded person, but he was not just an individual crank. The nineteenth century, though still in its first decade, was fast developing the opinion that many old English ballads were too coarse to be sung in their original versions. Still more curious, older people who had once found these songs perfectly acceptable now complained of their vulgarity. John Aikin, a doctor and a literary man of some ability, was one of those whose views had kept pace with the growing strictness of the age. When, as a young man in 1772, he had published an anthology of verse, he had not considered it necessary to delete any lines from his selections. But in 1810, when Aikin revised this edition, he bowdlerized his original text and proved to be almost as censorious as James Plumptre. He now spoke of the "prevalent coarseness" in the poetry of Ben Jonson, and when he printed Suckling's lyric, "Why So Pale and Wan, Fond Lover," he excluded the last stanza, probably because of the line:

> The devil take her.

Aikin also altered a poem of John Donne, explaining that his language was "far from elegant or refined." The original version of this poem runs as follows:

> Send home my long stray'd eyes to me,
> Which, O! too long have dwelt on thee,
> Yet since they have learn'd such ill,
> Such forced fashions,
> And false passions,
> That they be
> Made by thee
> Fit for no good sight, keep them still.

It is difficult to understand what Aikin could have objected to in this stanza. Nevertheless, he changed it, beginning at the third line, to read:

> But if from thee they've learned such ill,
> To sweetly smile
> And then beguile
> Keep the deceivers, keep them still.[23]

Aikin's revisions show that Plumptre merely acted in the spirit of his time. There was further evidence of this in the reception accorded his anthology. One might expect, especially at a period when many critics were notably satirical and abusive, that Plumptre's collection of songs would have evoked a volley of stinging remarks. But nothing of the sort occurred. The reviewers who had so bitterly attacked Coleridge and Wordsworth appear to have passed over this work in silence, feeling contempt for it, perhaps, but not daring to express their sentiments. The Evangelical magazines also neglected to comment upon the collection of songs, probably because the editor was not an Evangelical. The two church and state periodicals reviewed it, however, and these strongly partisan organs had nothing but praise for Plumptre's efforts. "It is impossible not to approve the spirit and principle as well as the taste and judgment which suggested this collection of songs," remarked the *British Critic*. The editors

[23] *Vocal Poetry*, ed. by John Aikin, London, 1810, pp. xlviii, 166, 215. Aikin's 1772 edition was entitled *Essays on Songwriting with a Collection*.

of the *Anti-Jacobin* were equally complimentary and urged Plumptre to provide further expurgated texts.[24] To this task the most industrious of the emendators soon applied himself, next producing a group of plays.

The English Drama Purified, which was published in 1812, was advertised as a collection "in which all the passages that have appeared to the editor as objectionable in point of morality have been omitted or altered." A three-volume work, it contained a total of seventeen plays, all of the eighteenth century. To be included, each play had to stress some moral principle, but hardly any of them satisfied all the requirements of Plumptre, and in almost every instance he found it necessary to delete a few passages or to alter certain scenes. *The Gamester,* for instance, could qualify only after certain changes had been made. Plumptre liked the play because it illustrated the evil of gambling, but when he published it, he altered one scene "which manifested too much the spirit of duelling," and another which showed one of the characters taking a draft of poison.[25]

Plumptre explained most of his revisions in the solemn prefaces which he wrote for each of the plays. In Nicholas Rowe's *Jane Shore* he changed the text because there was too much passionate love-making. He also altered the references to fate, emending such a line as "Fortune, I fear sir, has used you ill" to read "The world, I fear sir, has used you ill." *The Conscious Lovers,* though included in the collection, was considerably altered, for Plumptre objected to the "absolutely indelicate" scenes between Tom and Phillis, to the use of duplicity and falsehood by young Bevil, and to the "disguises and impostures" which Myrtle and Tom engage in.[26] Yet Richard Steele, the author of this play, had been one of the principal reformers of his time. When he introduced his sentimental comedies, they seemed completely decorous, and people applauded his fine

[24] *British Critic,* XXX (Aug., 1807), 194 ff. *Anti-Jacobin,* XXII (Oct., 1805), 167 ff.
[25] *The English Drama Purified,* Cambridge, 1812, I, 14.
[26] *Ibid.,* I, 88, 114; II, 148 ff.

moral sentiments. But not even Steele, except in an expurgated version, could satisfy the much stricter requirements of James Plumptre.

Other plays were freely clipped and pruned to make them suitable for inclusion in the collection. From Goldsmith's *Good Natur'd Man* Plumptre omitted the passages in which Olivia and Leoline practice deceit. He also deleted Croaker's jokes about earthquakes, explaining that the subject was "too serious and awful" for general ridicule.[27] Some of the plays abounded in errors so egregious that only the most drastic revision could purify them. Describing his treatment of John Home's *Douglas*, Plumptre wrote:

Those passages in the speech of Lady Randolph which savour of murmuring at the dispensations of Providence, the too-heroic ardour of Douglas, the speeches respecting fate as the ruler of the affairs of men, the invocations of created beings, the adoption of popular superstitions, and the suicide of Lady Randolph, it was absolutely necessary to remove.[28]

Needless to say, this process of purification by emasculation often weakened the dramatic effectiveness of the plays, though readers who could not suffer them in their original form were probably grateful for the expurgated edition. On the other hand, there were some, notably the very strict Evangelicals, who would refuse to open even a purified collection of plays. When Plumptre published his *Discourses on the Stage,* in which he expounded the theory that the drama, if cleansed of all its corruptions, could serve to promote morality, the *Eclectic Review* severely censured him. Nothing could reconcile the editors of this Evangelical magazine to believing that the stage could ever be anything but vicious and unlawful, and they were shocked that a clergyman should endeavor to defend the theater.[29]

Plumptre next published *A Selection from the Fables of Gay* and a second volume entitled *One Hundred Fables* by various authors. He had been encouraged to prepare these texts, he

[27] *Ibid.,* II, 257, 281.   [28] *Ibid.,* I, 260.
[29] *Eclectic Review,* V (Nov., 1809), 1031.

remarked, after reading Mrs. Trimmer's complaint that many fables were immoral. Dr. Lettice, writing in the *European Magazine*, had also objected to some of the old fables and had suggested that someone should purify those by Gay. Having undertaken this task, Plumptre assured his readers that he had been careful that "nothing should remain which can cause a blush on the cheek of modesty or grieve the heart of piety." [30]

Finally, in 1826, Plumptre brought out a "revised and corrected" edition of *Robinson Crusoe*. If today this famous child's book seems completely innocuous, it did not always appear so to critics. Several years before Plumptre published his version, Maria Edgeworth had expressed the opinion that the story might have the dangerous effect of inspiring in young readers a taste for adventure.[31] Mrs. Trimmer, who endorsed this view, further complained that in the second part of his novel Defoe had favored Roman Catholic doctrines. "At least," she added, "the Romish priest is exhibited as the perfection of ministerial character." [32] Plumptre, agreeing with these ladies, had still another objection: he had detected an inclination on Defoe's part to favor a belief in predestination, or fatalism. When he prepared his edition of *Robinson Crusoe*, therefore, he omitted the passages that he considered in any way offensive.

The publication of *Robinson Crusoe* was the crowning achievement of Plumptre's career as an expurgator. With the exception of the *Fables of Gay*, which reached a sixth edition in 1849, none of his texts appears to have sold very well. The failure of his works to attain a wide circulation might be attributed, in part, to the fact that readers were not very much interested in the old songs and plays which he printed in his miscellanies. But, and this was perhaps the more important reason, Plumptre was such a snapper up of unconsidered trifles that even the Victorians probably felt that he was unduly squeamish.

30 *A Selection from the Fables of John Gay*, Huntingdon, 1823, "Preface."
31 *Practical Education*, I, 336.
32 *Guardian of Education*, III (July, 1804), 297 ff.

THE EXPURGATORS OF SHAKESPEARE

The eighteenth-century critics generally had the highest regard for Shakespeare. They admired his plots, they appreciated his poetic genius, they affirmed that better than anyone else he had held the mirror up to nature, and they considered him one of the finest moral writers of all time. Believing that literature should be strongly didactic, they placed a particularly high value upon Shakespeare as a moralist. Dr. Johnson, to be sure, complained that Shakespeare too frequently "sacrifices virtue to convenience." Nevertheless, Johnson heartily endorsed the prevailing opinion that the individual precepts found throughout the poet's works were unexcelled. These precepts were frequently published as extracts, in order that a person who wished to study Shakespeare's moral philosophy need not be distracted by his plots and characters. This practice reflected a tendency in the eighteenth century not to disparage Shakespeare as a poet or dramatist, but to esteem him, above all else, as the universal instructor of mankind.

The typical reader of the early eighteenth century was probably not offended by the unvarnished Anglo-Saxon terms he encountered in Shakespeare, for contemporary writers had not accustomed him to polite euphemisms. As the century progressed, however, people were becoming more conscious of delicacy, and the editors of Shakespeare occasionally paused to reflect upon the vulgarity of his language. Thomas Hanmer, who published an edition of the plays in 1744, was one of the first to refer to the "ribaldry" found in Shakespeare. He particularly objected to the scene in *Henry V* where the French princess receives a lesson in English, so much so that he expurgated it from his text. Scenes of this kind were frequently omitted on the stage, but Hanmer was probably the first editor of Shakespeare ever to delete a passage for moral reasons.

Some years later, when he was commissioned to prepare an edition of the plays, Francis Gentleman considered the idea of publishing an extensively expurgated Shakespeare. He decided against this plan, however, for various critics, whom he had consulted, advised him that it might appear "an over-strained piece of prudery." [33] The text which he finally published in 1774 reproduced the plays in the cut-down acting versions then used in the theater, but Gentleman assured his readers that he intended merely to provide a companion for the playhouse, not a "reformed edition." Far from removing the passages which he considered offensive, Gentleman called attention to them by printing them in italics and commenting upon them in footnotes. From these remarks he appears to have been more concerned about indelicacy than most editors of his time, but he does not shy at words like "bawd" or "leaping-houses," and he reveals none of the extreme prudery manifested by the early nineteenth-century expurgators. The fact that he freely discussed the question of indelicacy shows the comparative liberality of his age. This practice would not have been tolerated fifty years later.

A more censorious view of Shakespeare, especially with regard to his language, had already developed by the end of the eighteenth century. One might infer this from the very title of an essay published by William Richardson. It was called "On the Faults of Shakespeare." Summing up some of the errors of the dramatist, Richardson remarked, "His rude mixture of tragic and comic scenes, together with the vulgarity, and even indecency of language, admitted too frequently into his dialogue, have exposed him to frequent censure." [34]

If people were beginning to take offense at some of Shakespeare's terms, it was partly due to the development of certain speech taboos and the introduction of polite euphemisms. But it was not simply the language of Shakespeare which was falling into disrepute. Although many revered his writings as much as ever, to some, notably the Evangelicals, he was neither a great dramatist nor a great moralist. Having a particular aversion for

[33] *Bell's Edition of Shakespeare's Plays*, ed. by Francis Gentleman, London, 1774, Vol. IX, "Introduction."
[34] *Essays*, London, 1784, p. 114.

the theater, the Evangelicals were especially bitter in their denunciations of the most popular of all dramatists, and the more
bigoted among them were inclined to the view that it was impossible for a writer of plays to be, at the same time, a great
moralist. Thus, as the Evangelicals became more numerous, the
opinion grew that, far from being the virtuous instructor of
mankind, Shakespeare was one of the chief disciples of the devil.
So pronounced was this prejudice by 1810 that Robert Southey
was not exaggerating its intensity when he wrote:

Poor Shakespeare, indeed, is an object of special abhorrence to some
of our worst bigots; there is a passage in the *Eclectic Review* which
describes his soul in hell, suffering from the evil which his works
continue to do in the world. The fiercer part of these professors
would no doubt consign those works to the flames as piously as they
have in their imagination consigned the author. . . . There is a
pithy and profitable tale in the *Methodist Magazine* of the conversion
of Mr. G. Burton, effected by seeing *The Tempest;* the last effect
we will venture to say that either author or actors dreamt of producing: "He was so struck with the wickedness of the players in mimick-
ing the works of the Almighty, in causing thunder and lightning,
that he was afraid, lest in the judgment of God, the house should
fall upon them and crush their bodies to atoms, and send their souls
to hell; and he was determined if the Lord would spare him to get
out of the place alive, he would dedicate his all to his service." The
stage being held in such abhorrence, it cannot be supposed that
Shakespeare will be tolerated.[35]

As Southey observed, this was the view which prevailed
among the "fiercer" Evangelicals. There was a more cultured
group of believers, however, who had some appreciation of
Shakespeare's genius. Although they, like their stricter brethren,
generally refused to attend the theater, they admitted that with
certain reservations one could *read* Shakespeare without being
corrupted. Hannah More, who belonged to the more tolerant
group, granted that Shakespeare had fewer faults than most of
his contemporaries and that some of his plays contained noble
and inspiring lessons. But she added, "Who will deny that all
the excellencies we have ascribed to him are debased by pas-

[35] *Quarterly Review,* IV (Nov., 1810), 507.

sages of offensive grossness? are tarnished with indelicacy, false taste, and vulgarity?" In order to avoid such passages, said Hannah More, the reader of Shakespeare must exercise the most careful discrimination.[36] But how was one to know what to avoid without having first wallowed in a quagmire of Elizabethan obscenity? The only solution was to have the plays in an expurgated text.

Thomas Bowdler is the person usually associated with the expurgated text entitled *The Family Shakespeare*, for his edition, first published in 1818, was the one best known to the Victorians. But he was not the editor of the preliminary edition of this work, containing twenty plays, which appeared in 1807. Several years later it was attributed to "one of Mr. Thomas Bowdler's nearest relatives." [37] Why this reference should be so vague is difficult to understand, unless it was a matter of delicacy. The first editor must have been either John Bowdler, a brother, who was the author of *Reform or Ruin,* or Henrietta, a sister, who had written some essays and verse. Henrietta seems to be the more likely candidate, and possibly the reason for preserving her anonymity was to shield her from any charge of impropriety for having studied the vulgarisms of Shakespeare so thoroughly as to qualify as an expurgator. At any rate the 1807 edition preceded Thomas Bowdler's text of all the plays by eleven years, and its appearance at a time when Plumptre was starting his series of alterations shows that prudery was already common by the first decade of the nineteenth century. Inasmuch as it contained the same kind of revisions as those made by Thomas Bowdler, however, it seems best to pass to a consideration of the complete *Family Shakespeare* and its editor.

Thomas Bowdler, born in 1754, belonged to a well-to-do and prominent Evangelical family. In his youth, before his conversion, he had spent considerable time on the Continent, where he enjoyed the society of sophisticated Englishmen like

[36] *Works*, V, 18.
[37] [Thos. Bowdler, the younger] *Memoirs of the Life of John Bowdler*, London, 1824, p. 319.

Sir William Hamilton. He developed a taste for more conservative friends upon his return to England, being frequently seen in the company of the Bluestockings, Bishop Porteus, and Hannah More. His conversion followed, and for the next several years Bowdler engaged in various Evangelical enterprises. He participated in the attempt to reform prison conditions, he served on the committe of Magdalen Hospital, and when Wilberforce formed his Proclamation Society, he became a member of that organization. Early in the nineteenth century he moved from London to the country, where he was to spend the remainder of his life. When he published his Shakespeare he was sixty-four years old, and one suspects that he undertook his expurgations partly to relieve the tedium of his retirement. His own explanation was that he wished to promote morality and to provide a text for the family library.

Reading Shakespeare aloud had been a favorite custom of his father, Bowdler said, and "such was his good taste, his delicacy, and his prompt discretion that his family listened with delight to *Lear, Hamlet,* and *Othello* without knowing that these matchless tragedies contained words and expressions improper to be pronounced." But relatively few people were capable of such ready discrimination, and Bowdler felt that polite circles would welcome an edition of Shakespeare which excluded "whatever is unfit to be read by a gentleman in a company of ladies." [38]

As Bowdler perhaps knew, reading aloud or listening to someone else read was fast becoming a favorite pastime. According to Hannah More, "among milliners, mantua-makers, and other trades where members work together, the labour of one girl is frequently sacrificed that she may be spared to read . . . to the others." [39] This form of entertainment was still more common among respectable families of the middle classes. In more prosperous households oil and gas lamps were being introduced, and, with better means of illumination, what pleasanter way

[38] *The Family Shakespeare,* London, 1847, 9th ed., "Preface to the First Edition."
[39] "Strictures," *Works,* VI, 93.

was there to spend a long winter evening than to sit at home with a book, or to join the domestic circle gathered round the fire to hear one member of the family read to the others? Yet no father wanted to stumble upon coarse or indelicate expressions when reading aloud to his daughters, and, as Bowdler had observed, it is something of an art to be able to skip judiciously. *The Family Shakespeare* helped to solve this problem, for it was so purified that one could speak the lines trippingly on the tongue, without occasion for pause or blush.

Bowdler was generally less severe than James Plumptre. When he published the same Shakespearian lyrics that Plumptre had so drastically revised, he let them stand without any alterations. Nor did he attempt to moralize Shakespeare. Unlike the fierce Evangelicals, he professed the greatest admiration for the poet. He granted that Shakespeare was the most illustrious dramatist of all time and that his works were "for the most part favorable to religion and morality." But Shakespeare had written in an age given to coarseness, and, though his works were less offensive than those of his contemporaries, many of his scenes were of such "a nature as to raise a blush on the cheek of modesty." [40]

Bowdler sometimes found it necessary to make deep incisions in the original text. Like Thomas Hanmer, he deleted the entire scene in *Henry V* in which the French princess converses with her waiting woman. He also excluded the tavern scene in *Henry IV, Part II,* because he disapproved of the low-life characters and vulgar language. Doll Tearsheet, one of Shakespeare's principal characters in this scene, was banished from *The Family Shakespeare* altogether. Not even a reference to her was allowed to appear in the text. Elsewhere the editor greatly abbreviated passages. In *Macbeth,* for instance, he cut the Porter's speech to less than a quarter of its original length.

As Bowdler admitted, the expurgator's task was not an easy one. He encountered many difficulties, especially in such a play as *Henry IV,* where it was necessary to consider the speeches of

[40] *The Family Shakespeare,* "Preface to the First Edition."

Falstaff and the scenes of low life. Bowdler explained his problem as follows:

Every person must be sensible that of all the historical plays, the two parts of *Henry IV* are the most difficult to render fit for family reading. To clear them of all indecent and indelicate expressions, without destroying the wit and spirit of Falstaff, and without injuring the narrative, is indeed an arduous undertaking; but I hope that I may remove many objectionable passages, though I may not be able to render the work perfect.[41]

The text as Bowdler published it was indeed far from perfect —even according to the standards of an expurgator. Whether through carelessness or stupidity, he failed to follow any consistent practice in expunging references which he considered profane. In *Henry IV, Part I* (Act II, scene 4) Falstaff uses the expression "by the Lord" twice in the same speech. The first time he says, "By the Lord, I knew you as well as he that made ye," and later, "By the Lord, lads, I am glad you have the money." In the first instance Bowdler leaves the line unchanged; in the second he deletes the opening phrase. Inconsistencies of this kind abound throughout *The Family Shakespeare*. "Zounds" and "S'blood" are sometimes omitted, though not always. "Marry" and "by'r Lady" Bowdler is inclined to leave in the text. He sometimes rejects "by the mass," but at other times keeps it. Still more curious was his apparent inability to distinguish between reverence and irreverence. Henry IV is certainly not profane when he says:

> I know not whether God will have it so,
> For some displeasing service I have done,
> That, in his secret doom, out of my blood
> He'll breed revengement and a scourge for me.

Nevertheless, when he printed this speech, Bowdler changed the word "God" to "heaven."

The same inconsistency characterized the attempts to remove what Bowdler considered coarse references. He usually deleted or altered such expressions as "ye fatguts," "whoreson," "geld-

[41] *Ibid.*, p. 377.

ing," and "leaping-houses." On the other hand, while he sometimes changed "wench" to "girl," he often let the original word
remain. In *The Family Shakespeare* Falstaff is made to say, "I
pressed me none but such toasts and butter, with hearts no big-
ger than pin-heads," instead of ". . . with hearts in their bel-
lies." From this it would appear that Bowdler, like the later
Victorians, objected to the word "belly," but again he is not
consistent, for he allowed Falstaff to use the word in *Henry IV,
Part II* (Act I, scene 2).

When confronted with *Othello*, Bowdler was genuinely per-
plexed. Much as he wanted to delete the references having a
sexual connotation, he realized that the play was so much concerned with sexual jealousy that a great deal of its import would
be lost if he omitted all the execrations that welled from the
impassioned Othello. His final solution to this problem, he
said, was to depart from his regular practice and to allow words
to remain which he had excluded from other plays. But as a
warning to his readers he added, "If after all I have omitted, it
shall be thought that this inimitable tragedy is not sufficiently
correct for family reading, I would advise the transferring of it
from the parlour to the cabinet." [42]

An examination of Bowdler's version of *Othello* shows that,
while no scenes are excluded and no situations seriously altered,
several whole speeches are omitted. One might expect to find
expurgations in the lines of Iago, who is one of the more
prurient-spoken characters in literature, but in addition to removing his more salty expressions, Bowdler cut speeches that
even the most delicate female might have read without a
tremor. The notably beautiful lines beginning: "Our bodies are
our gardens to the which our wills are gardeners" found no
place in *The Family Shakespeare*. Possibly the editor rejected
this passage because it contained a strong affirmation of the
freedom of the will. On the other hand, he may have considered
the word "bodies" too offensive to appear in print. The latter
explanation seems to be the more plausible one, for Bowdler

[42] *Ibid.*, p. 880.

deleted the phrase with the word "body" from the speech in *Romeo and Juliet* in which the nurse says of Romeo, "though his face be better than any man's, yet his leg excells all men's; and for a hand, and a foot, and a body, though they be not to be talked upon, yet they are past compare."

Despite its many absurdities *The Family Shakespeare* appealed to the prudish taste of a large section of the reading public. One may judge its popularity from the fact that by 1831 it had reached a sixth edition. So far as delicacy was concerned, Victorian standards had already triumphed. There was further evidence of this in the attitude of the critics. Even Francis Jeffrey, who had frequently heaped abuse upon the romantic poets, had nothing but praise for Bowdler. After recommending his text as one in which "no offence is offered to delicacy," he wrote in the *Edinburgh Review:*

We have only further to observe that Mr. Bowdler has not executed his task in anything of a precise or prudish spirit; that he has left many things in the text which, to a delicate taste, must still appear coarse and reprehensible; and only effaced those gross indelicacies which everyone must have felt a blemish, and by the removal of which no imaginable excellence can be affected.[43]

Encouraged by the favorable reception accorded his Shakespeare, Bowdler next edited Gibbon's *Decline and Fall of the Roman Empire.* From the time it was first published this work had been the subject of controversy, chiefly because of the sections dealing with the early history of Christianity. These parts, including the famous fifteenth and sixteenth chapters, as well as several others, Bowdler excluded from his edition. "The history of the church," he wrote, "is not intended to form part of this work." [44] He also rearranged several other chapters, explaining that he wished to have the history follow a better chronological sequence. All this was done in a spirit of mixed vanity and humility. In his introduction Bowdler said that he hoped the time would come when his edition, without its prefaces and

[43] *Edinburgh Review*, XXXVI (Oct., 1821), 52.
[44] *Gibbon's History of the Decline and Fall of the Roman Empire*, ed. by Thomas Bowdler, London, 1826, Vol. I, "Appendix."

notes, would be read as the authentic one. Although Gibbon had been dead for only thirty years, Bowdler ventured to assert that if the great historian could speak for himself, "he would say that he desired nothing more ardently than the laying aside the former editions of his history, and trusting his fame and reputation to the opinion which posterity might form of him and his talents from the perusal of that portion of his writings which will be found in the present publication." [45]

The revised edition of Gibbon was published posthumously, for in 1825 death abridged the career of Thomas Bowdler. Other expurgators had already appeared, however, and before he died Bowdler must have seen an edition of Shakespeare which contained even more drastic deletions than his own. The editor of this volume, which was printed in 1822, was the Reverend John Rogers Pitman, later domestic chaplain to the Duchess of Kent, the mother of Queen Victoria.

Pitman's *School-Shakespeare*, as the title implies, was intended for juvenile readers and more especially for young ladies. "Immoral language has been carefully excluded," said the editor, "so that taste may be cultivated without offence to delicate and religious feelings." [46] Dividing *The School-Shakespeare* into two sections, Pitman devoted the second part to reproducing brief extracts of some of the less frequently read plays. Only three scenes from *Troilus and Cressida* were printed, and from these several lines were deleted. *The Comedy of Errors, The Merry Wives of Windsor, Henry V,* and the other plays that appeared in this section were so reduced that in no instance did the selections occupy more than a few pages.

The plays in the first part of *The School-Shakespeare,* though more complete, frequently had whole sections excluded. The text of *Henry IV, Part I,* for instance, omitted three entire scenes as well as dozens of lines from other scenes. As one might expect, the most frequent deletions occurred in the dialogue of Falstaff and his companions. Sometimes, however, Pitman expurgated

[45] *Ibid.,* Vol. I, "Introduction."
[46] *The School-Shakespeare,* London, 1822, "Advertisement."

lines to which, it would seem, no one could possibly object. One is baffled to explain why a clergyman should delete a reference to the Atonement of Christ, especially when the lines are particularly beautiful. Nevertheless, Pitman must have had some reason for disapproving of the lines in *Henry IV* in which the king proposes to go on a crusade, for from this passage he expunged the part referring to "those holy fields,"

> Over whose acres walked those blessed feet,
> Which fourteen hundred years ago were nail'd
> For our advantage on the bitter cross.

More understandable, since *The School-Shakespeare* was intended for polite young ladies, were some of the other expurgations. Bianca, the courtesan in Shakespeare's *Othello*, was neither listed in the *dramatis personae* nor allowed to appear anywhere in the play. As a result the text omits the important handkerchief scene between Cassio and Bianca. Pitman also excluded the various bawdy references of Iago and the more disillusioned speeches of Othello. From *Antony and Cleopatra* he deleted, in addition to several whole scenes, many lines in which the characters discuss the subject of love. Mardian, the eunuch, is never referred to as such, though he is allowed to appear as one of Cleopatra's servants. The Queen of the Nile, it would appear, did not need the same degree of protection as the young ladies who were to read Pitman's mutilated Shakespeare.

Pitman was not only more censorious than Bowdler but took pride in that fact. When he introduced his volume, he explained that, though he was acquainted with *The Family Shakespeare,* he could not give it his unqualified approval. Many of the plays in that collection, he wrote, "were injudiciously altered; and few of them were sufficiently purified from coarse and profane expressions." [47] Thus it happened that, in a sense, even Bowdler was bowdlerized.

[47] *Ibid.*

PART THREE: 1820-1830

CHAPTER ELEVEN

VICTORIANISM

IN 1815, after twenty years of warfare, England was at peace. Its position among nations was established, and its leadership was not to be disputed seriously again for another century. As the empire grew, Englishmen took pride in the extent and wealth of their possessions, in the magnificence of the English fleet, in the glory of their civilization. From the time of Waterloo, moreover, Englishmen prided themselves also upon another kind of superiority—their moral excellence. To many the defeat of Napoleon seemed the triumph not only of might but of virtue. "It is to the cultivation of moral qualities that England is indebted for her power and influence," asserted the *Morning Chronicle* in 1815, "from the want of them France may be mischievous but she never will be great." [1]

Nationalism based upon a belief in the ethnical superiority of the English race was already centuries old, but nationalism based upon a belief in the moral superiority of the English over the lesser breed of men was relatively new. The conviction that the English were a chosen people, elected to enjoy the fruits of virtue at home and to rule over palm and pine abroad, was peculiar to the Victorians. Even they made no such claims for their ancestors, for it was clear that virtue and morality had only recently triumphed, after years of struggle with the forces of evil.

One had only to compare the standards of the previous century to understand this. Looking back, one realized how recently

[1] Quoted in Élie Halévy, *A History of the English People in 1815*, London, 1924, p. 394.

the nation had been steeped in corruption. The view of former
times was revolting, to be sure, but it best evidenced the triumph
of the new century. Even in the first decade there were signs of
improvement. Virtue had not yet triumphed completely, but the
worst bogs of wickedness had been left behind. As the pilgrims
climbed the steep paths of righteousness, each glance backward
spurred them on. With the rounding of the first quarter of the
new century, the goal was in sight. A chosen people had reached
their promised land.

To those whose memories went back to the last century, it was
apparent that vast changes had occurred in society since their
youth. But what had produced these marvels? When they tried
to answer that question, they could not agree. Partisanship often
prejudiced their judgments, and the complex character of events
was baffling. Actually, of course, no one circumstance was responsible for the new order. Conditions had changed because
various forces had combined to alter public opinion. The conservative reaction to the French Revolution, the Evangelical
revival, the influence of aggressive societies and propagandist
literature, the role of the model female, Sunday schools and
monitorial systems, censorship and the stifling of free opinion
—all these, combined with other circumstances, had mutually
contributed to the growth of stricter standards. Even the industrial revolution had played a part, for more rapid means of
communication and the mechanization of industry had undoubtedly hastened the dynamics of a changing society.

Gradually the impact of these various influences had altered
public opinion. There had been resistance at first, and some of
the changes had been foisted upon an unwilling public by the
persistent efforts of a few. But opposition slackened as more
people accepted the conservative social doctrines, and during the
reign of George IV public opinion had come to favor the new
standards. Henceforth it was to be the most powerful factor in
their maintenance.

Reviewing a collection of letters which had been written in the
eighteenth century, a critic exclaimed:

What a contrast to existing manners do these volumes present. Surely, if we have not become more virtuous, we have become more decorous; in language and outward appearances, at least, we are improved, and perhaps that is all, for human nature is pretty much the same in all ages.[2]

But was it just a change in outward appearances? Opinion differed when that question was raised. Scott, commenting upon the social transformation that had occurred since his youth, said that men of the upper classes no longer dared "to insult decency in the public manner then tolerated; nor would the wildest debauchees venture to imitate the orgies of Medmenham Abbey." Higher standards of integrity existed in public life, for men were "now under the necessity of being actuated, or at least appearing to be so, by nobler motives than their predecessors proposed to themselves." These changes Scott attributed chiefly to the "more general diffusion of knowledge and improvement of taste." But Scott was not sure that better manners meant better morals. "We are not now, perhaps, more moral in our conduct than men fifty years ago," he wrote, "but modern vice pays a tax to appearances, and is contented to wear a mask of decorum."[3]

When Francis Place read this statement, he felt that it was contradictory. Disagreeing with Scott, he said:

The word "tax" itself is proof that vice has diminished, since to save appearances many opportunities to be vicious must be passed by, which would be seized with avidity were it not necessary to preserve appearances. Thus the habit of being vicious is not so confirmed as formerly, and vice like any other pursuit is increased by habit.[4]

Place and Scott belonged to different social spheres, and their disagreement appears to have been owing largely to the inclination of each to think of conditions prevailing in the particular stratum of society with which he was most familiar. Both agreed that people would no longer tolerate the flagrant public conduct of former times. But a greater change had occurred in some

[2] *Literary Gazette*, no. 374 (March 20, 1824), 177.
[3] *Miscellaneous Prose Works*, Edinburgh, 1827, III, 516.
[4] B.M., Add. MSS 27,828, pp. 53 ff.

ranks than in others. It was most evident among the middle and lower classes, the sections of the population which Place knew best, though, as he admitted, there were some, especially among the poor, who were not much more concerned about the amenities than their eighteenth-century ancestors had been. These individuals remained ignorant, profane, and profligate, but they now constituted a separate group, for the more respectable members of the working class refused to associate with them. The latter, having cultivated better manners, were nearer to the lower middle classes, and the middle ranks formed the most solid phalanx of social conservatism.

The habits of the aristocracy and of the gentry had probably changed least of all. In these exalted circles, where Scott was most at home, one was not so vulnerable to public opinion. The possession of a title or wealth allowed one to pass as "respectable" without deferring to the popular moral and religious shibboleths of the time. But owning a gig was not sufficient to make one respectable; it took a coach and four. Anyone of the lower or middle classes who denied "the popular faith" was shunned "as if he had caught the plague from some infectious lazarette," wrote John Wade, but a "lord or gentleman of £10,000 a year may admire Voltaire, Diderot, or Spinoza without being expelled out of the pale of social communion." [5]

Still, when all reservations have been made, the evidence shows that by 1830 the standards of most Englishmen were remarkably different from those of the preceding generation. Moreover, despite the cant and hypocrisy of the times, and a prevailing tendency to emphasize appearances, there had been a genuine advance in decency. The manners destined to survive for almost a century were something more than a fad. They were often the expression of deep-rooted convictions. The time had passed when clergymen hastened through a sermon to go fox hunting and people paused only briefly in church on their way to the alehouse. England had become a religious nation.

By 1830 Protestantism was probably a greater force in the lives

[5] *Extraordinary Blackbook*, p. 78.

of the English people than it had ever before been. The effects of the religious revival, however, were observable long before that date. At meetings of the Eclectic Society it had been the custom periodically to propose the question, "What are the present appearances of true religion in the world?" For years the clergymen belonging to this Evangelical organization had answered the question by grim assertions that irreligion prevailed, but at a meeting in 1810 the reply was, "We live in an uncommon day." After a century and a half, religious enthusiasm had once more been revived. "It is the most astonishing change in the public mind ever known," exclaimed one clergyman.[6] And so it seemed to others who rejoiced in the return of piety. Celebrating its tenth anniversary in 1811, the *Christian Observer* remarked:

The circumstances with which we are most forcibly struck is the different aspect which the Christian world exhibits at the present moment from that which it bore at the commencement of our course. Nor is its aspect altered only; it is improved beyond the fondest dreams of a visionary. If one could suppose some calm, calculating Christian Observer to open his eyes, after a ten years sleep, on the passing scene, would he not find himself in a new creation?[7]

If the Evangelicals were inclined to take all the credit, there were some who felt that one among them had been especially responsible for the new spirit in the religious world. The person thus singled out was Hannah More. Among the various individuals who complimented her as the high priestess of reform, none paid her a more flattering tribute than Miss Jane Porter, who wrote to Hannah More in 1815 as follows:

I need only call to the mind of Mrs. Hannah More, what was the state of morals and religious opinions among all ranks of persons in this country twenty years ago! The poor were in profligate ignorance —the rich in presumptuous apostasy. I cannot give the latter a milder name; for I remember that at about that period (then a very young person), I burst into tears at a large table after dinner, from horror and pity of some persons present, who were scoffing at religion without a reprimand from anyone. Such conduct now would not be

---

[6] *Eclectic Notes*, pp. 476–77.   [7] *Christian Observer*, X, "Preface."

tolerated a moment in any company; and the one I speak of was what'was called a most respectable circle. You were then, dearest Madame, "sowing seeds in the Lord's vineyard." And the pious Mr. Raikes of Gloucester was "bringing little children into Christ," by the opening of Sunday schools. From you and from him, under heaven, I date the regeneration of the people of this country. Your pen addressed the young, the old, the high and the low. And most happily your former literary fame was a bright forerunner to your promulgation of the Gospel. It made it fashionable to read your works; and by that word, they passed into all hands, and gradually infused their contents into all hearts.[8]

Mrs. More herself was hesitant about conceding the triumph of religious and moral reform. The cause was her stock in trade, and she kept on publishing pious works. Disturbed by reports that came to her, she continued to express alarm at the course of events. When she heard that history and science were being taught to the poor, she condemned the "ultra-educationalists" for carrying instruction to "preposterous" extremes. Upon learn- in at the close of the war that English families were travel- ing in France again, she was sure that England would be exposed to an epidemic of French manners and corruption. Some of the voyagers visited her upon their return, however, and for once she heard something favorable to the French. Her visitors as- sured her that "they are imitating all our religious institu- tions." [9]

Mrs. More was equally gratified by the news coming from that other stronghold of Jacobins across the sea. "You would be surprised to see the masses of books, pamphlets, etc. I have re- ceived from America," she wrote to one of her correspondents in 1823. "I do not naturally love republicans, nor the coarse man- ners which belong to them; but these people appear really to be making such rapid advances, that they seem determined to run with us the race of glory." Mrs. More was too good a Tory to concede that a nation which had adopted the political principles of her old enemy, Tom Paine, could excel her own country in

[8] William Roberts, *Memoirs of the Life and Correspondence of Hannah More*, III, 431.
[9] *Ibid.*, IV, 174–76, 85, 159.

"the race of glory" and finally, impelled by patriotism, perhaps, she admitted that the religious revival in England had succeeded far beyond her early dreams. In 1825, when most of the first-generation Evangelicals were dead and she herself was eighty years old, she observed, "It is a singular satisfaction to me that I have lived to see such an increase of genuine religion among the higher classes of society. Mr. Wilberforce and I agree that where we knew one instance of it thirty years ago, there are now a dozen or more." [10]

The religious revival which the Evangelicals had launched was no longer a matter of party or sect. All branches of Protestantism participated in it, and there was no great distinction between the true Evangelical and the pious churchman. To be sure, a distressing problem still awaited solution—the question of plural livings. Many clergymen of the Established Church received inordinately large revenues from several parishes. This system of "spiritual polygamy" had, in some quarters, made orthodox ministers unpopular. Public opinion was awakening to the injustice of the system, however, and was soon to insist upon a reform.

But the revival, after the death of Wesley, had never been so much a matter of clerical zeal as of lay enthusiasm. It was the laity, for the most part, that distributed tracts, supported the various societies, and read the religious books and pamphlets. It was the laity, or a section of the laity, that had made religious zeal a fashion, and the change in their attitude really marked the success of the revival. As early as 1816 Jane Taylor wrote:

> How customs and opinions change their place!
> Religion now, is scarcely in disgrace:
> Her outward signs at least will even raise
> Your credit high in these convenient days.
> Fashion, herself, the cause of virtue pleads,
> Becomes chief patroness of pious deeds,
> And lets us e'en pursue without restraint,
> What once had stamped us *puritan* and *saint*.[11]

---

[10] *Ibid.*, p. 217. A. M. B. Meakin, *Hannah More*, London, 1911, p. 391.
[11] *Essays in Rhyme on Manners and Morals*, London, 1816, p. 145.

There can be no doubt that tract distribution, visits to the poor, attendance at meetings of the societies, and other fads were largely responsible for restoring religious enthusiasm. Nevertheless, although true spiritual ardor had probably declined since the death of Wesley, it had not completely degenerated, and the manifestation of zeal in the nineteenth century was often sincere. To be sure, the self-righteousness of the Victorians accounted largely for their sense of moral superiority, expedient interests often motivated their noble professions, and their stern moral code made little provision for true charitableness. At the same time, however, the nineteenth century was marked by a certain idealism which was part and parcel of the religious life of the times. It was not a great spiritual epoch, and its failure to cultivate spiritual values was the chief indictment brought against it by such contemporaries as Newman, Ruskin, Carlyle, and Arnold. Yet these men, and many others, owed much of their own idealism to the religious climate of the Victorian period, and their insistence that man does not live by bread alone helped to restore certain values which the previous century had too often neglected.

Although the nineteenth was not a great spiritual century, its piety was clearly manifest long before the accession of Victoria. A great church-building movement had been started in 1817, when a society was formed to raise money for additional places of worship. In the following year Parliament contributed £1,-000,000 for this purpose and later added to the sum. Altogether 212 new chapels and churches were built between 1818 and 1824 from various private and public funds.[12] Even with these additional buildings it was sometimes difficult to accommodate Sunday worshipers. Meanwhile the clergy found that their duties had become more arduous. The old practice of holding two services on Sunday had been restored, and in many communities three or four services were not unusual. Certainly the

[12] W. L. Mathieson, *English Church Reform, 1815–1840*, London, 1923, pp. 18, 128.

later Victorians never observed the Sabbath more rigorously than did the people described by Sir Richard Phillips when, in 1828, he wrote:

Sunday in Nottinghamshire is a peculiar day. Before nine o'clock I found trains of people returning from morning service. By half-past ten, I saw every sect in motion, proceeding to churches or meetings. From half-past twelve to one, they disperse to dinner; and at half-past two or three a large proportion of them are again in motion towards their places of devotion. At five they return to tea; and at half-past six, form anxious trains to various evening services. At half-past eight, the bustle is over, but in many families the day is finished by prayers and hymns at home. Such is the regular Sunday practice of many. Others attend but twice; but of the ultra religious community, consisting of many hundred families, three attendances per day is usual, and in many, the circle of four is made as above mentioned. At some chapels there are four services, but the rigid devotees who belong to the establishments which have only two or three services interchange their attendance at places where their religious zeal can be indulged.[13]

PUBLIC CONDUCT AND AMUSEMENTS

Sunday amusements were, of course, forbidden, but even on week days the upper classes as well as the common people disported themselves in a quiet and restrained manner, for the English had curbed much of their former boisterous spirit. Drunkenness had vastly diminished. One might deduce this from statistics, which show that, despite a more than doubling of the population, there were fewer places licensed to sell liquor than in the eighteenth century.[14] But the recollections of people who remembered the old days provide the most vivid contrast of conditions. Francis Place, who made several observations upon the greater sobriety of the working classes,[15] believed that the drinking habits of the upper ranks had improved as well. Upon this subject he offered the interesting testimony of the Reverend

[13] *A Personal Tour through the United Kingdom,* London, 1828, no. 2, p. 195.
[14] B. Webb and S. Webb, *The History of Liquor Licensing in England,* London, 1903, pp. 80 ff.
[15] See above, chap. vii.

Robert Knipe of Oxford, whom he describes as a "well-bred gentleman, a man of the world, a travelled man, and a magistrate."

Knipe came from Cheshire, where "in his youth he was intimately acquainted with the principal gentry of the country." In those days, he said, "fox-hunting, drinking, bawling out obscene songs and whoring was the common delight of these people," who, whenever they met at one another's houses, made it a practice to "get beastly drunk." Upon these occasions they indulged in pranks that equaled any found in the novels of Smollett. One time, after getting a visitor completely sotted, they seated him facing backwards upon a horse, which they then drove through the town so that the mob could enjoy the spectacle of their hapless victim. Knipe remembered another occasion when these gentlemen pranksters fortified the wine of a temperance-minded young man. When he was thoroughly drunk they pulled down his breeches, stuck a plaster on his buttocks, and sent him home, completely insensible, by his servants. Such hoaxes, said Robert Knipe, were perpetrated not merely by youths of college age, "but by the middle-aged and old men, men of large-landed property, of great influence in their country, and fathers of families." But times had changed. "They are all gone now," Knipe told Place (January, 1827), "except one or two of the youngest who still remain stupid, drunken, fox-hunters, and they get drunk alone or in some other company than that of their equals in rank and property." [16]

Profanity and obscenity, though common formerly, were heard much less frequently. After reading some letters written during the eighteenth century by people of social distinction, a reviewer remarked, "We cannot help wondering to see the wits and beauties of what is called the Augustan period of our literature using expressions and making allusions that would almost shock the delicacy of Billingsgate, and certainly offend the moral sentiments of St. Giles." [17] Francis Place also noted

16 B.M., Add. MSS 27,827, pp. 108–11.
17 *Literary Gazette*, no. 374 (March 20, 1824), 177.

that there was a remarkable decrease in swearing, and Lucy Aikin confirmed his opinion. "I am told that no member of a mechanics' institute ever utters an oath," she observed, "and even coachmen and cabmen shock the ears less than formerly." [18]

One no longer heard the bawdy songs and the picaresque ballads which had delighted the eighteenth-century populace, and to Francis Place this was one of the most remarkable signs of greater public decency. The old street songs had started to disappear, he said, when the Association for Preserving Liberty and Property had forced the loyalist songs upon the professional ballad singers. Then, in the first decade of the nineteenth century, the Society for the Suppression of Vice had prevented hawkers from selling street ballads. Dibden's sea songs had taken their place, and a new generation grew up which had never heard the vulgar ditties of the past century.[19]

Still, one might observe that the religious tracts which now constituted a large part of the reading of the masses had similarities to the songs celebrating the lives of criminals. The ballads usually contained an account of the criminal's career, his confession of guilt, and his speech on the gallows. The tracts, when they described the life of a sinner, traced his progress in the paths of evil, told of his regeneration, and concluded with his deathbed speech. Both satisfied the taste for morbidity inherent in human nature. But the tracts, of course, were never bawdy, and their readers no longer considered highwaymen as heroes.

There were other signs that among the lower classes rowdyism was giving way to respectability. Gone were "the cutter lads and flash young men with peculiar dress—rollers at the cheek, striped silk stockings, numerous knee strings, and long quartered shoes." Gone, too, were the more notorious resorts of rogues and whores, such as The Temple of Flora and The Apollo Gardens.[20] Taverns remained, but the rough-and-tumble games formerly played at public houses were no longer popular. Other interests engaged the working classes. Many of them attended adult schools

[18] *Correspondence*, p. 306.   [19] B.M., Add. MSS 27,825, pp. 144 ff.
[20] *Ibid.*, no. 34.

or mechanics' institutes, or spent their evenings at home read-ing.[21] They were becoming so genteel, in fact, that one writer felt that they were bordering upon effeminacy:

The amusements of the people have changed with their character. The athletic exercises of quoits, wrestling, football, prison-bars, and shooting with the long bow have become obsolete and almost for-gotten, and it is to be regretted that the present pursuits and pleas-ures of the labouring classes are of a more effeminate cast. They are now pigeon-fanciers, canary-breeders, and tulip-growers.[22]

Meanwhile the upper ranks had become almost as subdued in public as the common people. Chalk Farm, Copenhagen House, and some of the other old resorts still existed in 1825, but despite the fact that they were now respectable gathering places, they had lost much of their patronage. In London, clubs opened reading rooms for their members. Chess had become a popular pastime; gambling had gone out of favor.[23] People still played cards, of course, but even when there were no stakes, card-play-ing was not so much in vogue as formerly. Comparing the ladies of her day with those of the Queen Anne period, Lucy Aikin remarked, "Then they played quadrille, now they read theology, and attend lectures, and gather pence for missions and Bible Societies." [24]

Social gatherings in high life were no longer occasions for mirth and gaiety. As early as 1815 people complained that as-semblies had become stupid and dull. Admitting this change, a writer in the *Edinburgh Review* explained that

Our very advances in politeness have an undeniable tendency to re-press all the extravagance of mirth or indulgence of humour which, at an earlier period, gave a variegated and amusing aspect to society. The end of our refinements, in short, has been to disabuse us of many mistakes and cure us of many affectations—to make smart talking and pretensions to wit and vivacity rather vulgar accomplish-ments, and to restore our original English taste for honest, manly good sense, and something of a cold and contemptuous severity of

[21] F. Place, *Improvement of the Working People.*
[22] R. Guest, *A Compendious History of the Cotton Manufacture,* p. 38.
[23] B.M., Add. MSS 27,832, section C; 27,828, p. 35.
[24] *Correspondence,* p. 308.

judgment. Artificial spirits and mere frivolous glitter, we believe, were never so little in request among us.[25]

There was, to be sure, less ceremony of a certain kind. Men had stopped wearing wigs at the time of the French Revolution, and gone with the wig were various formalities. Many early Victorians rejoiced in the fact, for they were inclined to associate the etiquette of Johnson's day with a corrupt society. "With the apparent show and polish of the former age," observed Joseph Farington, "much brutality was mingled, and great and general licentiousness prevailed in all ranks." A "more rational and refined" age had discarded both the ceremony and the coarseness, he said, with the result that "convivial intemperance is no longer the prevailing fashion of our social meetings; and the current familiar conversation is purified from the taint of indecency." All this was generally true, but early Victorian etiquette was far from being so simple and unaffected as Farington implies when he adds, "Perfect freedom of manners has been reconciled with perfect decorum." [26]

The characters in Jane Austen's novels are very much concerned with propriety, and, writing in the first decades of the nineteenth century, Jane Austen was undoubtedly portraying the standards then current among polite people. It has been remarked that the gentlemen who appear in her novels are seldom referred to by their first names. They are almost always Mr. Darcy, Mr. Bingley, or Mr. Collins. This type of formality, according to Tom Moore, was much more common than it had been in the eighteenth century. Writing in 1825, Moore observed that one of the most significant changes in recent decades was the virtual disappearance of the old custom, formerly "prevalent among men of high station, of calling each other by such familiar names as Dick, Jack, Tom, etc., a mode of address that brings with it, in its very sound, the notion of conviviality and playfulness." [27]

[25] *Edinburgh Review*, XXIV (Feb., 1815), 397.
[26] *Memoirs of the Life of Sir Joshua Reynolds*, London, 1819, pp. 66–68.
[27] *Memoirs of R. B. Sheridan*, London, 1825, p. 217.

The bards of passion and of mirth were dead, and with them had passed the whole era that was merrie England. At times in eighteenth-century taverns might have been heard the semblance of rollicking Elizabethan laughter, but by now even the echo was stilled. Summing up the prevailing tone of society in the new age, Moore wrote:

The natural tendencies of the excesses of the French Revolution was to produce in the higher classes of England an increased reserve of manner, and, of course, a proportionate restraint upon all within the circle, which have been fatal to conviviality and humour, and not very propitious to wit—subduing both manners and conversation to a sort of polished level, to rise above which is often thought to be almost as vulgar as to sink below it.[28]

THE THEATER

One amusement which particularly suffered from the change in manners was the stage. During the first half of the nineteenth century the public seemed to have lost interest in the drama and the playhouses were almost deserted. Not only Drury Lane and Covent Garden, but the provincial theaters as well were so poorly attended that it became hazardous financially to keep them open. Various reasons have been given to account for the decline of public interest in the drama. Historians of the theater explain it by the failure of the times to produce good dramatists, the fact that Drury Lane and Covent Garden were too large for effective presentation of plays, and the objection of playgoers to the presence of prostitutes in the lobbies. These circumstances explain in some degree the poor attendance at theaters, but the most important reason would appear to be the blight which the moral reformers had cast upon the drama.

Strict Evangelicals, it should be remembered, boycotted the theater altogether. Others, not so strict in theory, followed their example, thinking it fashionable to do so or perhaps fearing the censorship of their neighbors. Since the beginning of the new

[28] *Ibid.*

century the theater had been moral to the point of dullness,[29] but no degree of strictness could reconcile those who considered the drama completely unlawful. They condemned it without qualification and avoided the playhouses as they would a plague. The *Morning Chronicle* (November 2, 1826), observing that hardly anyone attended performances given at the provincial theaters, blamed Methodism and its adherents for the unpopularity of the stage. But the other Evangelicals were equally responsible. Their leaders had repeatedly told them that the theater was a vicious institution, and the rank and file were inclined not to question this dictum.

But what explained the nonattendance of less pious members of the upper classes? According to Francis Place, one no longer saw many of the "nobility and people of fashion" at the theater. When seats were occupied, the audience consisted chiefly of "small gentry, clerks, and attorneys." [30] Undoubtedly it was the innocuous character of the plays to which the superior classes objected. Many who had no moral scruples against the theater found it dull, for producers had grown extremely timid, afraid of offending the critics and the more prudish section of their audiences. Upon this subject the *Edinburgh Review* made the following comment, "Fastidiousness and hypocrisy have grown for many years, slowly but surely, and have at last arrived at such a pitch that there is hardly a line in the works of an old comic writer which is not reprobated as immoral, or at least indecent." [31] Such was undoubtedly the true situation. Standards in the theater had been growing progressively more strict for several generations, but in the period of George IV they reached extremes of prudery. Francis Place was interested to read that Sheridan had expunged "some licentious expressions" from Congreve's plays and had emended the plots of *The Old Bachelor*, *Love for Love*, and *The Way of the World* before produc-

[29] Allardyce Nicoll, *A History of Early Nineteenth Century Drama*, Cambridge, 1930, I, 14 ff.
[30] B.M., Add. MSS 27,833, pp. 21 ff.
[31] *Edinburgh Review*, XLIX (June, 1829), 317.

ing them for a late eighteenth-century audience. "No alteration
of these plays," said Place (1829), "and more especially the two
first, could now make them endurable." [32]

As for contemporary dramatists, the Examiner of Plays saw
to it that their works were pruned of anything offensive to delicacy before they reached the stage. John Larpent, who was re-
puted to be a Methodist, held that office until 1824. He was
known for the strictness with which he judged plays submitted
to him and for the number of excisions he demanded. George
Colman, who succeeded him in office, was no more tolerant. This
surprised many, for Colman was a man of the world and one of
the most sophisticated of the eighteenth-century dramatists. His
own plays had sometimes shocked the relatively tolerant audiences of the preceding generation, and at least one of them had
been censured by the Lord Chamberlain. As Examiner of Plays,
however, Colman insisted upon the same sort of emendations
that Plumptre and Bowdler had made in their expurgated texts.
He would seldom permit a reference to Scripture. Any allusion
to God, even the term "Providence," he deleted, and he regularly returned manuscripts to their authors with expressions
such as "damn," "hell," and "ye heavens" marked for omis-
sion.[33]

Colman had not been converted. Even in his old age he had
the reputation of using extremely coarse language. But he knew
that standards had changed since his youth and that the public
would no longer tolerate indelicacy on the stage. Upon one occasion, however, he apparently underestimated the prudery of
a nineteenth-century audience. Francis Place, who considered
the extreme censorship of the stage ridiculous, noted this instance with glee. "Even Mr. Colman," he wrote, "the severest of
all censors, has at last shown that he is more licentious than a
playhouse audience." To prove his point, Place produced a
clipping from the *Literary Gazette* (July 20, 1833). This item

[32] B.M., Add. MSS 27,831, p. 224.
[33] Nicoll, *op. cit.*, pp. 17 ff. F. Fowell and F. Palmer, *Censorship in England*,
London, 1913, pp. 155 ff.

states that a play called *The Convent Belle,* which had apparently slipped by Colman, was condemned by the audience upon its first presentation for "too much freedom of speech." The management thereupon withdrew the play temporarily until certain *double entendres* had been deleted.[34]

From such comments it would seem that the moral climate of the period was largely responsible for the lack of interest in the drama. The theater failed to attract two important sections of the population—those who considered it unlawful, and those who felt that prudish restrictions had made it too dull to be entertaining. That section of the people which did patronize the theater insisted upon moral plays, or plays that at least gave no offense to delicacy. Needless to say, they got what they wanted.

Still another reason for reduced attendance at the theater was the rival claim of the hearth. Reading aloud to the family circle, a favorite pastime, saved the price of theater tickets and the expense of hiring the carriage which was almost a necessity when one attended Drury Lane or Covent Garden. With a scornful glance at the past, a writer in the *Quarterly Review* explained that the drama was "originally intended and adapted for a state of society in which reading is not a general accomplishment of the people." What was a farrago like *Hamlet,* he might have asked, to a good, sound moral tale like *The Dairyman's Daughter?* "We are now a nation of readers," he added, "much more so than any other people in Europe—and that, we strongly suspect, is the principal reason why the theater is more neglected among us than anywhere else." [35]

A NATION OF READERS

Without doubt reading had become the favorite occupation of leisure time. The introduction of Sunday schools had served not only to create millions of new readers, but to stimulate in the middle classes, who had always been literate, a desire for more education. Thus many who had formerly passed their time

34 B.M., Add. MSS 27,833, pp. 117–18.
35 *Quarterly Review,* XXXIV (Sept., 1826), 355.

playing cards or other games had now become prodigious readers. Monthly periodicals no longer sufficed to appease the hunger for information and entertainment, and the new weekly magazines which appeared at this time attained a wide circulation. Books were everywhere in great demand, and popular authors reaped large fortunes from the sale of their works. Readers who could not afford to buy books could generally borrow them from the popular circulating libraries or from those maintained by the Sunday schools. The latter, of course, specialized in moral and religious works. Writings of this kind were also circulated by the book societies which the clergy in recent decades had instituted for the convenience of their parishioners. Even in the small community of Bedford, said Sir Richard Phillips, each sect had its own reading club, with the result that this little town could boast of three or four hundred serious readers.[36]

Now, with a population nearing fourteen millions, approximately half the nation could read. That fact alone distinguished the new generation from any previous one, and upon it were contingent many other characteristics of the time. One effect of the increased size of the reading public, ironically, was to lower its literary standards. In taste, in the ability to judge what was excellent in literature, it was vastly inferior to the smaller reading public of the eighteenth century. Then, readers had prided themselves upon their discrimination. The study of Greek and Latin literature had provided many with touchstones of criticism. They knew the best English writers of later times, their interests were catholic, and they demanded a certain excellence in what they read. Now, though much larger, the reading public consisted of many people of inferior taste. A great number of them, even among the middle classes, had attended school for only a short time. They had no criteria by which to judge the worth of a piece of writing and, having no standards of their own, they were easily induced to accept the Evangelical canons of criticism.

Furthermore, the generation marked by a great expansion in

[36] *Op. cit.*, p. 8.

the limits of the reading public was distinguished also for the restraints imposed upon freedom of expression. Reading was controlled and directed in a fashion never before known. An exorbitant tax limited the circulation of newspapers to a small section of society, and the prosecution of unorthodox opinion checked the free dissemination of ideas. Meanwhile a hungry reading public was supplied with a diet consisting largely of Evangelical porridge. Although literacy had opened the door upon a new world for the masses, it was, for most of them, the narrow world of the religious zealots and moral reformers. Few of them were to know the realms of gold explored by the youthful Keats. The goodly estates of classical literature, the western islands of fairyland, even the kingdoms embracing many realities of their day were not for them. If they formed new opinions, they received them from the demesne carefully restricted by self-appointed warders.

The taste for Evangelical literature had eventually pervaded all ranks of society. Even among the upper classes there were many, like Lord Melbourne, who read theology and biblical criticism for pleasure.[37] The invention of steam presses early in the nineteenth century would, in any event, have increased the supply of books, but only a profound change in the temperament of readers could explain the great demand for moral and religious works. In 1825 the Religious Tract Society published 10,500,000 books and tracts. In 1827 the British and Foreign Bible Society produced 294,006 copies of Scripture, and in the same year the S.P.C.K. supplied the reading public with a total of 1,461,752 tracts, Bibles, and other works.[38] These figures, moreover, represented the issue of only three of the many societies producing similar works.

The Evangelicals had at first pressed their literature upon the reading public, but compulsion was no longer necessary.

[37] L. Strachey, *Queen Victoria*, New York, 1931, p. 85.
[38] Wm. Jones, *The Jubilee Memorial of the Religious Tract Society*, "Appendix"; George Brown, *History of the British and Foreign Bible Society*, London, 1859, I, 112; *Two Hundred Years: The History of the Society for Promoting Religious Knowledge*, p. 198.

Many people had come to prefer religious works. This was evident from the demand for books in the secondhand market, upon which one writer observed:

There is not a stall in London where the passenger may not learn of its proprietor that the religious department of literature is his most extensive and profitable business, *The Whole Duty of Man*, *The Pilgrim's Progress*, *The Holy Living and Dying*, and the *Book of Martyrs* are to be found in every alley in London; and I have the authority of the first divinity booksellers in asserting the advance in value of old divinity, already the most extensive class of books. The increase in modern divinity, I think, I may be allowed to consider amply proved.[39]

With respect to secular literature the most striking characteristic of the reading public was its strong disapproval of indelicacy. It considered some situations too improper for discussion. It tabooed words and expressions which had once appeared in the vocabulary of the most respectable authors. Standards of taste had always been subject to change from period to period, but never before had good taste in literature been so easy to define. To the typical reader of the Victorian era it meant simply freedom from any degree of coarseness. By 1825 this criterion was well established. Contemporary writers had learned to comply with the strict demands of the reading public, and no reputable publisher would have dared to print a book which dealt with indecorous situations or contained gross language.

From the time of Chaucer readers had been accustomed to meeting in books certain four-letter Anglo-Saxon terms. These words, most of which referred to the processes of evacuation, could be found in literature until the very end of the eighteenth century. Then suddenly they had disappeared from print. The public would no longer tolerate the simple verbs referring to normal functions of the body, and in some circles it was considered indelicate even to call the physical organism a "body." As late as 1795 the Reverend Rowland Hill, when writing a pamphlet, had not hesitated to use the word "whore." Thirty

[39] *Vindiciae Britannicae*, p. 379.

years later a respectable author would have avoided this noun. Even that long-lived and traditionally conservative newspaper, the London *Times,* had occasionally printed vulgar bits during the first years of its existence. For example, the issue of July 24, 1790, contains a plain reference to a man urinating on a letter to show his contempt for it. This item, had it appeared in the *Times* of 1825, would have resulted in the cancellation of subscriptions all over England.

To use a phrase of Samuel Johnson, people had grown "more combustible." In 1777, when Boswell told him that Lord Hailes had referred to some poems of Prior as "impure tales," Johnson replied, "Sir, Lord Hailes has forgot. There is nothing in Prior that will excite to lewdness. If Lord Hailes thinks there is, he must be more combustible than other people. . . . No, Sir, Prior is a lady's book." [40] The common reader of the early nineteenth century would not have agreed with the great moralist. Poems like "The Ladle" now seemed extremely improper, and in 1816 Alexander Chalmers, writing in the *General Biographical Dictionary,* said of Prior, "In his tales we find much indecency, and his works, collectively are not a suitable present from a decent giver." This critic placed several other famous writers in the same category. Shakespeare was distinguished for "the licentiousness of his language," he remarked, and in the writings of Swift there were "the greatest indelicacies." [41]

The most daring book published in 1825 was the *Memoirs of Harriette Wilson.* It was a gossipy account of the life and adventures of a woman who had been the mistress of several members of the nobility. Insofar as it exposed prominent people and revealed some intimate aspects of high life, the book was unusually frank for the period. But it contains none of the grossness found in the *chronique scandaleuse* of the eighteenth century. Even when speaking of her indiscretions, Harriette was most discreet in her language. Her circumlocutions, indeed, would have done credit to a lady of quality. Nevertheless, al-

[40] Boswell, *Life of Johnson,* III, 192.
[41] *General Biographical Dictionary,* XXV, 333; XXVII, 386; XXIX, 67.

though it was widely read, this volume of memoirs was considered extremely shocking. To begin with, the publisher, J. J. Stockdale, had had an unsavory reputation, and his daring to print such a work involved him in several costly suits for damages. Meanwhile the author, fearing recriminations from the people she had exposed, fled to Paris to escape prosecution.[42]

There was, to be sure, a certain amount of trafficking in frankly pornographic works. According to Francis Place, a few hawkers and an occasional bookshop in the poorer sections of London still dealt, though very furtively, in such literature. But there was little demand for books of this kind. When a couple of venders, specializing in pornography, opened shops in Regent's Quadrant and the Opera Arcade, they failed, said Place, not because they were prosecuted, but "from want of customers." [43]

As a student of manners, Francis Place was particularly impressed by the growth of delicacy since his youth, and his notebooks are a valuable source of information on this subject. Some of his judgments, to be sure, are needlessly severe, for Place, more than he realized, was influenced by the strongly censorious attitude of the times. But even when one does not agree with his interpretations, his facts about writers and publishers may generally be relied upon. Place frequently observes that no reputable publisher doing business in the reign of George IV would dare to reprint various works which had once circulated freely. A poem like the "Scarronides" of Charles Cotton contained so many offensive terms, he said, that "it would be a disgrace for any respectable bookseller who should print it, and no such bookseller, were he to print it, would find a sale sufficient to cover expenses." [44] This statement was undoubtedly correct, for Cotton's *Burlesque Poems,* though popular early in the eighteenth century, had not been reprinted since 1765. Many works formerly enjoyed by the upper classes were now considered as vulgar as the eighteenth-century street ballads. Yet the

[42] B.M., Add. MSS 27,825, p. 101.   [43] B.M., Add. MSS 27,824, p. 54.
[44] B.M., Add. MSS 27,825, pp. 20 ff.

public for whom these books were originally written had seen nothing offensive in them, nor had the authors or publishers intended that they should. When the well-known firm of J. and J. Rivington printed *A Philosophical Dialogue Concerning Indecency* in 1751, they had had no thought of pandering to coarse appetites, Place observed, but even "if the gross expressions it contains were all expurgated, Messrs. Rivington would not now consent to have their names on the title page—neither would any other respectable bookseller." And so it was with a number of eighteenth-century books. No publisher of any standing would have dared to bring out a new edition of the *Political Register* of 1767, the *Miscellaneous Works of John Bancks,* or *The Adventures of William Bradshaw.*[45]

How could one account for the changed attitude of the reading public? Place believed that it was owing largely to the changed circumstances of life. A picaresque tale like *The Adventures of William Bradshaw, Commonly Called Devil Dick,* when it was published in 1754 had not offended readers. They knew that there were hundreds of desperate criminals in London, and they saw nothing unusual in Devil Dick's career of lying, cheating, robbery, and debauchery. "Many persons in those times went through a series of low, vulgar, infamous adventures, which no one goes through now," wrote Place, "and the tale, which without exaggeration might be told of them, could only be paralleled now by collecting the incidents from perhaps fifty miscreants." [46]

Both the tone and the substance of literature were bound to be different, Place argued, for readers and authors of the early nineteenth century lived in a different world from that of their ancestors. Because the events in *Devil Dick* now happened much less frequently and because the language employed in this book was no longer the language of everyday life, the early Victorian would be inclined to think that the author was going out of his way to be sensational or vulgar:

45 B.M., Add. MSS 27,825, Sections X and ff.
46 *Ibid.,* pp. 106–7.

This it is which constitutes the difference between society now and then. When such things were common, they of course were thought less of, and the morality and general conduct of all ranks being also exceedingly lax when compared with the moral and general conduct of people of similar classes now, will explain how it was that such gross books were written and addressed to the youth of the middle classes of society, and why it was not then thought disgraceful to eminent booksellers to publish them.[47]

Literature had not ceased to hold the mirror up to life. It still gave a true reflection of it, but life itself had changed, and the mirror caught a different image. After all, *The Dairyman's Daughter* was a true story, and the heroine of this pious tale had as many prototypes in actual life as Devil Dick had had in the lawless eighteenth century.

Despite its general validity, however, this theory does not account for the excessive squeamishness of the Victorian reader nor for the revulsion against some of the most exemplary writers of the past. Something more than a mere outward change in circumstances had occurred. The thoughts of men were different. But far from being "widened with the process of the suns," the thinking of the Victorians was, in many instances, definitely narrowed. Almost no writer of the previous century, except the early leaders of the revival, escaped censure when examined under the Evangelical microscope. Each blemish was magnified, with the result that slight lapses from rectitude became enormities. Furthermore, those who held the microscope viewed conduct with such a prejudiced eye that they frequently misjudged as vicious what men at almost any other time would have considered laughable if not commendable. Even Dr. Johnson, symbol of all that was best in the eighteenth century, did not escape. After reading Johnson's "Prayers and Meditations," the Evangelical Arthur Young wrote in his diary:

His religion seems to have been against the very grain of his soul, and all the tendencies of his mind to have arisen from his understanding only, and never to have been truly in his heart. Company, and engagements, and indolence kept him from church from Janu-

----

[47] *Ibid.*

ary to March. He scarcely ever got to it in time for service, and he aimed in his resolutions to take the Sacrament only three times a year; he does not name a book (the Scriptures excepted) that was likely to give a right turn to his devotions. . . . 'Tis well his mind was morbid, for he seems to me (from his work) never to have been converted.[48]

The Evangelicals were not alone in this practice of sitting in judgment upon their predecessors. Frequently those who had no sympathy with the religious teachings of the revival, having been influenced by its stern code of conduct, were quite as severe as the Evangelicals. Even Francis Place, a skeptic who disliked the Evangelicals, shared, quite unconsciously, their strong bias. He believed that there had been a great advance in decency, as undoubtedly there had been, but he failed at times to see that decency was carried to the extreme of prudery. This was the more curious because Place was capable of detecting priggishness in others. He hated cant, and when George Colman, the Examiner of Plays, had imposed a strict censorship upon the theater, Place had denounced him as hypocritical.

Place himself was no hypocrite, but, like many men of his time, he had risen from the lower ranks of society and, as a member of the new bourgeoisie, he developed much of the seriousness that characterized the Victorian middle classes. It is observable, for instance, in his comment upon a familiar incident found in Boswell's *Life of Johnson*. Two young friends, Topham Beauclerk and Bennet Langton, knocked at Johnson's door at three o'clock one morning. Appearing in his shirt, Dr. Johnson greeted their proposal that he join them in a ramble with: "What, is it you, you dogs! I'll have a frisk with you." He got dressed and the three started out on an excursion to Covent Garden, where they found the greengrocers unloading the fruits and vegetables that had been shipped from the country. After astonishing the tradesmen with their efforts to assist in the work, Johnson and his young friends retired to a tavern for a bowl of punch. Finally, to top off the morning, they went for a row on

[48] *Autobiography of Arthur Young*, ed. by M. Betham-Edwards, London, 1898, pp. 421 ff.

the Thames.[49] To the modern reader this amusing adventure clearly shows Dr. Johnson's essential humanity. But to Francis Place, who cited it as an instance of the low taste of the eighteenth century, such conduct "in a man of renown, a religious man, well-connected with eminent men" seemed completely indecorous.[50]

Place's comment upon another escapade in which Johnson was involved is equally interesting. When Goldsmith produced *She Stoops to Conquer,* some of his friends, fearing that the play might not prove successful, decided to give it their encouragement. Several of them, therefore, including Johnson, the Burkes, and Sir Joshua Reynolds, attended the performance on the first night. Acting as a claque, this group led the laughter, with the result that the audience responded to their enthusiasm and the play was a success. The reaction of Place to this incident surprises one. Instead of praising the good-natured loyalty of Goldsmith's friends, he termed the affair "mean," "indecorous," and "fraudulently deceptive." It would "be impossible," he said, "to collect such a company for such a purpose now." [51] So far as the last statement is concerned, Place was probably right. But his own comments upon the conduct of Dr. Johnson, coming from a generally objective observer, are still better proof that the seriousness of the reformers had become general. Victorianism had arrived.

The first three decades of the nineteenth century had come to a close, and the nation was on the brink of a new era. Tennyson, though referring to the Middle Ages, may very well have had his own age in mind when, in 1833, he wrote,

> The old order changeth, yielding place to new.

Byron, Shelley, and Keats were dead, the older romantic writers had completed their best work, and a new generation of poets, more at peace with the world and with themselves, were tuning their lyres. They, too, could write in the romantic vein, telling

[49] Boswell, *Life of Johnson,* I, 250–51.   [50] B.M., Add. MSS 27,827, p. 127.
[51] B.M., Add. MSS 27,827, pp. 121 ff.

over again medieval tales and expressing thoughts that lie too deep for tears. But most of them possessed a kind of moral earnestness unknown to their predecessors. In Tennyson, in Browning, and to a lesser degree in Arnold, one sometimes detects an almost Evangelical note, as if the poet was faintly remembering from his nursery days the lessons which he had probably read in Mrs. Sherwood and Mrs. More. There was also in their works a suggestion that the moral virtues had arrived at a higher level than they had ever before attained.

The man of common clay, seeing about him a multitude of changes, was convinced that civilization had reached the crescent promise of a brighter day. He saw smoke floating over the industrial cities of the north, he heard the hum of machinery, and at night he watched the flames of smelting furnaces against the sky. Men were leaving the fields for the factories; women were deserting their spinning wheels to tend power-driven looms. A thousand new and marvelous products—store clothes, machine-made shoes, kitchen-ware, household gadgets, improved plows, fine cutting tools—were now on the market. Even more awe-inspiring to the ordinary man was that wonder of wonders, the new railroad, which in 1830 began to carry passengers between Manchester and Liverpool.

Still, in some ways, the industrial revolution was a less curious phenomenon than the revolution in manners. Science and invention, though progressing rapidly, had not as yet greatly changed the economic pattern of life. In 1830 only 20 percent of the population lived in cities of more than 20,000 inhabitants, and the typical worker was not a factory hand but an agricultural laborer. Even in London, where small businesses still predominated, printers, tailors, cabinetmakers, and the like formed a more numerous group than the employees of large industrial concerns.[52] Thus the economic existence of the average Englishman did not differ very greatly from that of his ancestors. His social existence, on the other hand, was distinctly changed, for the typical workingman was better educated than his grand-

[52] J. H. Clapham, *An Economic History of Modern Britain,* I, 66 ff.

father, more law-abiding, and much more concerned with the amenities.

Far-reaching, too, were the political reforms of the time. One bill after another was brought before Parliament to reform municipal government, the laws discriminating against Catholics, the corn laws, the system of poor relief, the penal code, and the factory acts. More famous, even, was the great Reform Bill of 1832, which extended the franchise to any householder who paid a yearly rental of ten pounds. The passage of this measure served greatly to increase the legislative powers of the middle classes. But they had, for years, been legislating upon conduct and they had already won their greatest victory by effecting what the Queen Anne moralists had rather quaintly called a reformation of manners.

Meanwhile England had been ruled by an eighteenth-century monarch who was a scandal to the nation. This distressed the early Victorians, and although they could not repudiate their lawful king, they had expressed their moral indignation toward George IV, the man, by siding with his queen when he tried to divorce her. Even his death in 1830 brought little comfort, for he was succeeded by William IV, another eighteenth-century product, who shuffled belatedly upon the stage long after the old comedy of manners for which he had so assiduously rehearsed was played out. But England could wait. At Kensington the Princess Victoria was growing to young womanhood under the careful surveillance of tutors who were training her to be a model female. She was not allowed to read novels. Like many young ladies of the time, however, she was supplied with the works of Hannah More.[53] Within a few years the nation was to come under the rule of a monarch so profoundly in sympathy with the new social order that her name would become the symbol of an era.

[53] L. Strachey, *op. cit.*, p. 45. A. M. B. Meakin, *Hannah More,* London, 1911, p. 395.

BIBLIOGRAPHY

THE FOLLOWING bibliography is intended chiefly for the general reader. It includes, for the most part, secondary works which may be obtained at any large library. Other bibliographical references will be found in the footnotes and text.

Abbey, C. J., and J. H. Overton. The English Church in the Eighteenth Century. 2 vols. London, 1898.

Adamson, J. W. English Education, 1789–1902. Cambridge, 1930.

Allen, W. O. B., and E. McClure. Two Hundred Years; The History of the Society for Promoting Religious Knowledge. London, 1898.

Balleine, G. R. A History of the Evangelical Party in the Church of England. London, 1908.

Baring-Gould, S. The Evangelical Revival. London, 1920.

Bennett, James. A History of Dissenters, 1808–1838. London, 1839.

Binns, H. B. A Century of Education. London, 1907.

Binns, L. E. Religion in the Victorian Era. London, 1936.

Boswell, James. The Life of Samuel Johnson, L.L.D. Edited by G. B. Hill. 6 vols. Oxford, 1887.

Bowden, Witt. Industrial Society in England towards the Close of the Eighteenth Century. New York, 1925.

Bready, J. W. England: before and after Wesley. London, 1938.

Brown, Philip Anthony. The French Revolution in English History. New York, 1924.

Bury, J. B. A History of Freedom of Thought. New York [1913].

Canton, William. History of the British and Foreign Bible Society. 5 vols. London, 1904–10.

Carpenter, S. C. Church and People, 1789–1889. London, 1933.

Clapham, J. H. An Economic History of Modern Britain. Vol. I, Cambridge, 1930.

Clark, Henry W. History of English Nonconformity. 2 vols. London, 1913.

Conway, M. D. The Life of Thomas Paine. 2 vols. New York, 1892.

Coupland, R. Wilberforce—A Narrative. Oxford, 1933.

Craig, Alec. The Banned Books of England. London, 1937.

Cunningham, W. The Growth of English Industry and Commerce. 2 vols. Cambridge, 1903.

Cunnington, C. W. Feminine Attitudes in the Nineteenth Century. London, 1935.

De Montmorency, J. E. G. The Progress of Education in England. London, 1907.

Dicey, A. V. Law and Public Opinion in England. London, 1914.

Dimond, S. G. The Psychology of the Methodist Revival. Oxford, 1926.

Dobbs, A. E. Education and Social Movements, 1700–1850. London, 1919.

Edwards, Maldwyn. John Wesley and the Eighteenth Century. London, 1933.

Fowell, Frank, and Frank Palmer. Censorship in England. London, 1913.

George, Dorothy M. England in Transition. London, 1931.

Graham, Walter. English Literary Periodicals. New York, 1930.

Graves, F. P. A History of Education in Modern Times. New York, 1913.

Gray, B. K. A History of English Philanthropy. London, 1905.

Green, Samuel. The Story of the Religious Tract Society. London, 1899.

Grubb, Isabel. Quakerism and Industry before 1800. London, 1930.

Halévy, Élie. A History of the English People in 1815. London, 1924.

Haller, William. The Rise of Puritanism. New York, 1938.

Hammond, J. L., and Barbara Hammond. The Town Labourer, 1760–1832. London, 1917.

Harris, J. H. Robert Raikes, The Man and His Work. New York, 1899.

Jones, M. G. The Charity School Movement. Cambridge, 1938.

Krutch, J. W. Comedy and Conscience after the Restoration. New York, 1924.

Laprade, William T. England and the French Revolution, 1789–1797. Baltimore, 1909.

Malcolm, J. P. Anecdotes of the Manners and Customs of London. 2 vols. London, 1810.

Mathieson, W. L. English Church Reform, 1815–1840. London, 1923.

Meakin, Annette M. B. Hannah More. London, 1911.

Nicoll, Allardyce. A History of Early Nineteenth Century Drama. 2 vols. Cambridge, 1930.

Nokes, G. D.   A History of the Crime of Blasphemy. London, 1928.

O'Malley, I. B.   Women in Subjection. London, 1933.

Overton, J. H.   The Evangelical Revival in the Eighteenth Century. New York, 1886.

Piette, Maximin.   John Wesley in the Evolution of Protestantism. New York, 1937.

Pole, Thomas.   A History of the Origin and Progress of Adult Schools. Bristol, 1814.

Pons, Jacques.   L'Education en Angleterre entre 1750–1800. Paris, 1919.

Portus, Garnet V.   Caritas Anglicana. London, 1912. A history of the Societies for a Reformation of Manners.

Power, J. C.   Rise and Progresss of Sunday Schools. New York, 1871.

Roberts, William.   Memoirs of the Life and Correspondence of Hannah More. 4 vols. London, 1834.

Rose, J. H.   Life of William Pitt. London, 1923.

Russell, G. W. E.   A Short History of the Evangelical Movement. London, 1915.

Slater, Gilbert.   Poverty and the State. London, 1930.

Stephen, James.   Essays in Ecclesiastical Biography. 2 vols. London, 1849.

Stephen, Leslie.   A History of English Thought in the Eighteenth Century. 2 vols. London, 1902.

——— English Literature and Society in the Eighteenth Century. London, 1904.

Stoughton, John.   Religion in England from 1800 to 1850. 2 vols. London, 1884.

Sykes, Norman.   Church and State in England in the Eighteenth Century. Cambridge, 1934.

Taylor, E. R.   Methodism and Politics. Cambridge, 1935.

Thomas, Gilbert.   William Cowper and the Eighteenth Century. London, 1935.

Townsend, W. J., H. B. Workman, and George Eayrs, editors.   A New History of Methodism. 2 vols. London, 1909.

Traill, H. D., editor.   Social England. 6 vols. London, 1896.

Trevelyan, G. M.   British History in the Nineteenth Century, 1782–1901. London, 1931.

Tuberville, A. S., editor.   Johnson's England. 2 vols. Oxford, 1933.

Tyerman, L.   The Life and Times of the Reverend John Wesley. 3 vols. New York, 1872.

——— The Life of the Reverend George Whitefield. 2 vols. London, 1876.

Utter, R. P., and G. B. Needham.   Pamela's Daughters. New York, 1936.

Wade, John.   History of the Middle and Working Classes. London, 1833.

Wallas, Graham.   The Life of Francis Place, 1771–1854. London, 1918.

Walpole, Horace.   Letters of Horace Walpole. Edited by Mrs. Paget Toynbee. 16 vols. Oxford, 1903–5.

Warner, W. J.   The Wesleyan Movement in the Industrial Revolution. New York, 1930.

Webb, Sidney, and Beatrice Webb.   The History of the Liquor Licensing in England. London, 1903.

Wesley, John.   Journal of the Reverend John Wesley. Edited by Nehemiah Curnock. 8 vols. London [1910–17].

Wheatley, H. B.   Hogarth's London. London, 1909.

Whitaker, W. B.   Sunday in Tudor and Stuart Times. London, 1933.

Wickwar, W. H.   The Struggle for the Freedom of the Press, 1819–1832. London, 1928.

Williams, J. B.   A Guide to the Printed Materials for English Social and Economic History, 1750–1850. 2 vols. New York, 1926.

Wright, L. B.   Middle-Class Culture in Elizabethan England. Chapel Hill, N.C., 1935.

Young, Arthur.   Autobiography of Arthur Young. Edited by M. Betham-Edwards. London, 1898.

Young, G. M.   Victorian England. London, 1936.

INDEX